"Binns' writing style is both canny and witty. In these pages, the author genuinely relates her suffering and how she safeguarded her son's welfare, and the book ends strongly on a ray of hope."
—*Kirkus Review*

"'Without Death,' St. Thomas Aquinas suggests, 'Life would have no meaning. Too difficult to know just what's what in all the happening that keeps happening.' Jane Binns, in her meaningful memoir *Broken Whole*, draws in purposeful parentheses around a lively percolating period of her life, expertly drawing out some fractured yet finely finished order from the daily chaos. Clairvoyant and courageously clear-eyed, poetic and prosaic, relentless and revelatory, *Broken Whole* is expert negotiating these paradoxical sutures and conveys, in breathtaking detail, a mean golden mean of the aforementioned meaning."
—Michael Martone, author of *Michael Martone* and *Brooding*

"In this post–Harvey Weinstein world, we're all hurt and wounded. *Broken Whole* is a courageous step toward a better tomorrow, when men and women can begin to be more honest, loving, and more forgiving toward one another. I laughed when my heart wasn't breaking. I'll never look at myself the same again."
—David Madgalene, author of *Call Down the Angel*

"In her relentless search for love, Binns is never afraid to take a detour for a little fun and a good story. As she navigates the lust, loss, and laughs of dating, her sharp eye and tongue are as often turned on herself as on the men she encounters. Searingly honest, Binns insists on finding hope amidst the heartbreak."
—Lisa Birman, author of Colorado Literary Fiction Award–winning *How to Walk Away*

BROKEN
WHOLE

BROKEN WHOLE

a memoir

by

JANE BINNS

SHE WRITES PRESS

Published 2018
Printed in the United States of America
ISBN: 978-1-63152-433-2 pbk
ISBN: 978-1-63152-434-9 ebk
Library of Congress Control Number: 2018945617

For information, address:
She Writes Press
1569 Solano Ave #546
Berkeley, CA 94707

She Writes Press is a division of SparkPoint Studio, LLC.

Book design by Stacey Aaronson

Quote from John Calvi printed with permission.

Names and identifying characteristics have been changed to protect the privacy of certain individuals.

For CAM

May you already know you are whole.

This is my recollection of events that took place over the years 2001 – 2014. I wrote this collection of essays to unravel a mystery, to stop wondering and hurting, and to laugh again at what was funny then and continues to be funny now. The names of everyone in these pages have been changed to protect the innocent.

PREFACE

I spoke my name three times and waited for the readers to begin. It was a Wednesday evening in 2002. I was thirty-five years old. Our class had just finished the opening meditation, and now we would begin looking clairvoyantly at each other. The process of reading energy validated the "readee" as well as the reader because what was seen was often a reflection of what was ready to be released. We then turned our attention toward letting go of what was not working for us anymore. Our teacher repeated what the readers were to look at: "Notice where energy is stuck when she speaks. Look at the fifth chakra, her communication space. Just notice what you notice."

"I see a picture of you when you were about three years old," one of the three readers said. "You are standing. You feel abandoned, afraid. When you feel this way, you freeze. You can't say anything. I can't see exactly what happened. You were little, and no one was there for you."

I held myself still. Her words resonated deeply, but I couldn't remember anything. I thought she had the age wrong. No memory came.

The readers offered a healing to help me begin the process of letting go of what made me freeze when I felt abandoned. I accepted. The purpose of the class was not to remember. It was to let go so each of us could be in present time at our current ages and not stuck in a memory from our lives that happened many years before. In fact, it helped if you couldn't remember, because then there wouldn't be attachment to the memory. We were told this often.

Too often, however, I needed to remember in order to let

go. It was like returning a book to the library, settled, back in its place on the shelf. I felt better if I knew what it was I was letting go of.

Later that night, after I had gotten home, I remembered. The memory played before me like a short film. I credited it for how I'd felt frequently in recent days: frozen, unable to speak, abandoned. And now those feelings and inability to react had a point of origin. Shock and relief overwhelmed me. I didn't know what to do with this information. I didn't know what to do next, or how to feel. I didn't know how to unwind and disentangle myself from my instinctive reaction of shutting down when I felt abandoned. I had had years of practice in responding the same way without knowing why. It wasn't going to be easy to simply let it go and create a new response. I had to first recognize the shape of feeling abandoned. I had to see what people and circumstances I allowed into my life and how this fostered the continuous sense of isolation or allowed me to trust.

This makes it sound as though I went about this in a calculating scientific manner, like I was excising a tumor and examining it for cancer. I didn't. While on the one hand I recognized the magnitude of this event and its impact on my life, on the other, I disregarded its reach and pretended I had indeed been able to let it go.

But the truth was, I couldn't.

In 2001, after twelve years of marriage, I left my husband. I was nearly thirty-four. Our son had just turned two.

My husband was a nice man. He went grocery shopping, he did laundry, he was steadily employed, he was loyal, and he was an attentive lover. He also had a refreshing sense of humor that came in surprising, inimitable flashes. This part of him, his humor, was an adhesive to which I returned time and again as a reason to stay over the years. When I doubted, laughter restored my hope that we could last.

We met at Big Ten Party Store in Ann Arbor, Michigan, where we both worked. We were students in college: he was attending the University of Michigan as a political science major, and I was finishing up at Eastern Michigan University with a degree in piano performance and a minor in creative writing. We used to stand in the beer-making supplies aisle and talk. I loved how he would look up and to one side just before he said something witty, and how his eyes twinkled as he did it.

I got to work by riding my bike. That and the city bus. Occasionally, my mother would pick me up. Soon enough, Matt began giving me rides home.

The night I asked him out on a date, he leapt up on the back counter where I worked and stretched his arms out while he sang. There was no way I was not going to love him.

After three months of dating, he asked me to marry him. It was my twenty-first birthday.

I felt happy and safe with Matt, but life on my periphery was in chaos. My sister had married two years earlier because she was pregnant, and my older brother had followed suit a year later. Our parents were in the midst of a divorce after thirty years of marriage. Dad had had an affair and didn't want to work things out with Mom. Everything I had known had been pulled up, the roots splayed and torn. Marrying Matt felt like a good shot at stability.

Before we had been married one year, we were in counseling to learn how to not exchange one-liners that escalated into barbed arguments. I got tired of him being sarcastic all the time. I wanted to be heard without him making fun of what I was saying. And it didn't matter how I phrased it, or which door I entered to explain this, I felt impatient that he wasn't understanding how important this was to me. It was a betrayal. My resentment at not being heard and our mutual frustration with our inability to shift away from this pattern formed a chasm between us.

After our divorce, I thought I would find someone quickly; I thought the enterprise of dating after our split would be a blip on the radar. I didn't expect to continue writing about my experiences for over ten years. I didn't consider myself to be masochistic, and I didn't consider myself to be dumb. I didn't have a goal, though, either. I believed that my next relationship would solve everything for me, the next adventure would answer a question I hadn't yet told myself I even had. I did enjoy telling my stories to girlfriends, however, many of whom suggested I write a book.

This book was born out of a desire to understand myself better through the trials and errors I made in relationships. Stubborn, cantankerous, and determined to leave no stone uncovered, I began my journey. And it didn't take me long to discover that the only road in was rough—albeit (thankfully) sprinkled with humor.

CHAPTER ONE

‑‑‑‑‑

Here, Not There

*O*ne night in January 2001, when it was Matt's turn to come up with something for us to do to strengthen our intimacy, I sat on the couch and waited. I watched him iron his clothes for the next workday. Then I turned on the TV. I was calm, and everything seemed simple, clear. I knew I would leave. I didn't know when, but I was too limp to hold us together any longer.

Later that month, I attended Andre Watts's concert by myself. The next day, Matt told me that was the loneliest night of his life. I shrugged. *What are you going to do about it?* I wondered to myself. I waited for him to suggest something, but he said nothing.

The fifteen-minute commute to campus was not enough time to finish crying. In the middle of a fine detail about quotes and parentheses, my voice quivered. My heart thudded, and I wanted to evaporate into the whiteboard. I was going to cry. I took deep breaths, which helped. I saw my students shift in their seats, fidgeting with the seams of their shirts, their heads down and turned toward a side wall. Then a few of them enveloped me. Their faces waited, full of kindness, patience. I told them enough of the story; they cared. I felt embarrassed that I was overtaken with blubbering, and at the same time I wanted them to see me raw. I wanted a rescue. I wanted someone to know what to do, because I didn't.

Occasionally, when I was traipsing through a grammar lesson, one of my students, Allen, made sideways comments about an especially good sentence I had written. Little by little, these comments edged their way into flattery and then stretched into elongated conversations after class in the hallway. It was harmless, then. My intellect was tickled; flirting reminded me that perhaps I was attractive and worthy. Nothing needed to come of it. I felt safe so long as I was his teacher and we stood upright in the hallway. I would not reach beyond the confines of the semester; it would destabilize things.

As the end of the semester encroached, however, lines blurred. I didn't want to stop talking to him. When he leaned against the wall outside our classroom, I imagined pulling his shirt out of his pants and rubbing my hands across his back and down. I wondered if he would like to kiss me. I wondered if *I* would like it.

We were consenting adults and old enough to make sound decisions, at least according to the law. But the libido makes miscreants out of the most rational, especially if a heart is aching and lonely.

I invited Allen to be in a book club with me. I wasn't formally a part of any such club; it would simply be the two of us. Our first meeting was at a bar. He asked me how it would work.

"I don't know," I said. "Usually whoever's in it decides on what to read and then they talk about it after they're done." I smiled and hoped he wasn't really thinking we would read books together, though I was pleasantly surprised when he showed me the book he had brought. He smiled and, as if he'd heard my thoughts, said we didn't have to read it.

He was forty-two and lean. He wore glasses, was bald, and had a Texan drawl that made me smile helplessly. He had a self-doubting gentility that was endearing and suggested seduction. I was attracted to his desire and attention. It didn't matter what he said. He could have told me that he had been a drug dealer, a porn king, or a con man who'd bilked people out of millions and I would have nodded kindly, entranced by the song of his intonation.

Allen looked at me when I spoke. He agreed or disagreed, he intellectualized his thoughts and seemed alive to mine. I needed him to bring me back to who I remembered myself as, back in the time before it all felt vacuous.

Mindful of the time that first meeting, we only visited for an hour and a half, and all of it took place at the bar.

He walked me to my car. We stood in the parking lot with muted fluorescent orange lights streaming in all directions above us.

"I want to have an affair with you," he said.

You want me? You want to have sex with me and to listen to me, to laugh with me? I couldn't refuse him.

"I'm never going to leave my wife," he continued. "I love her. I'll always cheat on her, but I love her."

I whisked away the clunk of defeat in his declaration that he would never leave his wife. I would not be saved by him. I quickly changed my objective. This didn't need to be forever, and I didn't need to know what it would be, either. Jittery, excited, questioning this was superfluous.

Allen arrived late the first time we were supposed to meet. He didn't know how to get to our meeting spot, a library. I didn't have a cell phone. I sat in my car. I got out and waited on the sidewalk. I looked at my watch. I got back in my car and opened a book. I read the same line several times. I thought I should leave but I was too excited. I didn't want to miss my chance with him, or to be seen as unreliable or untrustworthy. I got out again and stood on the sidewalk.

I heard his truck at the same time I saw it. I smiled and waved, pretending this wasn't unusual. Friends met at the library all the time, just maybe not to park a car and break a vow.

We drove to a hotel. He paid for it and mumbled something about forty dollars not being too bad for ruining your conscience. He mused about how many wandering couples the desk clerks saw in the middle of the afternoon on a Saturday.

I felt embarrassed at how loose his underwear was around his thighs. He was vulnerable and fragile. This moment was real. I kissed him to remember and forget why I was there.

I was surprised by the size and shape of his penis. I reasoned that of course it would be different, but I hadn't seen any penis besides Matt's in twelve years. I climbed on top and acted like I felt something when in fact I didn't feel much of him at all. That did not keep me from enjoying and exhausting myself thoroughly by late afternoon.

We picked up my car and drove to a side street a few blocks from my house. I got out and sat with him in his truck.

"I'll miss you. Thank you for spending the afternoon with me." Allen smiled.

I wanted to keep him talking—wanted to keep feeling that blurry intoxication at the sound of his Texan drawl—but I didn't know what to say. Thoughts of my twenty-month-old son's needs, and Matt having tended to them all day butted against the thinning bubble of what I had just done. "I'll miss you, too," I told him. I didn't want to leave. The evening loomed in front of me.

I drove home feeling triumphant. A line had been drawn. I was no longer drowning in feeling invisible and mute. I had reached toward another to save myself.

Shortly after I arrived, my friend Joan called and invited me to dinner with a few other friends. I asked Matt if that would be okay; I had been gone all day, after all, leaving him to take care of Shane on his own.

"Sure," he said, and he didn't even look tired or irritated. If he felt any misgivings about continuing to care for Shane by himself, it did not show.

My betrayal of that innocence strung a cobweb of guilt around me as I kissed him good-bye.

At the restaurant, I looked around the large table and

wondered if any of my friends suspected I had had sex that afternoon with someone other than my husband.

I felt high and so grateful in those first few weeks. I had abandoned misery before it could destroy me. I felt desired. It was as though I had been dragging myself through the desert for years, and finally I could stretch and linger in an oasis. I felt refreshed, electric with possibilities for who I could be and how my life could be lived. Each of us being married made figuring out where and when to meet a challenge, but I was too excited to fret over any of it. The effervescence of freedom to feel buoyed me. I was ready to have it all.

I made up stories about what I was doing or where I was going. I would "feel the need to sketch or paint or write all day," when really I was meeting Allen at a Park 'N' Ride and then convening in a nearby field. I brought my sketchbook and journal along for cover. As our waywardness continued, I did in fact long to draw and write, but I lacked the patience to let myself be still.

The irregular drumbeat of our philandering grew more hurried and feverish with each visit. Inklings of impending disaster appeared; it was starting to get expensive. We did not live close to each other; he lived in a nearby mountain town, and I lived in Denver. The time away from our other lives, and the money we were spending to make it possible, was adding up.

I thought I could keep it from Matt until I figured out what to do, and I did—for a month.

I knew he knew when we lay in bed in a spoon position and he would not curl completely against my back. His arm lay like a log over me. I couldn't hear him breathe.

He admitted that he had read my journal. I had been keeping it upstairs in the attic, where I often went to write during Shane's afternoon naps, but I had gotten lazy or tired and left it next to my side of our bed. His story was that he was chasing after Shane, who ran into the bedroom and flipped open my journal to scribble in it. Matt took it away from him and started reading. I never quite believed this story, because Shane was too fat at nearly two years to run *that* fast, and he wasn't ever really a scribbler. Besides, there were never any scribble marks to be found in my journal.

But I felt too ashamed to be angry that he'd read my journal.

"Was it fiction?" Matt asked.

I could have lied. He gave me an obvious, legitimate out. I could have been working on a short story about a woman who has an affair. But I couldn't lie, and I didn't want to. I wanted to see what he would do.

"No," I said. I couldn't look at him directly, but I was watching him in my periphery.

"That explains why you've been gone so much." He looked down, away from me. His eyes retreated.

I could not undo this disappointment. I wanted him to yell at me or protest or ask why this happened. His silence was far worse; it forced me to look at the impact of my actions without the distraction of his anger.

Matt and I had seen six therapists individually and as a couple by this point. I had suggested, cajoled, or instigated all of those visits.

In August 2000, we brought Shane with us to counseling because we couldn't find a babysitter. He was sixteen months—old enough to stand but still wobbly when walking. He deftly flipped CDs off the bookshelf onto the floor. Matt quietly told him not to, but the counselor said not to worry about it. A whirlpool of dissonance, tinged by a quiescent hope, that we had spun round and round in for years hovered like an unwelcome specter. I didn't want to laugh at Matt's sarcastic commentary anymore. I silently expected him to show me that he cared enough this time to carry us. It was obvious to me that I had supported us through all of our ups and downs, into our previous engagements in therapy and back out into our relationship; it was his turn. Though I was tired at the thought of one more round of therapy, I showed up to do my part.

Our therapist had encouraged us to devote two nights of

the week to our relationship and advised us to get a babysitter on a regular basis, so we could go out on our own. She suggested that we each design activities to facilitate a connection and intimacy.

We did this for a few months, though many times I had to remind Matt of our intention to follow through with this.

On a couple of our outings, I considered whether or not I even liked being around him anymore. I could no longer ignore that I was the one who asked most, if not all, of the questions that sustained a conversation. If he did ask me something, it was in regard to a topic that had come up days before, something I had long since forgotten about. This dynamic had gone on for years and had whittled me down; I was ravenous for validation and restive in its absence. I felt guilty for wanting to feel connected and seen. I felt guilty that he could not satisfy my desire. I felt lower than dirt when he yelled that everything was always all about me.

Allen never had any intention of letting his wife know of his wandering, but once the cat was out of the bag for me, I was less cautious or concerned. I didn't care what anything cost anymore. I had survived Matt finding out. Even more so, I had survived unveiling it to my mother. I had hurt someone she loved, someone she liked more than me. She loved me because I was hers, but she loved him just because. She questioned me, saying that relationships were hard work and sometimes boring. She questioned me five years later, too.

"Why did you leave? I didn't want to pry. I didn't think it was my business."

It wasn't, but I marched through the frustration at never feeling like I could tell her in the first place and explained, "I felt empty, Mom. I got so tired of feeling so lonely when he was sitting right next to me."

This she understood. I had grown up watching my mother talk while my father read the newspaper, rarely acknowledging a word she said.

⁂

In June, I moved out to an apartment a block and a half away from our house. Allen and I continued to see each other when we could. He went on vacation with his family in late July. I asked him to please call and wish me a happy birthday in August. He didn't. The only thing I received from him was a postcard with a tiny smiley face on it. I kept it in my dresser for a couple of days and took it out frequently to discern any cloaked meaning. A few days later, I ripped it to shreds in a tearful fit.

He didn't even say he was sorry. He had stepped back from me. He was going to stay with Diane but wanted to be friends with me. Sure, I agreed. But what was that? Did that mean we'd be intimate without strings attached? The ever-popular friends with benefits? Maybe that would work for him. He still had the safety of his marriage to return to. I didn't know what I had or if I dared define anything in terms of a possession any longer. It seemed the bottom was likely to fall out of anything at any moment. Nothing seemed like it would ever feel certain again.

After some weeks of that murky friend territory, I told him I couldn't do it, not right now, which of course meant I didn't know when I would be able to, if ever.

I got tired of seeing Allen around campus. I felt branded and scarred anew when I made out his saunter and bald head. Sometimes, when I got close enough, I would ask him when he was going to graduate. Surely, it would have to happen soon.

It did, and four years later he moved away—without Diane. Every now and again he sent me jokes or chain email; they were pokes to see if I would nibble. Most of the time, I deleted them. He would send me an authentic "How are you?" from time to time, too; to those, I would reply.

I heard from him in 2009. He was in a poor town in a southern state, teaching elementary school. He had always wanted to go where he was needed and to give back to the community. He had felt like he was wasting his life being a carpenter. A series of journal entries were attached in an email. The report was grim. He struggled with what he was doing there.

One entry, written on his birthday, began with: "Another trip around the sun, another year older, but hardly any wiser. Today I wrestle with many of the demons I have seen in the past—over-indulgence, lack of commitment to people, feelings of guilt and despair. I am a poster child for Prozac."

His writing meandered into his personal life and his reflection about two women he had been seeing. One liked sex, whereas the other one was provocative and mysterious, and absent (too much). He mused that together they made the perfect woman.

He wove in and out of questioning the meaning of his work at the school. He wrote that a doctor had seen something on a chest X-ray, but he never explained what the outcome was. He noted that he had returned to drinking after having been sober for several years.

One paragraph was only one sentence: "If you have something worth living for, you will have something worth dying for as well."

I put his journals in a folder and tried not to remember that I had once encouraged him with his writing. He had a wry wit and could cobble a sentence together decently. I tried not to remember that I had once been one of the two women he was caught between. I didn't want to see that so little had changed for him. I wanted to expunge his last words: "Like it or not, we'll always be connected." I didn't know what that meant to him. For me, it meant he was the bridge out of one phase of my life into the next.

Connected? Yes, we were. I couldn't change that. It was immutable. An uncomfortable mix of regret and relief disheveled me. I never told myself that it was okay to hurt Matt, but at the time, after having spent years dancing in a sticky web of hope and disappointment, I hadn't thought about what he might be feeling, and I'd naively believed that what I did wouldn't matter. There were days upon hours and months when other people's judgment of what happened factored largely into how I saw myself. I felt helpless to defend any of my actions.

I didn't release myself from these shackles of doubt and self-hatred until the day Matt and I met for coffee, four years after our separation. He told me that all he could do in the beginning, after I moved out, was blame me. He couldn't see that he had done anything wrong or made me want to leave. He admitted he'd gone to see a therapist of his own volition, and he'd told this therapist to make him stay with it and to not say he was done with his sessions if he hadn't really done the work.

I felt raw all over again. I felt manipulated and betrayed. All those years I had dragged us into therapy, and Matt had only been putting a good face on, promising to do better without intending to try.

Two days before we met for coffee, when I had gone to pick up Shane from Matt's house, I'd met Matt's girlfriend. This was a first. We had never presented a new someone to one another. I felt shocked, deflated, and enraged. She introduced herself to me. I stopped myself from saying, "How ya doin'?" and looked past her. I hurried Shane to get his shoes on. Friends later asked me what my problem was: after all, I'd been separated for four years and divorced for three.

Part of my problem was the fact that a year after we separated, I'd asked Matt if he would like to meet a man I was dating before I introduced him to Shane. Matt yelled that he didn't care who I dated, and that was the last time we'd had a conversation about this. Being slammed for trying to do what seemed right was one thing, but the greater insult was that meeting his girlfriend reminded me of the lack of respect Matt had consistently shown me during our married life. How after we made love I had to either go get a towel myself or ask him to get one—he never thought ahead and had one there for us. Or how when I cried, he would just sit there. He wouldn't hand me a box of tissues or hold me without me telling him to do so.

Shane had a birthday party at his preschool the day after I met Matt's girlfriend. We both planned on being there. I had gotten no sleep the night before, because I had woken up to write. I felt so sad and heartbroken, again, and writing seemed to be my only salvation.

I focused my attention on Shane during the party; when the event was finally over, Matt left ahead of me and I relaxed. I kissed Shane good-bye and told him I would pick him up later. But when I walked out, I found Matt waiting for me.

Immediately, he apologized for "springing" his girlfriend on me the day before.

"That's the nature of the landscape now," I said. "Whatever."

"I'm sorry," he said. "I shouldn't have done that." And then he asked me to have coffee with him the next day.

Matt confided during our meeting over coffee that he had been thinking about reconciling things between us; he said he believed that things happen the way they do for a reason.

I didn't know what to say to this, so I said nothing.

A few hours later, I told him that I had grown past any interest in being with him.

I felt relieved he was finally seeing a therapist and was admitting to culpability in our problems, but it had taken too long. For years he had been telling me that I needed to accept that he was his father's son. It wasn't that I now finally believed this; I had simply become apathetic. I didn't want to see him again for months, but there was Shane's parent-teacher conference to attend the next day and a birthday party at the end of the week. Above all else, we were parents, and this came ahead of feeling as though I wanted to run away.

Staying in my marriage would have killed me. It broke my heart that I had tried, and it wasn't going to be enough. I couldn't bear the thought of my son absorbing my misery. Matt was tired and frustrated, too, but he would have blindly continued and hoped that things would eventually straighten themselves out. My affair shone a bright light on the fact that I wasn't going to pretend I could save us anymore.

Matt and I told our last therapist that above everything else, we wanted to keep our child's interests at the center of all of our decisions. By and large, we held true to this. We didn't do it perfectly, but we did keep our arguments between us and try not to engage in them when Shane was present. We participated equally in his school and sports activities.

In 2007, our eight-year-old started asking questions about why we didn't live together anymore. He said that many things would be easier for him. He was persistent and wanted to know what had gone wrong that his mom and dad didn't live together. I told Matt about this and we decided to go out and have dinner with Shane one night.

When we got back to my place, we all sat on the couch and Matt explained to Shane that Mom and Dad didn't live very well together. We had fights.

Shane looked at Matt. "Mom said you used to leave the empty milk carton out on the counter. Is that what happened?"

Matt laughed and then said, "There was more to it than that. Mom and I tried very hard to be married but it just didn't work. Sometimes I blame myself. I think that I didn't try hard enough. Mommy and I are friends. I think that when you have a baby with someone that you always love them, and that's true for me."

I took Shane's hand in mine.

"But we've been living in different houses now for a long time," Matt continued, "and even if we were to try it again, it wouldn't be easy, because you get used to living on your own and it's hard to go back. The important thing for you to know is that none of this is your fault. We love you very much and always want what is best for you."

After Matt left, Shane and I held each other and cried for a little while. Shane asked me why I was crying, and I said, "Because Daddy said some very nice things."

I called Matt the next morning and thanked him. I told him I loved him too.

༺

Several months after this, Matt drove himself to the emergency room for a kidney stone.

I got a call early in the morning and met Matt and Shane at the hospital, the same place where Shane had been born eight and half years before.

Matt asked Shane to wait outside his room, so he could talk to me alone. I had brought Shane his breakfast; I asked him to go out into the hallway to eat it.

"I don't know how to tell you this," Matt said.

My face flushed.

"They did a routine CT scan and found a tumor on the other kidney." He pinched his eyes with thumb and middle finger. "It's huge. The size of a softball."

I felt hollow and uncertain. Should I hug him? Dread and anger blipped on my radar. *You fuckin' don't take care of yourself and look what happens. Now I'm going to be left with Shane by myself.*

"What did they say? Are they going to remove it? Do they know what it is?"

"I don't know." He started to cry.

"Do you want me to call your family, your mom?" I didn't want to, but as far as I could tell, Matt currently had no girlfriend.

"Uh. Yeah. That would be great. I can't deal with anyone's histrionics, now."

"We'll figure it out. I'll take Shane. We'll work it out."

Matt had appointments with an oncologist and urologist. They didn't know what the tumor was; the prognosis was that it was not cancerous, but it would have to be removed because of its size and attachment to the kidney.

Matt's mom, Pam, came to stay with him for two weeks. She arrived a day before the surgery. Matt's brother Rob came too.

We all went out to dinner the night after Matt's surgery. Rob sat with Pam across the table from Shane and me.

Rob said he had been so freaked out when he got Matt's call.

I immediately turned Shane's attention toward the kid's menu maze and started asking him questions about what he could see there. I was furious at Rob for being so open about his feelings with Shane present. None of us knew what this was going to be, and I didn't need any help in nurturing Shane's fears. As far as he knew, he simply was not going to be staying the night at his dad's house for two weeks.

That first night, Matt was pale and flaccid. His wit pierced through his grogginess, however, immutable as ever. His youngest brother had sent a "Get Well" balloon arrangement, and when he called to see if it had arrived yet, Matt slurred, "Hey man, my balloon says 'Happy Bar Mitzvah.' Did you get a special deal 'cause there was only one left?"

We all laughed.

I remembered why I had loved him and stayed with him for twelve years. His sense of humor had been glue for what wasn't there between us, including the fact that he rarely laughed at my witticisms. I believed I wasn't capable of being funny because I wasn't funny in the same way he was. I had resolved that I was the serious one between us, but this chafed and echoed a dissonant clang because my friends consistently laughed at my observations.

Several weeks after I moved out, I asked him if he'd thought I was funny.

"You have a fine sense of humor," he said.

Yes, I laughed at everything you joked about, I thought. "I always wanted you to be the one to see and appreciate me for who I am," I told him.

He said he couldn't talk about this now; his realtor was about to call him, so he needed to get off the phone.

That was a typical response. Just when I thought we would have a substantive conversation about a topic that meant something to me, it would be dampened by an urgency for him to attend to something else.

I glanced at him in the hospital bed. I couldn't help but grill myself, again, about whether or not I had done the right thing in divorcing him. The sight of him in the thin blue gown prompted a fresh review. His vulnerability provoked a maternal response, easy to embroider as love. Would this have happened if we had still been together? But it didn't matter that we weren't married. This technicality did not come with a moat that prevented me from being involved. More importantly, I needed to know where all of this was going. I had to be involved, because I was freaking out. I obsessed over how I would handle being a full-time single parent. How would I deal with the death of my son's father? I began planning. I cursed myself for not having enough money saved. I wondered how much life insurance Matt had. I wondered what would happen to Shane if something happened to me, too. What would his life look like then? The questions shot in rapid fire, piling up unanswered, unresolved.

I believed everything would be all right. He had made a joke. We all laughed. I wanted to leave but I felt obligated to stay. I didn't want to get sucked back in, however. I didn't want his brother or his mother believing we would be getting back together because of this. If I said nothing and they said nothing, the notion would have to go away.

I told Matt to reach out to people, to tell them what was going on and so he could know that he was cared for. I suggested that he contact his ex-girlfriend, Karlin. She could be a friend, I believed.

There was nothing wrong with the kidney that was removed; the one that remained, however, had cysts all over it. The reports indicated they were benign. The Mayo Clinic and Stanford Medical disagreed on the pathology of the tumor. They agreed that Matt had a rare form of cancer that attacked fat cells, liposarcoma. They disagreed on a course of treatment to thwart any further growth or threat. Matt and his oncologist decided to err on the side of caution and go ahead with a six-week treatment of radiation. Matt would go in first thing in the morning for ten minutes, five days a week.

I held my breath during all of this. I solicited support

from family and friends. I asked them to call him. Whatever frustrations I had with Matt about his choices regarding our son, I knew I did not want to parent Shane by myself. It was irrefutable. I wanted Matt here more than I wanted him gone. He was a good dad to Shane. It wouldn't hurt to have people show concern for him.

Many did call or write; it helped me to share this struggle with those who'd once had regular contact with him.

The uncertainty gnawed for months as check-ups were scheduled. I would panic until results came back. After a year of a clean bill of health, I stopped worrying.

Months before Matt was diagnosed with cancer, in the spring, during a Field Day event at work, I hit my head. I was supposed to bend over and spin around a baseball bat five times and then run, but I face-planted after spinning. I thought I was all right at first, but within an hour I felt sick. My boss insisted I go to the doctor.

I drove myself to the appointment feeling dizzy and a little nauseated. The doctor asked me a series of questions: what day it was, who was president, if I found a letter with a stamp on it on the ground, what would I do with it? It was Friday, May 4, 2007; George W. Bush was president; and I would put the stamped letter in a mailbox.

"Is there anyone who can stay with you tonight? An adult?"

I shook my head. "I'll be with my eight-year-old son."

"The first twenty-four hours are the most critical in case the brain hemorrhages," the doctor said.

As she took notes, I started to cry. I looked in the direction of a basket of children's books.

"Aw. You're upset at the yellow ducky," she said. Her long braids flipped against her back as she wrote out a referral to the hospital for a CT scan.

I didn't know her. It had been over a year since I had set foot in that doctor's office and the practice had changed physicians. I paid for health insurance out of my own pocket, so I got to choose who I wanted, and this group had been close to where Matt and I lived. I had been too lazy to find anyone closer to my new home. Besides, I had liked the doctors. But I would never return to her again. Her clunky attempt at empathy was insulting. I had no time for anger or for reacting to the fact that I was hurting and alone. I needed to pick up Shane from day care. I needed to get the CT scan. I needed to not hemorrhage in the middle of the night.

I called Matt from the day care and told him what was going on. He was alarmed and asked if I needed him to take me to the hospital. I said no, believing that it was nothing and I would be fine. I didn't tell him the doctor had recommended that another adult stay with me overnight. I didn't want to say, "I need you." I couldn't let him care.

After talking with Matt, I listed off the people I wanted with me, and who should want to be there. Jack was the man I had just started dating, but he lived in Illinois. We had been dating only two weeks. He would have gladly come, but I felt awkward about asking him. Another man was Steve. I had known him since 2001, and I had just returned from camping with him in Tucson. We were on-again-off-again lovers and friends. We were lovers while I was with him in Arizona, an interlude that blurred and conflated more than clarified, leaving the door open for me to seek more reliable companionship from someone else. I forgave Steve for his ambivalence but dismissed the idea of asking him; I didn't want to put him in the position of rejecting me. Besides, if I was going to give things with Jack a fair shot, I needed to leave Steve out of it.

Though my sister and younger brother lived in the Metro area, I rarely spoke with them, and when I did, they always made it painfully clear how busy they were. Either one would have come, likely, but our infrequent contact bred hesitation. It did not occur to me to call a girlfriend and ask her to take me to the doctor's appointment, or hospital, or to stay the night, either. I didn't want to believe a concussion could be serious. I didn't want to ask another single mother to rearrange her evening to accommodate me. I knew how hard it was to do anything last minute when it was your turn to have the kids. I did not want to try to convince anyone of something I wasn't certain of myself. My doctor's inability to be authentic allowed me to dismiss the episode as trivial. Not to mention that the rejection in the words "I can't" would have been worse than dealing with this on my own. The bump on my head needed to amount to nothing, plain and simple.

Shane and I made it to the hospital without incident. As we looked at the CT scan together, Shane said he thought my brain looked gross. The radiologist saw nothing abnormal. Relieved, we went home.

At about two in the morning, I was famished. I fixed myself a hamburger and ate it ravenously. Peaks of sudden hunger persisted for a couple of weeks. I gained fifteen pounds in a month.

I began physical therapy through workman's compensation. My shoulder and neck had bunched and twisted in the fall. Once a week, I met with a doctor who asked about dizziness, memory loss, sleeping, and eating. I was advised to take frequent breaks from sitting at my desk in front of the computer: work for fifteen or thirty minutes, take a break for twenty. I heard blood pulse through my head, and a steady buzz alerted me when I was tired or hungry. I felt as though I had a built-in alarm system. For weeks, it felt like clamps were pulling at the muscles behind my eye sockets. I shied away from large groups of people. The hubbub and cacophony made me bristle and wore me out.

The dizziness stopped after two months but the buzzing in my head persisted when I felt tired or hungry or was coming down with an illness. I could only tolerate a crowded room for about fifteen minutes before the drum beat in my head began.

I wanted Matt to ask me how I was. I wanted him to offer to take Shane for longer periods of time, so I could rest. I wanted him to know what I needed without having to ask him. In the moments of his fragile and uncertain health, I was his advocate, shoulder, and friend. But I was always that way with him. The fact that we weren't married and that I didn't have to do anything didn't factor in. I could be there, and I was. What I had always hoped would be different was his ability to respond to me in a way that showed he understood my vulnerability and angst and would reassure me by putting an arm around me and handing me a tissue.

Matt knew how to say he was sorry. It was the delay that wilted me. No amount of yelling or discussion in even tones long after an event shifted his reaction time.

I did believe Matt when he told Shane that he still loved me. I wondered if someday, when I needed a hand to hold, Matt would sit down and offer me his. I wouldn't be afraid, and neither would he. We would be here, not there.

CHAPTER TWO

Crevice

I'm so glad you joined our class, Jane," Steve said as he leaned against the kitchen wall.

I liked his long arms and large hands and that he wasn't that much taller than I: five foot ten. He had a round face, a straight, broad nose, and succulent lips curtained under a Fu Manchu mustache—handsome. The only flaw was his blond hair. I never understood what all the fuss was over pale yellow hair. For me, it placed behind bald or black. Red made me falter, and brown I accepted because it was just like mine.

His gravelly voice was gentle and didn't rush. He laughed with our teacher, Patrick. It felt good to be around people who were smiling and happy I was there. I wanted to take that feeling home with me. I needed it to last longer than a ten-minute tea break during a meditation class.

Home was an apartment with hollow walls and creaky floorboards. My neighbors were mostly Section 8 folks, who did not work and had no concept of day or night. My bedroom abutted the living room of one neighbor. She had the TV on 24/7. I was told her kids had been taken from her. She was high on drugs most of the time. I saw her on a weekend visitation with her kids only once. I called the Resident Manager and the police about her several times because of noise. She retaliated by turning up the TV and taking packages that had been delivered to my door. I eventually succumbed to knowing it wouldn't matter what I did. It was a test of wills.

My upstairs neighbor had trouble sleeping and would soothe himself by pacing and strumming his guitar. I talked to him one night and he stopped playing his guitar in the wee hours, but I could still hear the floor creaking above me with his rhythmic footfall.

Shane did not stay overnight with me during the first three months because I couldn't afford to buy a bed for him. When I bought the pull-out sofa, we slept together on it for the next ten months. Shane was two. His dad and I had separated in July of 2001.

I sifted through muddied feelings and could conclude nothing that seemed like it would be believable to anyone else. I felt as though I had made a problem where none existed. How do you explain to your family who loves this man you married that you're leaving? I couldn't, so I didn't.

Things had gone from bad to worse when I started teaching when Shane was nine months old. I hadn't ever believed I could love a job, but teaching brought out the mischievous side of me. I was seen. I meant something to that sea of wondering, waiting eyes. I came home excited and wanting to talk about it and then felt crushed that Matt would riffle through the mail, or iron the clothes for the next day, or get up and leave before I finished talking.

I felt as though I didn't exist. I had no more fight left to defend being with him. We had wound up in the same place too many times.

The meditation class was suggested by friends. I had nothing to lose. I hadn't seen Allen in four months. The class began in November 2001, five months after I moved out.

I didn't expect to meet anyone. I didn't expect to not meet anyone. I needed something, but what, I couldn't say. Judgment engulfed me. Every breath was an insult. I didn't know who I was. I only knew I couldn't go on being married to my son's father. Having a charming, blue-eyed, well-built man look me in the eye and say he was glad I had joined the class filled in a hole. A promise of tomorrow arose. I felt wanted, tethered.

At the conclusion of the six-week meditation class, Steve and I exchanged phone numbers, and he invited me to call him to talk about my impending divorce if I wanted to.

𝒲e met for tea at a Barnes & Noble. I skip-walked next to him. He looked at me steadily as he told me he had been married for eighteen years before he divorced. "How long had you been married?"

"Twelve years."

"That's substantial," he said sincerely. I felt right about something for the first time in months.

We found a table, and I sat down while he got in line to buy our drinks. I held myself in close, trying to contain jitters. The seam of his jeans cocked and rippled as he shifted his weight to one leg. He was beautiful, so sexy, and interested in me! Never had someone as good looking as he given me a second look. I never believed myself to be enticing or powerful enough to attract someone I believed many longed for. I wanted to hold him, to feel his hand in mine.

He set the drinks down.

"What do I owe you?" I asked.

"It's my treat," he said. "But this isn't a date."

"Okay. Thanks." I wasn't going to argue syntax. He was across the table from me, and I had untold hours ahead just to be with him.

My marriage, Shane, the affair, counseling, teaching, telling, hiding, and denying surged from me like mountain snow run-off in May. Steve had a steady gaze. He nodded and laughed and knitted his brow with concern. His responses were perfectly timed, unrehearsed. Three hours passed so quickly. My arms flung out with emphasis, my voice rose and fell excitedly, ecstatic! I had an audience. More than that, instantaneously I felt connected to Steve, a bond beyond physical attraction. He could see all of me. I felt electric and grateful, and I was willing to sell my soul if it meant keeping this feeling alive. This is what I had been waiting for, this is what had been missing in my marriage and from my family.

He heard and saw me, and it was effortless. I didn't have to plead or beg or cry or yell because support wasn't there. It cost nothing. No one was mad at or judging me.

Two weeks later, he invited me over to share Christmas dinner with him. He prepared the entrée, and I brought a cherry pie. He had charred the steaks, but I ate happily because I was near him.

When time came for dessert, he was effusive. "Hmm. Hmm! My God, I have never tasted such a flaky crust. You put Marie Callender's to shame. This is better than my mother's. If I didn't know better, I would ask you to marry me. Just kidding. Hmm."

Electrified, I stored this away. He would be mine.

After dinner, he sat on his futon and I sat in a rocking chair across from him. He turned his head away from me as he spoke.

"I can't see you," he said. "I'm drawn to you. You're a bright light, and I could bask in that. You don't want to be with someone like me. I'm horrible with relationships. I've been married three times. The first time I got married was before I left for Vietnam. We ended it six months after I returned. Sally. We traveled all over the US when I got back but we both knew we were kidding ourselves. I was too broken, and I can't share that with anyone. No one understands. I don't expect them to, but I can't keep it all inside either. She went on to marry some Mormon and they had seven kids. She still keeps in touch with my sister. How insulting is that? The second marriage lasted a year and a half. Erin. And then there was the boys' mother. Monica. Eighteen years. I took care of our boys. I went over there every day after I moved out. The court still wouldn't give them to me. Colorado is against fathers. The courts are pro-mother. I drove back and forth, putting sixty miles each trip on my truck."

It felt wrong to interrupt him. I hated it when I was interrupted because it took so much effort for me to say what I meant in the midst of conflict or angst. But I couldn't help feeling as though each word was a nail sealing me inside of a steel box. I held myself still as he continued.

"Brad was thirteen when I left, Marcus was seven. And I left them with her! It's not right. They should be with me. Brad has a drinking problem, and she doesn't even see it. He's crying out, and she can't even see that! Marcus didn't sleep in his own bed the first two years I was gone." He heaved a sigh. "I have a daughter from when I was a senior in high school. We gave her up for adoption. And I'm pretty sure I have another son from a brief dalliance with a woman from Denver General. I saw her in traffic once and she pointed at the backseat to a boy who was the right age from when we'd been together. He looked like he could be mine. But she never called to say for sure."

I thought maybe he was finally done, but he forged on. "I'm horrible with money. When I have it, I spend it all on things that don't even matter. I'll give it away. And if that's not enough to send you packing, I have a daily marijuana habit—addiction, really—that I don't intend on quitting. I've been doing it for thirty years. It takes the edge off and gives me a little bit of peace."

I didn't shift in my chair. Startled, horrified, I held my breath. Frozen, speechless. He was abandoning me? Why? How? I was astounded at his clarity. How did he have that? How could he say that he didn't want to be with me after he made me feel so invited and wanted? I refused to hear it. I didn't understand how he could unbraid me so easily with genuine attention and simultaneously push away, retreating away from a connection. I was not going to stop seeing him until I understood. It was that simple for me.

I could not be angry. He had asked me to speak during our first meeting, and he'd listened when I did so. Gratitude bubbled up insistently, pervading all disbelief and allaying all fears. I would find a way for us to continue getting to know one another. I had hungered for someone to ask me about me for as long as I could remember, and I would not allow it to be stripped from me the moment after it arrived. I needed to be heard as much as I needed capillaries to circulate blood.

And despite his litany of reasons, these things were not insurmountable. We could still be something to each other. I only needed someone to be that sounding board, reflecting me back to myself; the rest of daily life I could handle on my own. It was quite simple, the way I saw it: he didn't need to do anything more than answer the phone when I called and get together for tea every once in a while. This would be enough.

I thanked him. I told him that it took a lot of courage to tell me all of those things and I admired him for it. I told him it was okay.

$\mathcal{I}$ called him sometime in the next week. Panic eddied, irrepressible. Who was I? What the hell was I doing leaving the father of my child, a good man, not an asshole? What was I going to accomplish in leaving? Why couldn't I stay? Why did I have to remind myself of why I left? Could I still make it work? No. Why did it feel so awful if I knew it was right?

Steve allowed for my pauses, my tales within telling. I wanted to unveil myself to him, peel back one layer after the other. I felt inspired to show him my naked, soft, and raw spots. For the first time in my life, someone was seeing the shiny, precious, funny person I felt too timid to believe in. I wanted to open her up in front of him. He had argued—substantively—that he was no good at relationships, but leaving him behind wasn't that simple. He was good at seeing me and, like an addict, I needed more.

The distance I now had from Matt did not feel free. My emotions flipped the pointer on my compass. Mornings were the worst; I fought with myself about getting up, facing my decision, and feeling judged. There were vacant spots where I couldn't name what I felt. I couldn't believe I had left. I couldn't believe I had done that. I couldn't believe no one had stopped me, not really. Everyone seemed to be watching me, waiting for what would happen next. I hadn't even doodled my next move onto a napkin.

$\mathcal{I}$ didn't call my parents for guidance. I didn't believe either one of them would be helpful. Their divorce still stung for Mom even though it was going on ten years old now. She still felt wronged. There wasn't room for me to vent without her steering the conversation back toward herself and why Dad betrayed her. It was difficult to not side with her since Dad had never been a fun and pleasant man to be around. He was sullen more often than not and usually grunted or uttered a disapproving "hmm" when Mom solicited a response from him.

In the first year after Dad left, I would call three, four, five times, leaving messages on his answering machine to please call me. He rarely returned a call; it was happenstance when he would pick up the phone.

"I miss you, Dad."

Nothing.

"Did you hear me?"

"Yes, I heard you."

I felt like Mom, begging for attention, pleading with him to respond in kind.

"Why didn't you return my calls?"

"I've been busy," he said. "Is there anything else?"

"No, I guess not," I said quietly. "When will I talk to you again?"

"I don't know. Just call me. A month?"

A month? I swallowed, squashing a gasp and cry. "I love you, Dad."

Silence.

"Don't you love me too?"

"Um-hmm."

I gave up. If I pushed him, would he never call me again?

He made it easy to believe in Mom's vociferous tirade after he left. I hated him those first couple of years and realized I didn't even know him. He had been an imposing figure in our house. Mom deferred to him despite his recalcitrance. I hated to see her give up any sense of herself to him and his unkindness.

It was only later that I was able to see her contribution to their storm. She hated keeping the house orderly. In a flurry of activity, all of us solicited, it would get picked up and cleaned when company was coming. Most of the time, we lived amidst clutter and stray piles of clothes, books, occasional dishes, and magazines. This aggravated Dad, who hated a messy house.

They fought about money a lot. It was a constant theme in their arguments. With four kids, one income for most of our young lives, and one person who miscalculated what was in the checkbook and one who never wanted to spend a dime, their explosions were frequent.

I had grown accustomed to their raised voices and outbursts by adulthood. It was the late arrival of their point of no return—or rather, Dad's point of no return—that shocked me most. When I got older I wished she had left him, especially for all the times he held up the newspaper in front of his face while she talked, and the times she would go into the bathroom after he had left for work and cry.

After Dad's crazy spell of moving out and abruptly disconnecting with all of us momentarily, he fell into his life with Delores, the woman with whom he had had the affair. He stayed with her for ten years, but they didn't marry. I never liked her, but mostly because she had helped Dad betray Mom. Still, even leaving that fact out of it, I found Delores a bit vulgar. She smoked and read trashy novels. Dad had stepped way down.

Mom went a bit off the map in her own way after the divorce by traveling with a long-time friend's cousin. They went to Australia, Hawaii, and London together. Ben was a hoarder and a spendthrift. They lived together for six months or less. A couple of years into their relationship, Mom found out he was still married to his first wife. That was it for her.

So I did not look up to my parents for how to be a thirty-four-year-old recently divorced woman. There was no one to emulate. I would have to figure it out on my own. I consulted a therapist, continued the meditation and clairvoyant classes, and vented to friends. I was functional for the most part. And three things were clear: I needed to care for

Shane, I couldn't go back, and I wanted what Steve offered—a person worth waiting for, listening to, and laughing with.

The need to care for a toddler forced me out of bed in the morning. It structured my day. Matt went to work in the morning. I walked the block and a half from my apartment to the house to be with Shane until Matt got home. I taught at night.

That was the routine until I needed more money. Then I requested more teaching assignments. I taught three classes at Metro State and eventually four at Community College of Denver. My students, round-the-clock planning, and grading kept me working hard. I didn't want to be dependent on anyone for anything, but I also wasn't going to argue with the divorce and child care dispensation that compensated me because I made less than half of what Matt made. I saved enough money each paycheck to set aside for living expenses in between semesters, because I never knew how many classes I would be teaching and therefore how much money I would be making in the next semester.

Survival was a new goal. So was feeling validated.

Those first few months after the meditation class, Steve and I would talk for hours on the phone. He opened up to me easily, as I did to him.

One night, I propped one hip against the bathroom counter, cradled the phone, and watched three-year-old Shane in the bathtub. The ceramic tiles were uneven, the paint an outdated green. Nothing seemed appropriate to say. I was startled, frozen—did he expect me to respond to him? I felt like I'd just been hit by a line drive. The subject had come out of nowhere.

Silence sandwiched between us until Steve spoke again.

"I hope that doesn't alarm you," he said.

"No, it doesn't," I lied. I didn't know what to say. I felt unprepared, on high alert for what might happen next. Maternal instinct kicked in and I felt I should not show my fear, believing that if I were calm, he would be too. Was this one of those stories I had heard where a friend tells another about wanting to commit suicide, hoping he will be talked out of it? Was he contemplating suicide right then? Would he kill himself when we got off the phone? Should I do something? Was this real?

"Have you ever contemplated it, Jane?"

"Yes, but I try not to. I can't, really."

"Have you ever thought about how you would do it?"

"No," I said. "It's more about just wanting the pain to end. I just want everything and everyone to go away. I can't stand it. Everything is too hard sometimes, but I can't because I feel guilty. I can't leave my son. I left my marriage for his sake. I didn't want him growing up watching me be unhappy."

"You're courageous and strong. I don't know anyone else who would leave when their kids were that young."

"The relationship was killing me. I felt stuffed, suffocated. That's no good for Shane. What does he learn from watching his mother be that way?"

"You say that you left for him, but you left for yourself, too. I couldn't have left when my kids were two. Do you ever think about going back?"

"Of course. But I can't. I have nothing left to give. You were a better friend to me in the first thirty minutes when we met for tea than my ex-husband ever was."

"That's harsh," he said.

"That's true," I said, "but I can't go back. My life is about going forward. Finding a different way. Fear of what is unknown is not the reason to not do anything. I had a teacher once tell me to write what you're afraid of. I think the same is true about life. Go toward what you're afraid of, discover it, stare it down. No. I'm arriving. I'm on my way."

"But it's so hard for you."

"Staying was harder than this is. I don't have money like I used to. Things were more stable and even, true, but I didn't have myself. I couldn't speak without him mentally being somewhere else. I'd rather be alone than sitting next to someone feeling lonely. That was terrible. There is no worse feeling. I tried, too. I dragged us into counseling four or five times. He used to talk about buying me diamonds and a fur coat, and I told him I didn't care about that. All I wanted was to feel connected. You can't make that happen. But I worked really hard at it. Finally, I gave up. I couldn't do it anymore."

Frequently, we would talk so long that his cordless phone would chirp, which meant of course that it was about to die. When that happened, he would call me back from the pay phone at the 7-Eleven down the street. There were many nights when we laughed at having to compete with the BEEP BEEP BEEP of the Pepsi trucks backing into the parking lot. We talked about philosophy, religion, art, and literature; emotional, metaphysical, and paranormal experiences; while our voices entwined in laughter, sadness, and sarcasm. It was so effortless and easy. I couldn't believe my good fortune.

I felt so open and turned on by this, it was very difficult not to want to be with him. And it was not one-sided; he was drawn to me as well. But he mentioned several times that he didn't trust himself.

His fingertips roved up and down my arms while he kissed me behind my ear. He folded himself down to gently teethe on a nipple and, moving down further, to tickle my belly with his mustache. He rose up to kiss me. He tasted sweet, clean. Returning to a nipple and then the belly, and kissing, in revolutions of electric caresses. He came inside, moving slowly in and out. His girth made me stretch. I ached but pulled myself up to feel his member press deeper into me. I couldn't help myself; I moaned. He stayed in while he sucked on one nipple and then the other. His index finger gently played with my clit. He pulled out and pressed my thighs wide, placing his lips and tongue over my labia. His mustache felt feathery, soft.

He wouldn't stay there long. Up again to kiss my lips or a nipple, behind my ear. Slowly in a harmony of senses, he finally stayed on my clit, licking and sucking until I shook and quivered. I had never felt that good. I felt so grateful to have someone touch me with such care, such reverence. I took him inside of my mouth to enliven him to hard, erect.

He turned his head away from me and said, "That's not even working. I can't. I feel too guilty about leaving my kids."

I stayed on him, licking him slowly, pulling him up.

"No one's ever done that to me before," he sighed, letting a little joy be heard.

For as much as we talked, we hadn't planned on sleeping together.

A few days later, while on the phone, he said, "You're my favorite, Jane. No one has ever touched me like you. You exude sexuality. It's beautiful and I'm drawn to it. But I'm so fucked up. I'm horrible with relationships."

I felt as though a wrecking ball had swung into my stomach. But I didn't hear, "We can't do that anymore at all." I heard, "We can't do that right now." I heard, "I want you." I heard, "Work with me, be patient." I didn't hear how or when or where. That didn't need to be defined right then.

I didn't initiate being with him again, then. I didn't know what having him in my life would look like. But I didn't want to let him go.

We resumed meeting for tea or breakfast and talking on the phone. I loved his interest in me. I loved the authenticity of his curiosity about me. I imagined how the events in my life would be seen through his eyes. I laughed to myself, excited to be able to tell him.

He wasn't always available, and he didn't consistently return my calls, however. I didn't like this at all and at first didn't say anything to him about it because I felt so grateful for the times when he did call me back and listen. I told myself we were not a couple, and as friends, he was allowed to be who he was and do what he needed to do. Furthermore, as long as we were *only* friends, I felt entitled to date someone else.

CHAPTER THREE

Phobias

*G*ary was afraid of many things and allergic to everything else. I kept track of these details because I am
like that, but I forgot, too, because it wasn't necessary to hold
on to them.

He drove fifty-five minutes on back roads from Parker,
Colorado, to visit me in Lakewood. If he had been willing to
take the highway it would have taken him only thirty, but I
wasn't alone and that was the most important thing.

Gary was the first person I officially dated after the ink
was dry on my divorce papers. We chose each other during a
night of speed dating. The concept appealed to my practical
sensibility: meet a lot of people in just two hours. For under
$50, how could I go wrong?

When I arrived, the men sat on one side of the room and the
women on the other, just like a middle school dance. There
were a few riotous souls who "cheated"—sat next to each
other and engaged in conversation prior to our abbreviated
pairings—but most people obeyed the rules.

I sat next to a woman who had laryngitis. She had just
gotten it that night but wanted to come anyway. I wondered
what guy would want to talk to a woman who couldn't talk
back. Maybe all of them. I reassured myself though that at

least one woman was out of the running. The room was short three men, so it felt like we might be clawing for the others.

I was interested in one guy immediately, just by the look of him. He had a beard and wore glasses. He seemed intellectual and liberal, a good start. He was also sitting next to a woman and they were talking up a storm, conspiring no doubt to ditch the whole thing and go out back. I hoped that perhaps they were coworkers or brother and sister, here to find "the one." I secretly hoped he and I would end up at a table together.

Another man caught my interest as well. He seemed to be older, in his mid-forties. He was a little round, had a receding hairline, and wore glasses. He also talked to a woman before things officially started, but he struck me as open and vulnerable. He laughed a lot. I edged into their conversation and made a sarcastic comment about the event taking place in an office building. They both laughed.

The facilitator doled out the rules: We would not meet everyone that night but would meet approximately ten people (eight if you were female, ten if you were male). The speed dating organization could not guarantee that anyone would find their true love. There would be breaks in between our meetings for snacks and drinks. Only first names would be revealed during the timed "date." At the end of the night, if you liked someone, you had the option of filling out a card and checking the box next to her or his name or going to their speed dating website and selecting names this way.

We had ten minutes with each prospect. We were given questions to ask, to help us get to know the other person.

The bell rang. I looked at the card and looked at my partner and another woman. We were a threesome. Because of the man shortage, we were clumped together for this first round. We laughed at the questions on the card: Do you have any pets? What do you do for a living? What are your hobbies? What is your favorite movie?

Ten minutes could seem really long.

The man in our group lived out in Erie. I had never heard of it. Where was that? After he told us, I wondered why he had come to Lowry for this. His short black hair was slicked back. He was a sales rep for some big corporation. I had nothing more to say to him.

The bell rang. Thank God.

I started asking the men across from me why he chose speed dating to meet someone. And what other methods had they used before? I soon discovered my questions were easily turned back on me.

One guy leaned way back in his chair. He wore skin-tight blue jeans. Strands of his thin, blond hair flapped against his forehead away from the matted mass around the rest of his head. I asked him what his favorite movie was.

"*Spiderman*," he said haughtily.

I wanted to laugh but asked him why.

"It was just so awesome. I mean, it was great. You know?"

I didn't know. I hadn't seen it. What grown man loves *Spiderman*?

I thought if he could stop tipping back in the chair or talking so loudly, I might be able to like him. I noticed, though, that he only asked me what I did for a living. He spent most of our ten minutes talking about himself.

I met with the guy from Erie twice. But I got him to myself the second time. We laughed and relaxed into our complete disinterest in each other.

I met Gary after our first break. He wore a plaid flannel shirt and seemed relaxed. His hair was cropped short, and he had a salt and pepper beard. I liked beards. Tired of the canned questions, I went to the heart of it.

"You have nice eyes. You look like you're deep in thought."

"I've been told I have sad eyes," he said.

"Are you depressed?"

"Sometimes."

"How long have you been divorced?" I asked.

"Let's see. Nine years."

"How long were you married?"

"Thirteen."

"Have you been in a long-term relationship since then?"

"Yes. Five years."

And then he turned the tables on me and asked how long I had been divorced.

"Six weeks."

"Six weeks? God. I don't think I would have been ready to date someone at six weeks."

"Well . . . I'm window shopping."

He laughed. "Still. I don't think I would have been ready by then."

"I was unhappy for a long time, though."

"How long were you married?" he asked.

"Twelve years."

"Twelve years? And you're at speed dating?"

"Well, I've been separated for ten months."

"Oh. Well . . . What do you do?"

"I teach college English. Writing."

"I'd better watch what I say around you then. Do you cut people down or get angry if people speak incorrectly?"

"No. I'm actually pretty easy-going. Talking is different than writing. I'm pretty non-threatening in general."

He told me that he sprayed lawns and trees for a living. He worked for himself.

At the break, I talked to Mr. Round and Receding Hairline, Tom. He was also recently divorced; his kids were young teens. He had been married for eighteen years.

"What are you going to do? You wake up one day and your wife wants to leave you. So you go on, right? I mean, it's not like I had a choice. I guess I could die, you know, but the pills are supposed to help with that."

I admired his raw emotion and sarcasm. After the desert I had lived in with my ex-husband, this was more than refreshing. I wanted to ball him up and take him home with me. I told myself I could take care of him. I could make the pain go away.

As the evening wore on, I cared less and less about anybody's name. Maybe that was part of the intent: you got so tired that you didn't give a damn who sat across from you. He was going to have to be pretty special for you to flicker an eyelash at him. I returned to the ready-made questions for support. It became really easy to think, *No way*. I had no patience for the corporate climber or the unemployed mountaineer. I wanted to meet the bearded liberal, and I couldn't even get close to him during the breaks.

The evening would end with me pining for him from only a few feet away.

I talked to Tom again; I even followed him to the restroom and waited for him. He hurried to find his coat and walked sideways away from me. His voice rose as he explained in a rush that he needed to get home and tend to his fourteen-year-old, who was home alone. A hundred bats couldn't have chased him out of there any faster.

Sunk, I held out hope that he could see I would love him if only given a chance and hoped he would check the box next to my name on his card.

I felt abandoned and eviscerated of any sense of myself. I had nothing to hold on to and nothing reached back for me.

I checked almost everyone's name when I got home. It was a numbers game. I decided the bearded liberal's name was Kevin and checked his name too. What the hell? Maybe someone would be risky enough to choose someone he hadn't met either. I checked Gary's name and then unchecked it. He said he got depressed sometimes. Ew. But I liked that he argued with me and that I had held my ground with him. We seemed to hear each other. I thought I could get along with him. I checked the box.

On Monday, I received an email that Gary and I had chosen each other. I was given his phone number and he was given mine. I called him Tuesday and we talked for an hour. His voice was deep and reassuring. He laughed easily. We made arrangements to meet for dinner that Thursday.

Over a plate of Indian food, he asked me where I was during 9/11. I thought he was so sensitive and vulnerable for asking that.

I had been home feeding Shane, who was two and a half years old at the time. Matt called and told me about the first plane. I turned on the TV in time to watch the second plane crash into the second tower. Shane watched as I cried. I turned off the TV quickly. I wondered at how tragedy brought people back together, and if Matt thought that might happen to us. I had moved out only two months before.

I didn't tell Gary about how the experience made me consider rejoining my ex-husband. I told him about feeding my son and about my car battery dying that day and getting jump-started by the owner of a store I frequented, and about having to get a new battery anyway, and going to school to teach that evening believing we would still have class.

He told me about a girlfriend breaking up with him a few days after this. She had "ripped" his heart out.

I nodded and watched self-pity mottle his face. I didn't like that look and wondered if he might crinkle in disgust over something I would say or do in the future. Still, I accepted his wound. It hadn't been that long ago, after all—nine months—and it had been a national tragedy.

I asked if she was his most recent girlfriend and felt relieved when he said yes—though I didn't believe she had been the last person he had slept with. My mother told me that she thought men had a harder time getting over a broken heart. I wanted to believe her, although her own experience said otherwise. It occurred to me men might move on quicker, but as soon as they settled in with someone, the grief seeped in. Gary had only dated his ex-girlfriend for six months. I looked past it, though, and told myself it was great that he could express raw emotion.

We went for a drink after dinner, but he didn't order any alcohol. He told me he didn't drink anymore.

Good, I thought. He had already taken care of this for himself. I felt reassured that I wasn't getting to know him as an addict.

He walked me to my car, and we made arrangements to go to the People's Fair in downtown Denver that weekend.

♌

The month of May yields unpredictable weather in Colorado. It can snow or rain or be uncomfortably warm. That Saturday downtown Denver reached the low nineties, even with an overcast haze around the mountains that shielded us from direct sunlight. I wore a sundress and sandals. Gary wore a broad brim floppy hat, shorts, sandals, and a T-shirt. I bought a broad-brim straw hat. It was hot.

We wandered around the Fair for a couple of hours and then went back to my apartment. Gary popped the trunk of his car in my parking lot and pulled out an overnight bag. I stared at it.

He smiled and said he had been a Boy Scout and had learned to arrive prepared.

I took his cue and smiled too.

I didn't know what I should feel or how I should react, so I went along with it. I didn't see any harm in his intentions, and the idea that he should have asked my permission only occurred to me vaguely. I didn't realize this had been omitted until I was staring at his overnight bag, and in that moment, I didn't have a voice for the flattery and anger that pirouetted in a corner of my mind. I wasn't prepared to express myself. I wasn't prepared to act. I felt stuck. The urgency of knowing I should say or do something could not melt my inability to speak. I retreated to the familiar territory of saying nothing.

Shame and self-loathing at having sex with someone I barely knew spawned a cord of anger that rippled through me. After Gary and I had had sex on my couch, first with a condom and then again without one, I asked him accusingly whether or not he had been tested for sexually transmitted diseases.

He pinched his fingers at the corners of his eyes as he closed them and explained in a miffed tone that as a result of having diabetes, he had to have his blood tested regularly. This sounded medically technical enough to be true; I was reassured. We had sex again and again throughout the night. He had a robust appetite; it matched mine. At age thirty-four, the tingling ecstasy of my sexual peak was coursing through me. I was sure I understood what an eighteen-year-old boy must feel like.

❧

One of the outcomes of my divorce was that Matt sold the house we had lived in. We split the net gain and I set my sights on buying a condo. I began looking in earnest six weeks after I met Gary. He suggested we go in on the condo together. I didn't say anything the first time he mentioned it. The second time, however, I told him that was not a good idea because we hadn't known each other long. He agreed and said it was mature not to rush into anything, though his downturned lips objected.

This was not the end of it. He enlisted my realtor to help him find a place of his own. I didn't question him, but I didn't understand why he needed this. He seemed happy where he was, renting a 600-square-foot house from his good friends and business partners who owned the property adjacent to his. He had a tiny garden, and he was out in the country. Maybe he couldn't stand the thought of a single mother with a toddler getting her own place when he didn't have one.

His credit and income were checked. Immediately there was confusion over his being paid by his business partners and the amount he paid in rent to them. A flag went up about whether or not to consider his rent as income or a deduction. It was an under-the-table arrangement and I didn't really understand it. The short of it, however, was that it got in the way. There wasn't sufficient paperwork for the money people to make it right, so Gary appeared to be high risk. He wouldn't be eligible for a loan without having a cosigner. I was afraid he might enlist me, so I asked preemptively about his brother or mother.

He dismissed them and ranted on and on about never being able to get a place. The world was against him.

The emersion of the victim in him, again, made me cringe. I reminded myself about what I liked about him and how my life was better with him in it because he thought I was pretty, he was not afraid of commitment, and he liked to have sex. I decided that he would stop feeling sorry for himself if he hung around me long enough.

He talked of going in for a vasectomy and having surgery on his deviated septum during these weeks of my search for a new home. I told him a vasectomy would be a nice thing for me. I wasn't using birth control consistently; occasionally I inserted a diaphragm or cervical cap, but a bladder infection was usually quick to follow. To prevent this, I had to chase the use of these devices with unsweetened cranberry juice, which was very effective after two days but was also extremely bitter. Gary didn't like condoms because they "had no feeling."

I took to monitoring my cycle and hedging my bets on the most and least likely conception times. I also employed two unconventional methods as a back-up plan: high doses of Rutin, a derivative of Vitamin C, which was to be taken right after sex and a day or more in addition, or ginger root in hot water a couple of days before my cycle was supposed to start. I enjoyed gambling like this at first, but the charm wore off as the realization that, no matter who did what, a pregnancy would weigh like an anvil in my lap. He would be able to leave if he wanted, and I would be stuck deciding how to deal with the blessed circumstance.

Gary was twelve years older than I and felt he was too old to become a parent. Shane was three then; I didn't want another dependent human, either. Besides, Gary wasn't exactly earning gold stars in his ability to interact with Shane.

I was taking evening meditation classes at the time and occasionally needed a babysitter. Gary offered to do this, which I appreciated, though my acceptance of his offer was not without reservations. Gary didn't have much experience with small children. His business partner had children around Shane's age, but Gary didn't watch them that often. There was also the general discomfort I had with leaving Shane with someone else, period. The fear that flashed to the surface always had to do with "what-if" scenarios. Gary was a sincere guy with good intentions, however, and Shane was a fairly easy child to interact with, so some of my fears were allayed.

The first night that I left Shane with Gary, though, Gary made himself comfortable in the living room while Shane was in the kitchen. I had to tell Gary to sit and play with him. When I got home that evening, Gary was back in the living room with the TV on and Shane was sitting nearby, disengaged and quiet.

"Were you watching TV the whole time?" I asked.

"No. No. Just turned it on."

I didn't believe him. He was engrossed in a sitcom he had been watching for a while.

I hated TV and didn't want Shane watching too much of it. I said nothing to Gary, though, mostly because Shane was sitting right there. I weighed my options. Two hours every once in while was not that much time, and I really enjoyed learning to meditate. Shane wasn't being harmed, but he didn't seem to like Gary very much either.

Gary's reminiscence of his own boyhood was provoked as he and Shane spent time together. Once, after they had been tossing a ball back and forth, Gary told me with tears in his eyes that his dad had never played catch with him. I listened, but there was nothing more to it. He was forty-eight and this still made him sappy? Why was he hanging on to this? I wanted something in his life to not be an open wound.

Talk of the vasectomy never materialized into action. The surgery on his deviated septum, however, was going to be scheduled after peak season in lawn care: December or January. I committed to helping him when the time came, but six months into our future was beginning to feel like ten years away.

My realtor landed me a sweet deal with a condo. The owners wanted to get out from under renting it. Their current tenants, two men in their early twenties, had trashed the place. They were willing to lop off $11,000 on the asking price or include that and have it fixed up to my liking. It didn't take long for me to do the math: I was going to be teaching six classes that would chisel exhaustion into my regimen for fifteen weeks—Monday from 6:00–8:45 p.m., a Tuesday morning class (8:30 a.m.), a huge six-hour break, and then three classes starting at 4:00 p.m. and going all the way until 9:45 p.m., Thursdays same thing, and then Saturday morning. It was worth the eleven grand to pick out new carpet, countertops, sinks, tile, and paint and have someone else take care of the installation for me. I had absolutely no curiosity about how to accomplish these projects. Besides, some things should not be complicated by having the incompetent toil with them.

It took only a brief amount of time to choose my colors. I went with a light gray carpet and extra thick pad, gray linoleum for the bathroom and kitchen, speckled counters (beige, peach, gray), off-white paint, and cream-colored sinks. I had moments of exhilaration while flipping through the palettes and samples. Never had anything, any place been completely my own. I wouldn't have to jockey for, argue over, or negotiate these 1,000 square feet. I relished my anticipation and excitement silently. I didn't want to rub it in that I was getting a place when Gary couldn't. I also didn't want him throwing water on my little flame of happiness.

I moved in the weekend before classes started.

Gary enlisted one of his workers, Tyler, and I had asked an acquaintance, Ron, who I knew from a church singles group, to help me move. Gary had a trailer that he hooked up to his truck, and Steve and I had exchanged vehicles, so I could use his truck, too, though he didn't help with the move himself because his shoulders had rotator cuff inflammation.

Gary, Tyler, Ron, and I managed to get everything from Lakewood to Southwest Denver in one trip. The move took the better part of the day and was capped off by moving my sofa bed. It had been put on the truck first so naturally it was last to go in, an unfortunate reality. A quick analysis unveiled that the bed would not disassemble from the sofa. So, minus the cushions, which were removable, the whole thing had to go up six flights of stairs, around three railings, and through my front door.

Watching the guys drip and heave as they brought up the sofa bed was one thing. Seeing it angled through the narrow doorway was another. It got stuck. They shimmied it back out and tried again. The front and screen door were removed. The light above the foyer was taken out. Another friend had shown up for this endeavor, so there were two men on either side of my couch, and yet none of them could get it through. I had visions of the sofa permanently sandwiched in the doorway. I sat in the living room quietly wishing they would pitch the thing over the edge down to the ground.

Finally, with all possible obstacles unburdened, they shoved the sofa bed inside. It ended up wounded and marred, scratches and white paint all over the wood frame. But I pretended everything looked fine. I couldn't complain, not after watching four men throw their backs into getting it inside on my behalf.

Gary left late that afternoon to drop off Tyler. Before he returned, Steve arrived to retrieve his truck and return my car.

I let Steve in and we walked out to the patio, which overlooked the street below. We leaned on the rail, and he mentioned that I should get chicken wire because the rail had gaps that Shane could easily squeeze through. I nodded, making a mental note to do that right away. I didn't like anyone telling me what to do, even if they had good reason, but I didn't resist this piece of advice. It was bad enough that I had broken up Shane's sense of family; it would be much, much worse if I were cavalier in my mothering and neglected to attend to something as simple as securing the patio so he wouldn't fall three floors below.

I wanted to stand closer to Steve. I felt reassured by his presence, like I had done a good thing and had nothing to be ashamed of for separating myself farther away physically from Matt. I no longer lived around the corner from him but rather twenty minutes away, in Southwest Denver. A small wrinkle in co-parenting Shane. Matt wasn't happy about this commute or having to calculate a mid-way point. I had to push hard against any trickling of guilt seeping in.

When Steve asked how the move went, I became animated and at ease, regaling him with the best the move had to offer: the drama of birthing the couch through the front door.

His eyes danced, delighted. He leaned toward me with one leg crossed over the other. His black T-shirt was neatly tucked into his jeans and he smelled like incense and herbal shampoo. I smelled like sweat and suddenly felt self-conscious. I stepped back a little and hoped his own fresh scents would mask mine.

"I'm sorry I couldn't help more," he said. "My shoulders would be talking to me now if I had, though. Did you have any trouble with the truck?"

"No, it was fine," I said, smiling. "Just took a little getting used to because it was so big."

We continued to chat with an effortless banter until Gary returned. When he did, he parked along the curb and craned his neck in our direction, glaring.

"Somebody looks pissed," Steve said, smiling.

I waved, pretending I didn't know he was upset that there was another man on my patio, a handsome man, looking happy to be there.

Gary stomped his feet on nearly all of the twenty-one steps up to my condo. I pretended I didn't notice this either.

Steve clued in immediately and headed to the door. As Gary walked in, Steve angled around him, barely allowing me to introduce them and stuck out his hand.

Gary shook Steve's hand reluctantly, keeping his pitted brown eyes on me, accusing. He stepped farther into the condo, and I thanked Steve again for use of his truck. Steve mouthed the words, "Call me," through the glass of the outer door. I smiled and mouthed back that I would.

"What was going on up here?" Gary asked.

"Nothing," I said. "He was just here to pick up his truck. He offered to come over to bring me back my car."

"Why did he have to come in?"

"Steve and I are just friends," I said firmly. "We were just catching up a little."

Gary looked pitiful as he donned his best puppy-dog sad eyes.

My face froze into neutral. I didn't want to show him how disgusted I was with his insecurity.

❧

As all the excitement and anticipation of settling into my new place petered out, I unpacked things as I needed to use them and tried to adjust to my horrid teaching schedule. When I wasn't riffling through boxes, teaching or grading papers, spending time with Shane, or attending a meditation class, I was with Gary. I never allowed him to sleep over when I had Shane and I never slept over at his place with Shane, but my parenting schedule changed up frequently, and as result I was with Gary three to four nights a week.

The only writing I was doing was feedback on students' papers. I needed to secure my emotional life, and until that felt okay, I couldn't bring myself to the page. I wrote with my students during free writing sessions, but these were more like Dear Diary entries. I had begun a novel but fought myself to find words, let alone believe in its purpose. I told myself I had been through a lot; I couldn't write because I was still feeling the after-shocks of the affair, separation, divorce, caring for my young son, and moving. Each of these was an item in a list of excuses, and I found it hard to forgive myself. A writer writes.

I wanted Gary to take meditation classes with me. He believed himself to have premonitions, so why couldn't he be more open-minded and curious? I wanted to be able to talk to him about what it was like to examine myself, acknowledge an area of vulnerability, and identify how to overcome it. I was learning so much about decisions, my family, and my ex-husband. I was peeling back layers of my life and understanding that I had made choices. I didn't need to succumb to anyone else's way of thinking. I could have my own ideas and not feel guilty about executing them. I was afraid that if he didn't come along with me that I was going to outgrow him. It had happened to quite a few people I knew in my classes. There was a tendency to get fixated on what you could metamorphose, and if the people in your life couldn't keep up with your transformation and greater understanding of yourself, you sometimes left them behind.

I talked to Gary about my fear. He balked; he didn't want that to happen. I said that I didn't either, but I felt uncertain. I couldn't help seeing who and where he really was as opposed to how I wanted him to be.

Gary didn't read books, and this bothered me as well. When we spent the night together, I read out loud occasionally, and I invited him to share this with me. "I like it when you do it better," he always said. He had no appreciation for the written word. I wondered sometimes if he really cared about *anything* besides the idea of ever-lasting love, his cat, and his garden.

The negatives against Gary were stacking up. He complained all of the time about his business partners, his work, aggressive drivers, his parents, his brother, his ex-wife, his ex-girlfriend, his health. I wondered if he complained about me when I wasn't around. He mentioned once that there were probably things about him that bothered me that I never told him. I said, "Sure," but it only made me suspicious about that checklist in his head about me. I wondered, too, if he was collecting misgivings like slingshot rocks, waiting for an opportunity to hurl them all back at me.

One night when I was at his place and couldn't sleep because he was snoring, I left the bedroom and went downstairs to the living room. I tried to sleep on the couch, but the whir of the ceiling fan annoyed me, and the blankets smelled like cat pee. Gary never noticed that his house smelled awful from the litter box because of his sinus trouble and deviated septum.

His checkbook was on the coffee table. I flipped through it.

Many of the items were for groceries and gas, but one, from just a few days earlier, was for liquor. Gary had told me he'd been sober for over two years.

I got up and began opening all of his cupboards and drawers. I was not quiet about it. A few minutes later, he called down to me and asked what I was doing.

"Looking for booze!" I yelled. "You wrote liquor in your checkbook!"

He came downstairs, rubbing his eyes. "I bought that for the guys after work because they had done a good job that day."

I didn't believe him.

"Come back to bed," he pleaded.

I acquiesced. I knew I would sleep better next to him than by myself on the smelly couch. I suspected he'd lied about when he had quit drinking, but I wasn't going to take it up with him right then. Shielded behind a sense of propriety and this not being my business, I waited for a more developed story of Gary quitting drinking to reveal itself.

The relationship's big, unblinking eyes stared at me. I could not convince myself any longer that this was simply casual. Gary had been entwining me for months in a sticky string intending to keep me near him, and he had succeeded. He would ask me if I was paying attention when we went clothes shopping. Could I remember his sizes? The same was true for groceries. Did I remember what he was allergic to? He'd even talked me into joining his cell phone plan.

The thickening sense of responsibility I felt for Gary and our relationship pronounced itself more when we went out to dinner or other social functions with his business partners, their kids, and Shane. The pretense of normalcy and community with people I couldn't relate to made me wish I was on another planet. When Gary wondered aloud if the boys would go to the same high school and play sports together, I squirmed.

On the phone after my teaching day had finally ended, he said, "Why don't you come on home?" He meant his place. I winced. He told me his mother would like me. He talked not so subtly of buying me a ring.

I didn't ever want to feel stuck again and being in a relationship didn't equate to safety. Was Gary going to be enough for me? I had learned that much from being married to Matt: no matter who I was with, I needed to accept him as he was and hope that we could learn how to evolve together. I was beginning to believe I wasn't suited for marriage. I liked having time to myself, and the thought of having someone around all the time made me uneasy. Could I strike a balance between having time to myself and being with someone else?

Halloween was approaching, and I set my heart on going to an annual dance that was sponsored by my church and a few singles organizations in Denver. It was a huge event. I thought it would be a great outing for us. I would get to see people I hadn't seen in a while because I had been spending all of my free time with Gary, and I would get to observe how he fared meeting my acquaintances. I needed a break from our island of two.

I had had no time to think of a costume until the very last minute, but I was determined to make sure it was like no other. I had plenty of cardboard lying around from my recent move, and I had enough clothes to dress in all black. I made a sandwich board and drew a treble and bass clef, and the notes to form a G chord, on it.

Gary arrived a couple of hours before it was time to go with his costume: a simple eye mask. I was disappointed that he hadn't tried to be a bit more creative, but I said nothing. Gary sat on the floor, propped against the couch.

"How are you?" I asked.

He sighed. "I'm really feeling the SAD today." He meant seasonal affective disorder.

I rolled my eyes and turned back to my project.

"You hurt my feelings just now."

"It just seems that you're always sad about something," I said. "It seems like the only thing you're ever happy about is me."

"I always get this way when it's cloudy out," he said, his shoulders slumped. "You hurt my feelings when you acted like you didn't care."

"Well . . ." I stopped.

We had reached a point in our relationship where he felt okay about baring all. He was willing to show me his warts and bruises. Matt had never shared very many true feelings with me. He made fun of anything that made him uncomfortable. I felt unprepared to be Gary's ear, sleeve, and shoulder. I didn't want to learn, either. Did I need to hear about every emotional moment?

"I'm sorry," I said—but I wasn't. A small fantasy flickered that perhaps he would be angry enough to go home and I would get to go to the dance alone.

The party took place in a large, multi-purpose room at a recreation center in Wheat Ridge. The room was appropriately dimmed. The eighty or more people milling about showcased an array of risk, imagination, or lack thereof. More men than women had opted out of wearing a disguise altogether. Most common costume among the women: the sexy witch, replete with mesh spider stockings, stiletto heels, a tight, short skirt, a low-cut blouse, gobs of makeup, and the trademark pointed hat. Some had encumbered themselves with a broom.

Gary and I looked for a table as soon as we made it in. He sat down, and I exchanged one of my drink tickets for a cup of cheap wine. I brought Gary a Coke.

I asked him if he wanted to dance and he said, "No." He only danced when he was drunk, and he didn't drink anymore.

"Don't you want to try it?" I asked. "Most of these people don't know what they're doing either."

He shook his head.

I got up and scanned the room. I walked to the other side, where the pizza and drinks were. I looked for familiar faces. Strangers asked me what I was.

"A G chord," I said.

Blank expressions and then weak nods, sometimes a doubtful smile, then a quick exit.

I wondered if my treble and bass clef were drawn incorrectly. Maybe most people didn't know how to read music— or maybe they thought this was a ridiculous costume, not even clever, just downright stupid. A G chord? Why a G chord? It didn't compute. I was no stranger to the incomprehensible costume—when I was with Matt, I had once gone to a Halloween party as an address label—but it had been a while since my handiwork had seen the light of day.

I continued to wander around the room. Surely there would be someone I could dance with, who could be fun enough for a few minutes?

One man tapped me on the shoulder and asked me if I was a G string.

I laughed with him and lingered a bit.

I remembered, though Russ had obviously forgotten, that we had talked on the phone after meeting at a singles game night back in April, before I met Gary. Russ had never called again, presumably because I was a single mother of a three-year-old. I remembered how he had failed to conceal being startled at realizing this. A divorced woman in her mid-thirties with no children *was* too good to be true. Russ epitomized the typical man at this dance: early to mid-fifties, kids out of the house, worried about his 401k, looking for a hassle-free fuck buddy.

I liked older men; I couldn't help myself. I had been introduced to men my own age and found them to be about ten years behind me. If they hadn't already been married and procreated, that's what they wanted, and I was about 80 percent sure that I didn't want to be in the baby-making market anymore. Many of them were self-centered and still expected privileges to be bestowed upon them because they were young and male. An older man, in contrast, had been around long enough to know that he wasn't always going to get his way. Egoism had been winnowed, and in its stead, humility peeked and nudged itself to the surface.

I meandered back to where I'd left Gary. He was moping over a bowl of pretzels and M&Ms. I asked him again if he wanted to dance, and he said they weren't playing the right songs. I left again.

I stayed away as long as I could.

A younger guy with long hair, clearly drunk, called me over. He slurred that he was a guitarist. My costume was "awesome." He slumped into a woman I assumed he had come with.

A brief longing flashed. He was younger than Gary, and he recognized my G chord. He was also not alone.

I had been recognized, though, and this was some consolation. Maybe I wanted to be with an artist or musician. Did I? I was playing the part of committed girlfriend with Gary but privately keeping my options open. I didn't want to be alone, and I didn't want to commit to anyone. I had a sinking feeling that this polarity was going to unzip me, and anticipating when that might happen wasn't going to soften the blow.

Gary's mother wore a polyester dress with thick hose. She stood four feet ten inches and had rounded shoulders. Her coiffed, jet black hair did not elevate her more than an inch. Her slight frame shuffled in low, patent leather pumps from her kitchen to the living room. Photos of Gary's brother and his family hung in her hallway. No photos of Gary hung or sat anywhere.

We stayed in the guest room at the garden level of her assisted living facility. Gary said she would love me because she had been a teacher and I was a teacher. He so desperately wanted to please her and for once be the favored one. His younger brother, Donald, had outshone him in every way: marriage, children, and money. I was the linchpin that was going to finally make his mother's eyes sparkle.

I counted the number of meals I would have to spend with Gary's mother, father and stepmother, and his cousin on Thanksgiving Day. The holiday was the reason for our visit to San Antonio. The expectation and attention on me buckled my shoulders.

I was the designated driver on Thanksgiving. Gary was afraid of speeding vehicles on the highway. His mother and her friend were too old to drive. But I did not know the road or the car, and I was overwhelmed.

"Turn here, turn here!" they yelled in a cacophony of voices.

I swerved onto the exit ramp between the construction cones. As I straightened out the wheel, I checked the rearview mirror. Gary's petite mother slid shoulder first into the door of the backseat. Her best friend, sandwiched in the middle—a woman two and a half times larger than Gary's mother—slid into her.

I checked the mirror, again. The women straightened themselves. Gary's mother put her purse back on her lap. She patted her curled hair and said nothing.

What did they expect? I wondered. I wanted someone to forgive me. Gary could only bring himself to look sideways at me while he sucked on a cigarette in the parking lot outside our room after we'd dropped everyone else off. I stared at him, wondering at the miracle of having gotten him on the plane, since he was afraid of flying, too.

The evening before we left, I had trouble making love with him. The air seemed to be getting thinner, the walls and ceiling closer.

I didn't know what to do. My fear of commitment was butting heads with my fear of disappointing someone who cared for me. His mother and father liked me. He hadn't introduced a girlfriend to his parents in a few years, and meeting the family was the first step toward becoming part of it. They were well-meaning people, and this thickened my guilt. This was serious. I had no doubt he would soon ask me to marry him, maybe even as a Christmas present.

I wanted out, but I felt it was important to wear a façade until the lines of confusion stopped squiggling and a flat, clear path presented itself.

Two weeks before I left for Texas, I had stopped by Steve's apartment for a visit. He'd fixed me a cup of tea, and we sat at his kitchen table.

"How's school going?" he asked.

"Fine. I'll be glad when the semester's over. I'll never do that again: Monday night, Tuesday all day, Thursday, and Saturday morning."

Steve winced. "You make busy people look slow."

I laughed. He understood. "How were the vegetables I gave you?" I had brought a sack full of the excesses from Gary's garden a few weeks before.

"I used a couple of the zucchinis, but I had a hard time using the rest because of who they came from. Those got tossed." Steve shook his head and smiled.

I laughed. "You could have made zucchini bread!"

Good. He was envious of Gary. That meant I still mattered to him. I left feeling buoyed.

I was special to Gary but that didn't matter to me as much as it should, and I was beginning to get impatient with myself for not speaking or acting on my own behalf. Why didn't I say anything and why did I feel obligated to him? Because he loved me?

I had not been choosy. We were together because he had met my minimum requirements: he'd been available, and I'd been afraid of being alone.

The end of my horrific semester was bookended with a knock-down, drag-out sinus infection. I made it to the last week and then my body revolted.

It was a Saturday, and my doctor's office was open in the morning. I needed a prescription, fast. I called Gary and he asked to accompany me. I waited for him. He made me late. On the way, he made a joke about my complaint that I would probably get a yeast infection as a result of taking the antibiotic. I wanted to kick him out of my car.

The office manager at the doctor's office gave me the script from her car before she peeled out of the parking lot.

When we got back to my place, Gary complained to me that I was not the same "these days"—that he wanted the old Jane back.

I didn't want to talk about our relationship.

"I want to die right now," I said. "I am miserable. I am exhausted from teaching six classes for sixteen weeks. I need a break. I'm sick."

He pressed on for a while. When I gave him nothing satisfactory in response, he asked, "Do you want me to leave?"

"Yes," I said firmly.

When the medicine kicked in a few days later, I felt

clearer, capable of acting on my own behalf. I sat at my computer and wrote Gary a letter that explained that my love for him was not as strong as his was for me. I went on for a page and a half, double-spaced, attempting to be gentle but direct. I dropped it off at his house, along with the Christmas presents I had been collecting for him over the previous couple of weeks.

He called as soon as he retrieved everything.

"But I love you. I was going to marry you."

"I know," I said. "I just don't love you in the same way."

"Is there someone else?"

"No," I said, and I was telling the truth—kind of. I certainly wanted to be with Steve again.

"Would you consider counseling?" he asked, sounding forlorn. "What we have together is great. You want to throw that away?"

"I need to see other people," I said. "I had just gotten divorced when we met."

"Dating is nothing but a bunch of heartache and sour grapes. I've been dating for thirteen years. You don't need to go through all of that . . . There's nothing I can do to change your mind?"

I felt bad, but I held my ground. "No, uh . . . no."

"Well. I guess that's it, then. There's another one that got away . . ." He sighed. "I want to give you your Christmas presents and your things that are here. I got you that cabinet you wanted for your bathroom, and I got things for Shane, too. Is it all right if I come over?"

We met the following week. He gave me my things and installed the bathroom cabinet. And when January came, I followed through with my commitment to be with him during his nose surgery. I brought him home from the hospital and sat with him while the anesthesia wore off. Doctor's orders were that an adult should be with him for up to twenty-four hours post-op. We had nothing to talk about, so we watched TV.

After a few hours of this, bored and antsy, I asked Gary if he judged me for having an affair before my marriage ended.

"Well, I don't think it was a good idea."

I wanted to hit him. How dare he judge me? He was the one who had lied to me: I had learned a few weeks before Christmas that he had actually quit drinking just one week before we started dating. After he got my call, he'd decided to never drink again. When he came clean about this, he had also confided in me that he "hadn't needed" therapy since he had been dating me.

A confidante and healer was not what I wanted to be in a relationship. I had beaten my head against a wall several times to generate an adhesive for my marriage. It was time to be with someone who could take care of himself without clinging to me. Gary loved me because the "healer" vapors were still all around me.

These thoughts chased after each other as I sat there. I forced myself to calm down, telling myself he was still drugged from the surgery and I had asked for his judgment. Why did I need his approval? I couldn't answer that—not then. But I couldn't stand that I was sitting there, showing up to care for him when I didn't care. The contradiction was irreconcilable. It mattered that he had lied to me, but it mattered more that I had lied to myself. Why was what he or anyone else needed more important than what I needed?

$\mathcal{I}$ saw Gary at church two years later while I was standing at the single parents table for our annual fair. He had lost weight and dyed his hair. He had come with an acquaintance of mine and friend of his, Joy. She leaned in and told me he had called and wanted to go to church that morning but didn't want to go alone.

After some small talk, Gary bent over, brushed his hand over the top of his head, and said, "I colored my hair last night."

"I always liked the silver," I said.

He looked at me expectantly several times during our chat. It was as though his head was on a swivel, searching for a look of longing in my eyes. An "I'm sorry, Gary, let's try it again" look.

I made an effort to dull my expression. I did not want polite kindness to be misconstrued.

When I had nothing more to say, I walked away, knowing that he was watching me.

CHAPTER FOUR

Again

I didn't ever stop talking to Steve the whole time I knew Gary. We didn't get together much, but I talked to him on the phone when I wasn't with Gary—which was quite often, since I had 50 percent custody and Gary never spent the night when I had Shane with me. Steve made me feel heard, and I talked myself into believing that as long as I had him to talk to, I could do anything else.

"I imagined being with you while I was with him," I told him during one phone call. "That bed in the guest room of the assisted living place where Gary's mom lived was awful. I imagined your hands on me."

Steve laughed quietly. "That's not really fair, Jane."

"I know. But when we were together, it felt so great."

"You did that. You made it that way."

"You did too," I said. "I miss that."

"I do too," he said. "Maybe we could try again. We're great friends."

"I don't want to hurt you or make you uncomfortable. Can't we enjoy this part of being together?" I asked.

We got together a few days later and began again.

Seen, heard, loved, I felt complete and so happy. Steve and I talked every day and got together two to three times a week.

71

I was still meeting with a group for meditation and clair-voyance classes on Wednesdays. Steve never took any more classes beyond the initial one where we had met, but he was always curious and wanted to hear me talk about what we had done. He was highly intuitive and between the work he did as a medic in Vietnam and then as an EMT, he had years of experience with reading people and situations. I was fasci-nated by his stories of watching people "slip through the veil" as they died. He told me the story of a long-ago friend, Dan, who could shapeshift and pass through walls. I had never known anyone who had watched this happen. I never dis-missed anything. There was truth in all beliefs. All perceptions held a vibration of accuracy, some at a brighter resonance than others.

Steve told me that Dan once took him on a harrowing motorcycle ride where he tipped the bike so low on one side, he felt sure they were going to crash. Dan told him afterward that that was the closest he could get Steve to death, and if he really wanted to die he should do it on his own time. Dan was tired of hearing about Steve's anguish over what he'd seen in Vietnam. Dan moved away, and Steve called him a few years later but Dan made it clear he never wanted to hear from him again. Steve had quite a few stories like that—of people leaving and never wanting to speak to him again. I didn't feel that way. I couldn't get enough of how he made me feel. He reflected back the best of who I was and the woman I liked being. I couldn't ever imagine wanting to leave him.

$\mathcal{I}$ called Steve when I got home from meditation. We ban-died about in our normal, easy-going flow of how we were and what was new.

"How was class?" he asked.

"Good. In the line reading, Pauline saw a picture of me when I was three and I felt abandoned."

"Do you remember that?"

"I didn't at first. As I was driving home, I did. Funny what you remember." Reflexively, I waited to see if he would interrupt. I felt slow to continue when I told a story, and most of the time whoever I was talking to took that as an invitation to speak. He didn't.

"My mom's red face as she yanked a white turtleneck over her head. She was mad and crying. She had taken her glasses off quickly and held them out while she pushed her head through and pulled the shirt down over her bra. It was late fall, I think. She already had her pants on. Rich and Melanie were there. They had to have been seven and eight. They were in their pajamas, crying, pawing at Mom, pleading with her to stay.

"'I'm going to leave and never come back! That's what you want? See how you do, then!' she yelled at Dad, who sat with legs crossed on the couch, eyes closed, and his fist punched into the jowls of his cheeks.

"'Don't go, Mom. Please. Don't go,' they cried."

Steve breathed quietly, listening.

"I stood a few feet away, watching. Frozen. I don't remember crying or joining my brother and sister in their protests. I remember thinking I did not want her to leave us alone with him. Not then. She did everything for us. Dad wouldn't know what to do. He had never taken care of us. Later, I wished she had left him. I wished she had risked that.

"I had heard them fight before. That felt familiar. But Mom threatening to leave and actually getting dressed by the door frightened me. I hoped she wouldn't go. Maybe I started to cry then, too. I don't remember anyone saying anything to me. It was over after five minutes. Mom told us to go back to bed. We did.

"They had other fights, too, and sometimes Mom would drive off to a parking lot or the grocery store and she'd sit there, waiting. She told me when I was older that that's where she'd go. Sometimes someone would ask her if she was all right. She always said, 'Yes.'"

"Wow, Jane. Thank you for sharing that with me."

"Sure. Well, yeah."

"How do you feel now?" Steve asked.

"I don't know. It happened. I can't believe I forgot that . . .

Validated? Funny how it all came back, like it had just happened."

"You were little . . . Maybe you do understand me. Maybe your trauma is not that much different than mine."

"Hmm. Maybe."

I wanted him to tell me how our stories matched in his mind, but I didn't want to ask. I needed to let my story be mine and not entangled in his. I felt bowled over, numb, with a creeping sensation of wishing I had kept it to myself. I felt exposed, as though a heavy curtain had been drawn back and I had been disrobing behind it. Putting words to it felt wrong and yet inevitable. I didn't know where it would lead. I wanted to take it back and pretend I didn't know. I couldn't think. It was too late: I had taken that little movie inside my head and put it in someone else's now. That made it real. And now I would have to do something with it. Or I could run into the arms of my relationship, pretending it didn't matter.

On Valentine's Day, Steve's largesse came to bear full throttle with gift giving. When I arrived at his place for dinner that evening, I found pink, red, and white packages with satin bows and sheer ribbons laced and draped over the five-foot-long table top that covered his fish tank.

I was alarmed and embarrassed. Who was all of this for? Was some of it for someone else?

Steve laughed. "Of course not," he said. "It's all for you."

It took me over an hour to open everything. Many of the boxes contained brassieres and panties in an array of colors: pink, blue, black, and white. There were G-strings, a sleeveless one-piece that opened below like a baby's onesie, and tan and black, thigh-high floral and mesh hose. I was overwhelmed. I treated everything as though it might turn to dust in my hands if I held it too long.

There were soaps, lotions, earrings, and perfume, too. I felt ridiculous opening box after box. It took him less than five minutes to open what I had given him: chocolates and a cherry pie. In his card, I referred to him as "My Betrothed."

"You know that's a term for people who are engaged, right?" he said.

"Oh," I said. "I thought it was a shmancy 'beloved.'"

"Well. It's specific to intention to marry."

I could sense him recoiling, and saw the brewing of an imminent retreat. I said nothing more about it, continued opening my gifts, and hoped that my misstep would not stencil itself indelibly on his brain.

My favorite gift was an eleven-by-fourteen-inch hand-made card with tiny roses glued in the four corners. He had hand-copied "The Lovers" by Kahlil Gibran. On the back-side of the card, he had glued a photo of himself from when he was seven and written an insignia imitating the mainstream greeting card manufacturers. His handwriting was beautiful. I was elated.

The last gift was in a small box. It was a red-and-gold-plated, heart-shaped container. Something rattled around inside.

"Open it," Steve said, grinning.

The blue sapphire was the primary stone and three diamonds were mounted on either side of it. The ring itself was white gold. It slipped around my finger; the stones jutted toward the floor.

Steve explained that he just wanted to give me the ring; it didn't mean what that usually meant. I felt relieved but confused. Was I inside his heart or not? Why had he given me so many gifts? It was way too out of balance to believe.

I couldn't reconcile his gift of the ring, and its tradition-ally accepted symbol of longevity, with his statement that it did not mean this. That befuddled me. I couldn't keep track of the number and ways Steve did this on a regular basis, but I was learning to be wary of any sign of commitment, be-cause a retraction and reversal always nipped at its heels in short order.

I didn't like the ring—it was too big and ugly. I mentioned my issue with its size, and Steve promised to go with me to pick out a ring I liked. I found a gold band with tiny diamonds along its edges all the way around, but Steve just told the jeweler we would think about it.

He had a vacant look in his eyes and kept his distance as we walked out to the parking lot.

"I don't need a ring," I said gingerly.

He said nothing. And nothing much more was said about it until months later, when Steve finally told me, "I wanted to lock this down. I told myself, this is a good thing. You got to keep her. Just like when I had my friends over right away to meet you. I wanted it to be solid."

I watched him look at the wall behind me as he talked. I wondered if he was going to ask me to marry him—for real this time. What would I say? I was flattered that he still thought about making a commitment to me in a more public way. But as quickly as these thoughts came in, I swept them out to shield myself from any further letdown. I was beginning to sense the outline of the tidal wave I was riding before I became capsized by its tumult. It frightened me, so I pretended not to see it.

I told him he liked to give on his terms only. I laughed as I told him, which took the edge off his angry surprise.

"Hrumph," he said. Then, "What?"

I panicked and assembled my words carefully, wondering if how I responded to this would be catalogued away and used as a reason for him to distance himself from me indefinitely. I laughed a little more and said, "You know. I think it's just easier for you to give when you want to. Maybe it makes you feel like you have to follow someone else's rules when they suggest something, or it makes you feel obligated if someone gives you something."

"I've always had trouble receiving," he said. "I don't deserve it."

CHAPTER FIVE

One-Date Wonders

Steve announced he was departing for Arizona and would not be taking me with him. It was only supposed to be a vacation with his friend Howard, but it felt permanent, and the wound was personal. I knew how much he loved the desert, and I felt pushed away from sharing that with him. Heartbroken at being thwarted, again, I went for broke. I would figure out what I liked and what I didn't; it would be like trying on clothes. No one would be excluded, and everyone would be considered. When my heart deflated, I'd contact someone new. It would be easy. I would never need to feel abandoned. I dreamed of meeting all of them, falling in love with one, and having it work out. I would be happy, and the rest of my life could continue.

I was sure I was going to marry the first man I met online. His accomplishments charmed me. A few days before our dinner meeting, he sent me photographs of new cherry blossoms against a royal blue sky. The angle was proportionate and artistic. He played the violin, too—in an orchestra, though it wasn't the Colorado Symphony.

Like a gentleman, John met me in the parking lot of the restaurant I had suggested— Vietnamese, my comfort food.

John was slight. He wore a white button-down shirt with

no T-shirt underneath. His hair was longish and curly. I liked this. His hands were clammy, cold. I would have to work at not staring at his nose. It was enormous—"the size of Rhode Island," I later told a friend. He couldn't help it. Would I hold this against him? I challenged myself to look past it, to focus on his hair or eyes.

We sat at a booth, and he handed me a CD of his orchestra's music. I thanked him but thought that, though sweet, it was odd.

He asked if I had eaten there before and I said, "Yes. I haven't had anything I haven't liked."

"I haven't been here for five years," he offered.

That's the last clear idea I remember coming from his mouth. Between the ordering of the food and the arrival of appetizers and soup, John talked nonstop. I had never sat across from someone and listened to them speak that fast and succinctly. I watched his mouth, hands, and arms as they flapped and flailed. He didn't do anything offensive. He didn't talk with food in his mouth. He used his napkin, and he asked me about my writing and my novel—but I only got out approximately seven words before he told me that his father had been an author of forty-one books and added associative details that I quickly stopped trying to track.

Toward the end of the meal, I separated my dewy skirt from the vinyl seat and rose to go to the bathroom. The quiet ballooned around me, but his voice ricocheted between my ears. The sound of peeing seemed too loud. I took my time washing my hands.

Back at the table, I asked John if he would like to share the tab and he brushed it away with an announcement that he had made $5,000 that day with a contract through his architecture firm.

I stuck out my hand to shake his, and he leaned in for a hug. Our shoulders barely touched; our arms formed a square.

I got in my car, happy to go home alone. It was the first time I'd ever appreciated the luxury of solitude in the absence of a man's company. I felt relieved—and guilty for feeling relieved. Wasn't I supposed to feel empty without a companion? I didn't, but I didn't feel comfortable admitting that to myself either.

An hour after John and I parted company, I realized I'd left his CD next to where I sat. I did not go back for it.

I wrote him an email the next day telling him that I felt we processed things differently and I was overwhelmed by our meeting, but I would still like to stay in touch. (I had to say that, didn't I?)

He wrote that lunch would be fine, sometime.

As a consolation for not inviting me to go with him to Arizona, Steve gave me money to go away on my own. He wanted me to have a good time even though we were going on separate vacations. I went to Georgetown with the intention of writing. I brought my novel with me but found myself so distracted with anger at Steve, I couldn't write. When a couple checked in next door and began fucking almost immediately, my insult gaped. The woman was loud and congratulatory toward "her man" as he banged her against the wall. I happened to be on the phone with Steve when this was going on, and I told him I was going to leave as soon as we got off the phone. He told me to be careful driving down the hill. "Don't drive too fast," he said. I hated him for giving a damn from six hundred miles away.

I felt panicked when I returned home, and I wrote John an email. Maybe I had judged him too soon. But when I vented to him about my Georgetown experience over email, his response was dispassionate. I felt like I had just been shoved off his assembly line of options.

When I started corresponding with someone else, I tried to forget about John. Several months later, though, he passed me as I walked downstairs on my way to a concert at Boettcher Hall. A woman in a white satin ballroom gown trailed behind him. Her face creased with anguish. She held her shoes. He had grown his hair out some and it flopped as he turned to snap at her. She ran a bit toward him. He threw a hand up and then down as though to shove her back.

It made me feel a bit better to see John uncomfortable

and unkind. He had done me a favor. His dismissal when I felt panicked didn't seem so miserly now. Had things gone differently, I might have been the one trying to keep up with him, carrying my shoes.

My sister stopped me when I had hardly begun and asked if she would have to remember his name.

"Kevin," I said. "Well, maybe. I had a good time. We laughed a lot."

I would write him an email late the next day and tell him that I enjoyed our dinner. He would write back and tell me there was no chemistry. I remembered noticing when I had gotten home from our date that a patch of skin above my chin was flaky and white. Was this the cause for his "no chemistry" comment? Because I didn't put enough lotion on after I got out of the shower? Had he not apologized for having to mop his bald forehead several times throughout dinner because he said he was nervous? What was I failing to understand? We'd laughed and made great conversation. And he'd paid for the meal—a good sign in these modern-time, split-it-down-the-middle first meetings.

I told a friend a few days later, "Maybe he wanted me to be taller. Or blond."

"Or to have a bigger nose and smaller breasts," my friend chimed in.

I calculated our height difference: he was six one or so and I was a mere five four. "I bet he met somebody else and pulled out that 'no chemistry' crap to get rid of me."

My friend laughed, but I felt the beginning of a shovel digging into my chest. I doubted my laughter, and his smile. Worse, he had not been the first to rebuff my interest. Kevin had fallen somewhere in the middle of this revolving door of online dating, and my enthusiasm for it was beginning to falter.

Within a few days of my date with Kevin, I agreed to meet Craig for dinner.

He worked as a newspaper photographer. The emails I received from him were thoughtful and enthusiastic. He described having spent the day outside and how perfect it had been. I saw the light glinting in jeweled segments through branches as he walked happily in wonder. He wanted to know all about me and mused whether or not I had the type of brunette hair that was highlighted with gold and red and drove him crazy. Perhaps chemistry would be a given this time since I donned a ready-made, natural feature.

He greeted me outside the restaurant. Curly rumples of brown hair sprang out from above his ears, squished indelicately beneath his baseball cap. He walked in an unassuming C shape, with one hand stuffed in his blue jeans. I wondered if he was too warm wearing a long-sleeve T-shirt—the sun seared us even in the early evening hour—but he seemed comfortable enough. His clothing said everything: no expectations.

Making him desire me was a bit of a challenge. Could I inspire a sparkle in his eye and get him to stand straight? He was five foot eight but hunched over enough that he seemed closer to five foot six—not tall enough for my taste, though I tried not to judge him for something he couldn't control. I wondered if the hat was going to come off during dinner.

Conversation was light and covered the usual things: how many kids, how often we saw them, how long divorced, and what kind of relationship we wanted with the other parent. These were my usual questions. I never wanted to waste time wondering what was what and who was where. It amazed me when I talked to other girlfriends about their suitors and they didn't know how long the guy had been divorced even after seeing him for a few weeks. "It hasn't come up," they would confide. "Why don't you ask?" I would always probe. "That affects everything. If he's newly divorced, you know he's needy and probably dating a lot. But if he's been through all that then he's more ready, choosy."

It didn't seem to matter to them like it did to me. It

helped me if I could see all the cards on the table. I was beginning to understand, though, that readiness was cloaked in a mirage of contingencies. The guy could be three years out from his divorce and say he was ready, but still speak with venom about his former partner. And what did this belief about his readiness say about me? How ready was I?

Craig informed me that he had two children—a daughter from a first marriage, who was in her late teens, and a boy from the second marriage. I asked how old his son was, a bubble beginning to balloon with a fantasy of our boys playing together.

"He's nine." He looked away from me. "He requires a lot of care. He's a quadriplegic."

"Oh." I nodded.

"So. We share. His mother and I take turns taking care of him."

"That must be hard," I said. "Do you get along with her?"

He shook his head no and looked exasperated. "Sometimes I just have to tell her, I'll call you back, okay? I can't do that right now! It's okay, though. Most of the time we get along fine."

Would I help him with his son? Would he expect me to?

We were about halfway through our meal when he said, "Oh. I know. I wanted to ask you what clairvoyance is."

I sat back in the booth and explained that I had taken some classes in meditation and using clairvoyance to see energy. I folded my hands. Why didn't he look that up in a dictionary? He had a bachelor's degree. What cave had he crawled out of?

"What do you mean, energy?"

"Well. I have done readings for people where they ask me questions and I tell them what I see."

"Oh. Do you see everything? Can you predict the future?"

"I have to direct my attention toward it. It's like turning on a faucet. I have to want to see something. I don't have it on all the time." I wondered if he thought I could see his son, whether or not he was going to die soon.

He turned sideways in the booth, away from me. He

wouldn't look at or talk to me for the rest of dinner. When the bill came, he said, "Why don't you cut it in half?"

I said good-bye to him in the parking lot. He put his hand up, gave a curt wave, and walked quickly toward his car.

My mother told me to stop telling people that I had studied meditation. I argued with her. They needed to know; it was something I enjoyed doing. She said, "They're going to think you're crazy. In fact, I'm afraid you're going to go off the deep end one day, myself. I wish you'd stop doing that stuff."

To this, I said nothing. Less was more, and it spared me a lecture. But she did have a point: maybe I shouldn't be so eager to share this with just anyone. This wasn't the age of witch hunts, but that didn't mean people felt okay about not being able to hide, either.

It hadn't occurred to me that I wouldn't want to meet someone until I came across Tony. We emailed a bit and then exchanged phone numbers. His favorite and only topic was sex—positions, games, toys, and more—we were mere minutes into our first conversation when he made this clear. He was a swinger and knew of a few places in Denver. I asked him about being checked for diseases, and he said he had been clean for the last five years. He laughed but I shriveled.

"So, tell me, if I stop you in the middle of the street on our first date, put my hand on your chin, and pull you toward me for a passionate kiss, what will you do?"

I laughed, excited that he wanted me, but it was not my happy, comfortable laugh. "It would be okay." Of course, that was the hypothetical, automatic, look-how-cooperative-I-am response, which smacked against a reflexive cringe.

He didn't want to tell me about where he had been to college or what movies or books he liked, or even very much about his fifteen-year-old daughter.

I left on vacation to visit a friend in California before Tony and I could meet in person.

I called him from the airport, and he told me I was a

decent person. "No, I have never been to jail," I told him, deadpan.

He laughed genuinely. "I look forward to your return."

"Yeah, I'll see you when I get back," I said—but the sound of his voice conjured an ooze seeping through the phone, something even turpentine wouldn't sanitize.

Being away settled it for me. The subject line of my email was "On Second Thought." I simply wrote, "We have nothing in common," and "Best wishes."

$\mathcal{I}$ became quite facile at decoding emails: who was desperate, who was fun, who was hiding, who was confident, who didn't care. Would I forgive misspellings? It was about meeting people, not about how they organized letters, I thought, secretly defending these might-be suitors. I often thought of what my mother said about spelling as I scrolled through the many men on display: "It is not an indicator of intelligence." She, of course, was speaking of school-age children, not grown men who could not justifiably say they didn't know how to look a word up.

Regardless, I forgave spelling. Kevin had had two master's degrees; his spelling was impeccable, but according to him, there was no chemistry. Correct letter order was not going to dictate attraction or good humor. Besides, if I made that a criterion, pickings would be much slimmer.

Mark worked for Comcast and lived with his parents—to help his dad, he said at first.

We did not email very much and that was fine. What he did write was rife with grammatical and spelling errors, though he commented that he was "triing." By this point, I had succumbed to the idea that good writer did not necessarily mean good match, so we met for coffee on a Sunday evening.

He looked a lot like Steve: blond hair, full, bushy, neatly trimmed mustache. He was thinner, though, and more cowboy. He had the boots, blue jeans, and buckle. I didn't know if I could get past any of this, but I sat and listened.

He was a talker.

I ordered tea and a piece of pie.

He asked if I ate dessert often, and I said, "Sometimes."

He prattled on about a woman he had met who had posted her sister's photo online. He was disgusted to discover when they met that his correspondent was a good hundred pounds heavier than the photo made her appear. "I told her I was angry, too. That's just not right. I mean, I can deal with a few pounds, and you can have dessert and you look fine, but that was mean!" He shook his head. "I'm a sensitive guy. You can take me to a chick flick and you might look over and see a tear in my eye. I'm not afraid to show that. I look like I would fit into the bar scene, but I like to go to the museum and I appreciate art. I'm a good guy, and it seems like you like to do those things too, so I wouldn't have any trouble doing that. I like doing those things. I look like a biker type, but I'm not, and a lot of women think I look good because of the way I look, but I don't want to be with just anybody."

The pie was mediocre. I couldn't see going to the museum with Mark. I couldn't see anything but Steve.

He paid for my tea and pie and walked me to my car. He gave me a hug and asked if he could kiss me. I offered my cheek. He hugged me twice more and managed to plant one on my lips. It was soft; he landed in the right spot.

He called me when he got home and said he was really glad to meet me and he hoped he wasn't being too forward by calling me right away. I talked to him for a few minutes. I didn't have any expectations, yet here he was. I toggled between resting on the pillow of his attention and wondering whether or not I should feel wary that he had hugged and kissed me three times and called to make sure I had made it home all right.

Mark called several times in the next few days. I garbled that I could only be friends and hoped that would scare him off, but it didn't. I told him I was not quite over someone else, and he reassured me that we could just go out and do things, no pressure. He could be a good friend. I knew how that would go. We would go to the museum, and I would want to call it good after an hour; meanwhile, he would be inviting me to get coffee and hoping for a leak in the flood-gates I was holding back. He would offer Kleenex and touch my hand. I would tell him a little or too much. He would press on for more, encourage me with a story of his own, and if I didn't give in, he would be frustrated and want to know what was wrong with him. And on it would go.

In one of our early phone calls, Mark unwound a yarn about his latest girlfriend. She would not leave him alone. He'd had to get a restraining order against her, and even that didn't keep her at bay, apparently. That was the real reason he'd moved from Colorado Springs and in with his parents. *What's worse?* I mused. *A guy in his thirties who lives with his parents, or the reason why?*

Did Mark have good intentions? Everyone totes a cara-van of experiences in tattered, misshapen packaging. I couldn't see clearly enough to judge his motives. I couldn't see clearly enough to trust myself. I couldn't see past his resemblance to Steve.

The summer meandered on with hope renewed as each new man crossed my screen. James was thirty-four, the father of a fourteen-year-old son. He did not want to have any more children and could not understand how I could date someone eighteen years my senior, as Steve had been.

"You're in completely different stages in your life. You're still working, and he's thinking about retirement." I couldn't refute this, but I couldn't embrace it, either. Getting up every day to meet a job did not define existence—not for me, anyway.

Our first date was at Sushi Den. He was tall and beauti-ful, with a square jaw and glasses. He loved football and looked as though he might have played some. He was articu-late though he had never finished college. I laughed with him; he was easy to talk to. Whittled down by multiple disappoint-ments, however, I expected to find fault and it didn't take long for one to appear: James had recently been laid off and was piecing his money together through construction work and odd jobs.

Many of the men I came to know were struggling to make ends meet or were spendthrifts. I didn't care about how much money I had so long as I had enough to pay my bills. A notable difference between me and these men was that I handled my pile of pennies very well. Despite his financial situation, money wasn't an issue between James and me. He freely treated me to dinner, though I asked if he wanted to split it.

He was intrigued by my meditation practice and my ability to read energy and wanted me to read him. I saw that things were going to break open for him soon with employment and a few other details, but the only thing I cared about was the fact that there were at least three or four other women around him, and one of those he was sleeping with. He didn't deny it. He laughed and was a little embarrassed.

I shrank into myself. I didn't want to compete. I offered a different package than the ones he might have with these other women, but would it be enough?

We continued to email each other. He wrote very explicitly about his sexual preferences—hair and its absence, having a "clear landing strip." I wanted to be that woman he was looking for, but could I be this? My protest was polite: I wrote that we should decide as a couple what works and what doesn't. His "yeah, but" was not enough and too much. Still, I wondered if it might work. Was it him or was I too tired to tell the difference anymore? Would being with him be worse than being alone? There was no safety in either one of these; each would be work. I wanted to put my head down.

James met me on the Auraria campus during my lunch break. I looked nicer than usual, wearing a dress. It was a beautiful late summer day. We sat on the grass. He wasn't hungry, and I had just eaten.

"What did you have for lunch?" he asked.

"I have to be careful about what I eat because I'm fighting candida," I said. It sounded awful, as bad as chlamydia; I knew it as soon the words plunked down between us. I couldn't suck them back, so I just kept explaining. "It's a pH imbalance in the body caused by too much sugar and yeast in the system, and it's a bitch to get rid of."

He nodded and remained still as a stone. Saying more would pit me deeper into the ditch, saying less would leave too much a mystery. I continued.

"Dairy aggravates it because it's inflammatory. So does sugar."

"What do you eat?" he asked. "How do you avoid that stuff? It's in everything."

Perhaps all was not lost. "Well. I eat a lot of rice and special bread. For a while I was only eating hamburger and lettuce. I couldn't even eat fruit. It's actually quite common for a woman in her mid-thirties to experience a pH shift. The body just can't do it anymore—you know, it just can't continue eating the same crap."

He wasn't close to me. He wasn't far away. He wasn't touching me. Was it over? I hadn't told anyone all of that before—not a guy, anyway. I wanted to talk about it, I couldn't help myself. The science of it fascinated me.

We parted company with the tentative plan of getting together after a metaphysical fair that was happening that weekend.

I emailed him Friday and didn't hear back from him by Sunday. I decided he was chasing the tail of another bunny. But then again, I thought, maybe he assumed I would simply call him when I was ready to get together. I was discovering that guys often assumed there wasn't anything more to be said; they simply expected a plan to roll out.

I gave up on James. He was too pretty, and I didn't want to be with someone who had so many other women who were getting to know him. I didn't trust him and wasn't interested in waiting around to see if that would change.

If I was going to feel cursed, it was going to be because of the name Matt—or at least because of the number of men I dated in my relatively young life who shared that name. My best friend and I would run down the list and I would code them for her: Guitar Matt, Detail Matt (he worked on cars), Architect Matt, Ex-Matt (ex-husband), and now there was this one.

"Are you serious? His last name is Keepers? He must be the one," my friend said, laughing.

I had long since abandoned my dream of marrying the next man I found online, but I hadn't lost hope in giving someone a chance. This Matt didn't have a photo posted on his profile, either, but I was not deterred. He had been witty in our email exchanges, and that was a foot in the door.

Our phone conversation went well. He was self-deprecating and had a knack for talking about himself in the third person in a way that wasn't annoying. He would slip it in midstream with different intonation, and I would laugh.

We met for dinner in Wheat Ridge. He had suggested Italian, and I knew of a Bistro on 32nd and Lowell. Besides, I had tired of the Vietnamese place and was beginning to think a change in scenery might break the string of my illustrious one-date wonders.

I didn't notice he was missing his front teeth at first. He kept it very well concealed while we ate; his hand always went up surreptitiously with the napkin. I could tell, however, that he had had a cleft palate, though he covered the scar with a mustache. He was gangly, and he wore his dark hair, which had touch of gray, short. I could see myself with him. He was attractive enough.

We puttered up and down the street after dinner. He spotted a shrine in an alley and walked over to it, close. He knew the saint whose statue was represented most abundantly and mumbled absently about being homeless and relying on this saint to keep him alive. He stumbled into telling me how his front teeth went missing. He had been through hard times: alcoholism; homelessness; not speaking to family. Perhaps he knew what he wanted now.

We stopped at a coffee shop for dessert. His hand folded against his cheek as he propped himself up across the table from me. His jeweled aquamarine eyes looked not expectant but serene. "So," he said. "Do you want to keep doing this? Seeing each other?"

I nodded. "I think so. Sure. Let's see how it goes."

"I'm very comfortable with you, Jane."

"I get that a lot," I said, smiling. This was no lie. Maybe he would be what I wanted. Maybe I should stop smiling when someone told me that, too.

It felt like a real relationship right away. He cooked for me, we shared the stories of our lives, and we watched movies. We even argued and listened and could forgive each other. I liked that he could become engrossed in something instantaneously. He soon had me believing I could disentangle my tether to Steve.

He showed up to my place one night right after work to go to a movie and smelled awful. I tolerated it but told him later that he needed to shower before we would get together for an evening. He told his therapist, who agreed with me. He acceded, and I let him shower at my place the next time; his work was not far from my place, and it would have been quite a feat for him to travel all the way home to Arvada and then motor back down for our outing.

It had been a long time since I'd been that open and easy with anyone so soon after meeting, but I did not sleep with him. Having forced myself to wait to be sexual with someone, I learned I could wait, and I did.

In the second week of our acquaintance, Matt confided in me. He was tender, sincere. "I like you, Jane. I don't want to hurt you or bring harm to you. I think we could have something together."

I did not feel good. I knew this was going to be bad. He was going to tell me something I didn't want to know. I started to run a mental checklist of whether or not I had touched or kissed him.

He had Hepatitis C. He had gotten it when he was homeless, he believed. He also believed he would not pass it on to me if we were careful—that is, if he wore a condom.

It didn't matter what he believed. The blossom between us had been seared. Numb with disbelief and his sharp, bright honesty, I said nothing. We sat at my kitchen table until the afternoon light went gray.

We decided to rent a movie. We watched it without speaking. He lay down on the couch midway through the movie, and I lay down behind him with my hand on his bony hip. I smelled his sweat. I wondered at his reassurance about acquiring Hepatitis C. It was transmitted through semen and blood, not spit. I knew I would get it anyway. My mutant body would not be able to ward it off. My immunity sucked. I couldn't risk it. I was having enough trouble trying to shake candida.

But I never said the words, "No, I can't do this."

We continued to get together. At lunch, once, he told me about a one-night stand with a security guard. She complimented him in the morning. "So, I'm pretty good." He shrugged and bit into his sandwich.

This was an argument? I should want this with him?

Subtle, direct, try as he might, I delivered my poker face. I would need more.

I kept seeing him. He was funny, he was introspective and sincere. He listened and had an opinion. He wanted great things for me. In the end, though, he was only company.

We had an argument we never finished about Steve. Matt knew the addict because he had been one. He knew the enabler and codependent lover because he had had one of those, too. He yelled at me once, telling me I would never bring another kind of man into my life unless I truly let go of Steve. I knew he was right, but I could not let him know that. "I *have* let go of him," I rebutted. "I hardly talk to him anymore!"

What I couldn't tell Matt was that I didn't want him, or anyone, telling me what to do about my grief over someone.

He apologized, but I never called him back. It would be easier to get over the things I liked about him than to listen to his self-righteousness again.

The summer exhausted me. People were not recyclable. If I were going to get involved with a man, I would have to accept him—quirks, flaws, past, all of it. I couldn't mix and match characteristics of one man with another. Relationship was capricious, animated, in flux, constantly. The equation did not always get solved or even balanced. By September, one thing was clear: I never wanted to meet or date that many men in three months ever again.

CHAPTER SIX

One, Two, Three, You're Out

It will happen when you least expect it. That is the maxim of finding someone to fall in love with that often gets repeated by friends who are already "hooked up." They usually tell a story of how they were simply doing what they loved and being themselves and then it happened.

This is not comforting to someone who is lonely. After the revolving door of rejection that was that summer, I had given up hope.

I wanted to cancel my subscription to the singles site. I had begun referring to it as the box store of dating: so many to choose from at low, low prices.

Then I wrote to Jason, and though I didn't expect to hear back from him, I did.

We corresponded over email only lightly and then decided to meet. There wasn't any point in dilly-dallying with email if there wasn't the illustrious "chemistry," which I was now convinced mattered significantly. And a great writer could be a dud in person. Not to mention that someone else could be doing the writing for him.

During our meeting, he drew me a picture of something that fascinated him and which he believed was profound psychically. It was tear-shaped, with several lines in it. I liked his enthusiasm for this eccentricity, though I had no clue what the drawing meant. He had a curiosity about things, and a sense of humor. I loved his red, curly hair and the way he held the pad of paper. I thought he might be okay: a nice guy who was looking for a companion. I would give him a chance.

We arranged to meet again for dinner.

He was a self-employed computer repairman who rummaged for parts at thrift stores. He was also very frugal and was often looking for a good deal. We had this in common.

I had known Jason for a week when my friend Cassie invited me to a Labor Day party at the Speak Easy, a newer bar on High Street. I accepted, though I told her I rarely went to bars. The last time I had set foot in one, I was married and out with my lesbian friends: a safe environment for me. It had been a long summer, though, and I was willing to try anything.

Cassie was supposed to meet friends there: a married couple (she was having an affair with the husband); a man she had tried to set me up with several months back, and who she still played with every now and again; and her mother.

We arrived early to find a table to accommodate everyone in our group. Cassie set us up with drinks. I tried everything she put in front of me, knowing full well I was going to be under the table in a matter of minutes if I didn't eat soon.

I ate and drank more and more. The bar filled up quickly. It turned loud. I turned red and warm from drinking. I vaguely heard that Cassie believed the bar to be haunted. It had been a brothel 150 years ago, so the lore went. She asked if I wanted to go upstairs later. I shrugged and nodded, a rag doll.

Monte and Lara arrived first. Cassie sat on one side of him and his wife on the other. I watched all three from across the table.

Cassie said they had an open marriage, but I didn't see Lara fondling or leaning into anyone else.

I followed Cassie to the bar. She waved her arm. "Take a look at everyone here. Pick out someone you like," she said, laughing.

I glanced around. "I don't know."

"Come on. Anyone."

All the guys looked beige or taken except for one who was sitting in a chair leaning against the wall.

His hair was shoulder length; his eyes were pensive and brown. He wore a brightly colored vest that he had not bought at Kohl's. He looked as though he was from across an ocean.

"That one?" Cassie asked as we stood at the bar waiting for our drinks.

"Mhmm."

"God, he is cute. I want him for myself, but I'll let you have him tonight. Go say hi to him! Go on." She nudged me in his direction as she carried our drinks. "It's easy. Say, 'H-e-l l-o. Do you want to dance?' You don't even have to give him your real name." She laughed. "Go on."

I turned to walk toward him, but he was gone. What the hell. "He's gone."

"He is. God. Where did he go?"

Then I saw him winding his way back to his stool, head down. My fingers cupped the inside of his upper arm. "Do you want to dance?" I blurted out.

He met my eyes. "Sure. Yes. All right. Good. I'll be right there."

"We're up here!" Cassie gestured toward our table.

I thought he wouldn't come. I thought he said yes but really meant no, said yes because it was an automatic thing to say. I sat down; my stomach flopped.

He slid his beer onto the table and sat down next to me. He held the mug with both hands and asked me my name and what I did for a living. It was impossible to hear anything, but we bowed into each other and created a bubble of words.

"Do you know how to dance?" he asked.

"I'm terrible," I admitted. "Do you?"

"My wife—ex-wife—was a great dancer. She taught me."

I watched him remember. He turned away from his beer and toward me, but not quite all the way. *Wife—ex-wife—* burbled to the surface. Which was it? Did it matter? This pretty boy sat next to me. He had shown up.

"Do you want to try it?" he asked.

"Sure. But I'm bad. I don't follow very well."

He took a firm grip of my hand and led me into too many bodies. I fell into and stepped on him, but he kept spinning and pushing me away and pulling me back toward him. Would I be sick?

"Not bad!" he said. "Try it again?"

"Okay." I smiled over at Cassie and her mother. My head was sloshy; I couldn't remember her mother's arrival. She had simply materialized.

"This time, follow me," he said.

I knew I wouldn't be able to do that, but I could close my eyes. To my amazement, I moved with him. I didn't tumble, hesitate, stop, or lead. As he twirled me, I saw Cassie's mother smiling and clapping. Cassie was happy too. I laughed and laughed. I could dance. I fell in love with his hold on me.

"One hundred percent better!" he announced.

We sat down. I was elated.

He was from the Czech Republic. He had been married for eight years and divorced for three. He asked if I would help him with his English. I smiled and said, "Sure," though I was wary. Men were either afraid of me because I taught English or they wanted to learn from me. Why did it have to be a hindrance or a commodity? But I couldn't say no to Andrej's accent or that pretty face.

We stayed late at the Speak Easy. The alcohol had worn off; the crowd had thinned. Monte and Lara lived just a block away, and they invited us over. Cassie's mother had long since departed, so it was the five of us.

Monte had crafted an artsy abode. He was an architect. Their place was a refurbished auto body shop, and the hanging lights and rippled steel sliding doors made me think of a nouveau riche loft. The ceilings were low in some places, with pipe fixtures still visible. These didn't detract from the overall effect, but it was drafty in there.

A bottle of champagne was opened, but I declined. I was cogent enough now that I was fashioning my escape plan. I had had enough of watching Cassie prance around Monte under Lara's nose with everyone pretending this was okay. I was tired, too. Andrej—Andy for short—was pretty, but I could see he was insecure. I would be okay with never seeing him again.

Cassie kept me there by telling them about my accomplishments. My biography had recently been accepted into *Marquis Who's Who in America.*

"Why don't they choose a guy like me?" Andy said. "I'm an American."

"But you're not a citizen," I said.

"I am. I took the exam. But they don't want a guy like that in there. A painter. It's probably only for people who teach, but that's not America. It's not just made up of people who read and teach. What about the working man? That's who should be in there."

I reconsidered my haste to leave.

"Don't you just hate her?" Cassie raised her champagne glass and smiled.

Lara asked how old I was and when I told her I was thirty-six, she quipped, "I hope to have my master's by then!"

Cassie sidled up to me. "He likes you. I can't even get him to have a conversation with me. Get his phone number." She handed me her pen and a piece of paper.

"We could talk some more if you like," I said to Andy. "Can I call you?"

"Or I call you," he said.

I stepped toward the door and gestured at Cassie that I was leaving.

"But it's early!" she said.

It was closing in on 2:00 a.m.

Andy followed me out.

"Do you need a ride home?" I asked. It was raining.

"I walked down here," he said. "A ride would be good."

On the drive to his house, he talked about his mother and what it had been like when he first came to the US. I hoped he would call me. I was reminded of the irrepressible sadness my long-ago Vietnamese boyfriend had possessed. It showered Andy and I felt drawn to the honesty of it.

9 didn't wait for Andy to call me. I called him two days later.

His voice looped in excitement. He thanked me twice for calling him. We made arrangements to meet that Saturday. I would drive to his place downtown.

I had forgotten to bring his phone number with me and only vaguely remembered where he lived, but I recalled part of the building name and that the circuit through a maze of one-way and discontinuous streets was discombobulating.

In the end, I managed to drive straight to his apartment building—I was even on time.

Andy came down dressed in slacks, a shirt, vest, and a jacket.

"You look nice, so dressed up!" I said.

"European style," he said with a shrug.

"I look casual," I said, feeling ashamed of my black jeans and striped long-sleeve shirt. I should have anticipated that he would dress up. I had been to Europe and had watched enough indie movies to know this. I'd just assumed he had bought into the American style, since he had been here ten years.

I shrugged it off. It didn't have to matter, but I sensed that it did to him, even though he said nothing.

"Let's walk!" he said. "I take you to a coffee shop. It's not far."

We wandered and meandered and then it started to rain. And it didn't last just a few minutes, like most Denver rains; it poured on and on.

We took cover under a bridge near I-25 and 20th. The water drizzled down the cracks and managed to mist us. He told me stories about his grandfather while we waited for it to let up. Andy got up to imitate him walking with a stick and yelling at his wife. I laughed until it hurt. I loved a good show. He was pensive, raw, angry, adamant, and doubtful—a great character.

We sat next to each other on the sidewalk; he invited me to sit in his lap. I was afraid I would break him. He was strong but not that much bigger than I. Tentative, excited, I felt hopeful. His legs opened to a V and I leaned back against his chest. I held myself forward though, self-conscious of being too heavy against him.

He wrapped one arm around my waist, and we stayed like that for a few minutes.

It did not stop raining but we started walking again anyway. We walked and walked and walked, straight and down, up, over, down some more, and then we were there, near the Platte River, at the coffee shop.

"I thought you said this place wasn't that far," I said.

"It's not," he said.

I was soaked and dripping and so happy.

We talked about playing music in front of people. I told him one of my notorious stories of when I was in college and had to perform in a recital as an accompanist.

"I was so nervous; the piano was shaking every time I put my foot on the pedal. Before we got out there, I could see that the wedge to hold the piano in place had been moved but I didn't do anything. I sat down and pretended that nothing would happen. It rolled and shook, and I almost ran the saxophonist over. I had to get a page-turner at the last minute. My teacher was standing backstage—he was just this little guy, smaller than me—and he yelled, 'Jane Binns! Are you ready? Do you have a page turner?'"

Andy laughed, entertained. "I know what you mean, girl. When I play by myself, I am sooo good, but if I play for you, I start shaking like a leaf."

The coffee shop was full of chess players and artsy types.

Andy called out to a guy two tables away who was laying out Tarot cards. "Hey! You do that? Are you good?"

The guy nodded. "I'm very good."

"Good. I need to get your number, man. Can you read me soon?"

"Sure." The guy rose and walked toward us. "You're not from the US, are you?"

"No. Czech Republic." Andy stuck out his hand as the guy approached.

They smiled and introduced themselves to each other.

I wondered how long they might chat, but as it turned out the guy had come with a young woman, so he hastened back to his seat. Andy got his phone number before we left. I liked that he risked socializing with a complete stranger in hopes of getting something he wanted.

We left the coffee shop and headed off in the opposite direction from where we had come. I was more curious than tired but did begin to wonder if I would ever make it back to my car. I had only the vaguest idea of where we were. Andy murmured something about going "this way this time," and I trusted that we would be circling the other half of the loop we had trekked before. At least it wasn't raining anymore.

We followed the Platte River and were on the sidewalk until it disappeared. The river had flooded. I looked back. Andy did not. He rolled up his pants, talking to himself.

"Is it okay that your shoes get wet?" he asked.

I nodded. They already were.

He guided us. The water was at least two feet deep. We fumbled over rocks. I slipped more than once but did not fall.

"This is great!" I yelled out happily. I heard it in my voice. I didn't care if the night slipped into dawn, if we walked until the soles of my shoes wore off, if I ever saw my car again. I remembered the delight of adventure when I was a teenager and walked downtown Ann Arbor by myself.

We stopped and looked out over a bridge. I asked him how old he was. He talked about the moon, the queen of emotion, and how his astrological sign was ruled by her. He said he was a Cancer. I guessed the date, but he would neither confirm nor deny it. He was pensive, not playful. I thought that because he had come over as an immigrant he was protective of this fact to keep himself safe. Perhaps someone was looking to deport him? No. He had been married for eight years to an American; he had his citizenship. I didn't want to play this game with him. I was annoyed.

I thought perhaps he wanted me to tell him how old I

was, so when he asked, I said I was thirty-six, which was true. But even this did not break the lock around his secret.

I learned sometime in the next week that he was thirty-nine and was a late-June Cancer, like Gary. I was beginning not to believe in accidents anymore.

We arrived back at my car close to 2:00 a.m.

He kissed me good night, and I wanted to climb right inside of him. The kiss pulled me into a stupor; my eyes lay heavy, surrendering to sleep, while my groin and chest were resuscitated to ecstasy. He released me twice and told me to go home. The second time, though, he said, "Girl, you better go. Otherwise I'm not going to care how messy my place is and invite you up. I haven't had anybody there in so long. Dirty house. A single guy. I'm not caring where I throw anything."

I would have told myself I didn't care right then. I was happy at the thought of a man cleaning his house for me too. But I finally left, and I was glad I didn't stay. I needed to know that I had enough willpower to go home.

I felt in love. I felt charmed—and guilty. I kept myself awake on the ride home by wondering what it would be like to date two men at the same time.

9 called Jason sometime in the next couple of days and went to his house for dinner. I helped him cook, we talked, I gave him a psychic reading, and then we went to bed. He wore a condom without my asking him to.

It was not awkward or clumsy. I felt as though he knew my body instantaneously. How could I not love this?

Andy and I met for a drink later that week. He kissed me long and pushed my hand over his hard, wide penis while we stood next to my car in the parking lot of The Speak Easy.

I loved the back and forth of two men for about two weeks. My head spun with comparisons about everything: sex, conversation, humor. Who had my heart?

Jason won out easily in the intellectual argument: He was educated, established, he had kids, he was looking to settle down, which I thought I could talk myself into doing again.

Choosing him made the most practical sense. He liked to talk about his feelings and insights. I loved his red hair and how he made love to me. He did frighten me, though, when he offered his house key after I had known him for only one week. I told him, politely, "No, I am not ready for that, but thank you."

Andy, meanwhile, inspired my bohemian nature. Nights with him rode the crests of adventure and passion. He was an artist and musician. He played guitar for me and sang; his soul pined and shone. He had claimed his life when he left the Czech Republic. His freedom and sense of obligation to no one lured me in. His tiny, 300-square-foot apartment was jammed with books and art. He could argue about anything and had something to say about everything.

He was also a wit and great storyteller. I was a sucker for his accent. He could have described the molecular structure of bentonite, and I would have hung on every syllable. As it was, he usually had me doubled over and cramping from laughing so hard. He once described to me how a friend had left his bicycle at another friend's house. He had needed a part for it to work well again and had asked the friend if he could leave it there. A couple of days after he left it, the guy checked on the bike to make sure it was still there and noticed the seat missing. He returned the next day and a wheel was gone. Each day he visited, the bike was missing one more part, until finally there was nothing left. Andy had marvelous pacing and gestures that accompanied the enumeration of the loss of each piece of bicycle. It was simple and pointless but conjured up this ever-hopeful and yet forlorn young man. It was too precious. I ached and tried to catch my breath.

Andy often complained of having smelly feet. I recommended that he take chlorophyll because I had heard that this was good for neutralizing body odor. I asked him if he thought it was working and he said, "Girl. I can't say it is doing anything for my feet because they are too far from my face, and I'm not going to lift and smell them. But you would think I've been living in the rainforest because my poop is as green as the Amazon!"

ꔹ

Andy came to my place the first night we would spend together. I told him I had a toothbrush for him and asked if he
had any condoms.

"No," he said. "You have a toothbrush but no condoms?"
He laughed. "What kind of woman invites a man over and
has a toothbrush but no condoms?"

I was ovulating, but I wanted him.

We got up for a drink of water after our first interlude,
and I told him I was ovulating.

He put the glass of water down and looked at me. "You
kidding me?"

"No," I said. "Does that make you nervous?"

"Sure, it makes me nervous that you tell me after we have
sex, when I can do nothing about it. You want to have a baby
with me? You want to have my baby? Go ahead!"

"This will stop it." I showed him a tablet of Rutin. "This
will keep the baby from coming."

It had never failed before, and I hoped it wouldn't this
time.

He shrugged.

We went back to bed and had sex again. I was horny, and
all I wanted to do was to satisfy this desire. I didn't want to
look at what it might mean to get involved with him, or to
put pressure on myself to choose him over Jason.

I told myself that having sex with one man who wore
condoms and one who didn't was the same as having sex with
only one man and was therefore safe. Whittling it down to a
common denominator of sex with or sans protection was so
inane I could never say it out loud to anyone else. Would this
simple equation shield me from the risk of catching a disease?
How were the numbers adding and subtracting themselves as
they marched in and out of my heart?

I quickly got tired and worried that one would find out
about the other. I would be on the phone with one and the
other would call. I was afraid I was going to slip and reveal

there was another man. It didn't occur to me to be honest with either one of them. I wanted each of them to be loyal to me; I knew I wouldn't tolerate another woman in their lives. I also knew this was unfair and dishonest, and there wasn't going to be any story I told myself that was going to justify it morally. I was dabbling in the land of heartbreak, but I wanted to play and juggle a while longer. It was exciting, and I had never done anything like this. I told my girlfriends that it was a good thing I wasn't big on calling out anybody's name when we were intimate. A couple said they tuned into my life for their weekly entertainment.

The two men were beginning to show who they really were. Andy criticized my dress, my hair, my rear, and my teeth every time we got together. I decided to let things slack between us, to see if he missed me. To see if he would treat me better if I weren't so available.

I focused on Jason.

He wanted to get our boys together right away. His son was two years older than Shane. I asked that we wait a little longer—a month. He agreed but had a sober look on his face.

We went for a walk near his house, and we stopped in the path. He put his arm around me and spoke of "when things calm down and are settled."

Was this it? He wanted to marry me? I told myself that he couldn't be serious, but I said nothing to him—I was waiting for him to show me more of who he was.

We took a drive to look at the autumn foliage near Evergreen. He spoke on and on about his ex-wife. She was turning his kids against him. He was convinced she was in love with a woman but wouldn't admit it. He'd left her but hadn't told her why.

We stopped for lunch in Idaho Springs. He turned the ketchup bottle down and beat it. It shot onto my pant leg in an array of clumps.

I laughed and laughed. I didn't care about my jeans.

The TV was on in the room where we ate, and he remembered how much his ex-wife liked to watch football on

Sundays. Her family loved it, too. They wore jerseys and hats. He never got into that.

He recalled another recent spilling incident in his life. He had opened a bottle of red wine at his last girlfriend's house and accidentally dumped it on her white carpet. It was no laughing matter to her. She had asked to call him a different name because he had the exact same first and last names as her ex-husband. They had gotten their boys together almost immediately, and his son, Ryan, had had a horrible time letting go of James after they broke up six weeks into it.

With this experience in Jason's recent past, I assumed he would see the wisdom in waiting to bring our kids together. But things were not happening fast enough for him.

I reflected to him on the way back home that his grief seemed quite raw and fresh.

"It's only been nine months," he said, growing defensive.

"Yes," I said, "but I am not raw."

He talked more about his feelings. He understood what it was to juggle a new schedule with the kids, along with the myriad of emotions that arose from being a divorced parent: competition, rage, sadness, defeat, guilt, and failure. I liked that he could understand these feelings but didn't like how easily he bled them out.

Could I stand to bear witness while he muddled through, all the while knowing that I was gaining distance on my own grief? I remembered I, too, had pined for a calmer life not too long ago. I'd been willing to do anything to make things feel settled, even if that included talking about marrying someone. The picture of stability had a powerful reach.

I was not patient enough to see if Jason could arrive at a centering within himself. I pulled back, though not entirely out. Would I miss him?

$\mathcal{I}$ decided it would be a good idea to spend time with a girlfriend. I picked up Cassie one Saturday morning and drove us up to Idaho Springs to go for a soak in the hot spring caves.

We laughed on the way. We talked of the men in our lives. My revolving door of suitors paled in comparison to the kaleidoscope of men spiraling in and out of Cassie's life. She was currently dating four men, only one of whom she considered a boyfriend.

In the caves, we sweated, and she told me sad stories.

She had been pregnant ten or more years back and had had an abortion. It had botched things for her for good. The fetuses had been twins.

I had already known that her father and her sisters' and brother's fathers were all different men.

I chimed in with my own sad stories but soon gave up. She won. And besides, I didn't want to compete with her.

We ate lunch in town and before the food had been laid down, Cassie drank two Bloody Marys. I watched her wide-eyed and thanked God I was the driver. She seemed happy after two drinks; I would have slithered to the floor, untouchable.

We headed down the hill back to my place. She tried to reach the boyfriend but realized her cell phone had no signal and no power.

"You can call him from my place," I said.

When we got inside, she held the phone with a blank look on her face. "I forget his phone number, I need to look it up on my phone," she said, laughing sloppily. "What are you doing tonight?"

I shrugged. "No plans."

"Do you have anything to drink?"

"All I have is my brother's hooch," I said. He made wine from his backyard concord grapes every year. It varied from year to year in taste but not in potency. A thimbleful made most everyone's eyes glaze over.

Cassie wrestled with the cork and poured eight ounces into a tumbler. She had that down in a matter of three minutes and was halfway through another glass when she suggested we rent movies and hang out.

She staggered and laughed at how strong the wine was.

I took the bottle from her and put it in the refrigerator.

On the way to the movie store, she asked me to stop at a liquor store so she could buy rum and root beer.

I waited for her in the car.

At the movie store, she sold me on three movies she wanted to watch again. She convinced me they were all good. I didn't care. I was mopey that neither Jason nor Andy had called, despite the fact that I didn't want them to. I wanted to be wanted by someone who was not still mucking through his divorce grief and who would not belittle me. I felt hollow.

When we got back to my place, I fixed us dinner. I was hungry, and I was sure Cassie needed food to sop up some of that alcohol.

We sat out on my patio and talked about writing. I had missed talking about writing with someone. Cassie said glowing things about me and said she wanted to be like me.

It was nice, but I didn't trust it. She had been marinating for most of the time we had spent together that day.

After we ate, she put in *Love, Liza*, one of Phillip Seymour Hoffman's early movies. I sat at one end of my couch and she asked if she could put her head on my lap. I put my hand on her back while she nestled in. I felt motherly toward her and relieved that she was finally settling down.

She made light commentary about the story, and I shushed her.

She giggled and apologized. Then she pulled at my shirt and lifted it.

I asked her what she was doing, and she stopped. Then she pulled and lifted some more, and I asked again, "What are you doing?"

She stopped before starting again.

She got as far as sucking on my navel. When I stopped her again, she begged me to try it with her. Promised that I would never want to go back to a man. "I'm good, Jane. I really am."

"I'm sure you are," I agreed. "But I don't want to."

"Come on. You'll like it. I promise. You've never had better."

"Get up," I said. "I'm going to take you home. Come on."

"No, I'm sorry," she pleaded. "I promise I won't try anything again."

"Get your shoes. Where's your purse? Come on. I'm going to get you home, now."

"Don't be mad at me. Are you mad?"

"I'm not mad. It's time for you to go home, though."

She watched me the whole trip back to her apartment downtown. She pleaded with me to forgive her, said that she was a stupid fuck and asked if we would still be friends over and over again. "Come upstairs with me so I can make it up to you," she said.

"Take it easy," I said. "Get a good night's sleep."

I watched to make sure she got in okay then headed over to Andy's apartment, which was only a few blocks away.

I knocked on his door but got nothing. He wasn't home.

I stared at the dark crack underneath the door and waited. Did I hear music? I wondered if he couldn't hear the knocking, or if someone else was in there with him. Another woman? *He's out trolling*, I thought. I felt hollow, and even worse knowing that anyone who might see me would see how needy I felt.

My hands fastened themselves to the steering wheel. I shook anyway. I had never shaken over anything. I tried not to cry.

I called Jason when I got home. It was close to 9:30 p.m.

I told him what happened with Cassie. He didn't say one word, not even an "Mhm." I asked him if I had called too late and he said, "Yes. Kind of."

"Is Ryan in bed?" I asked.

"Yes."

"I'm sorry . . . I'm upset, and I need someone to talk to. I'll talk to you later." I hung up quickly.

I waited for him to call me back to say that he was sorry that he'd had a crappy night, but he didn't. I had me all to myself. I believed I should feel sad but what I felt was confused. I didn't know what to do with myself. I felt panicked, foolish. There was no safety in company. I already knew this from my married life, but why wasn't it different with someone else? Why wasn't the one I wanted there for me when I needed him to be? What person who is splitting her time between two men genuinely wants to be with one of them full time?

I was abandoned, frozen. I felt no one could see me. Jason was mired in his grief and wanted to set up his life, so it had appeared that he had moved on, and Andy was distracted by appearances. Neither one of them was right for me. They were parts of what I wanted in someone, but they were not the whole. The hope I'd had to have a girlfriend to do things with had just vaporized. It was two hours later in Michigan. It was too late to call my mother. Besides, I was too far down in my own muckmaking for that. I didn't want to deal with anyone else's judgment. This wasn't fun. There was no jubilance in desperation. A relationship with either one of these guys was not going to save me. I was lost. Who would define me?

I gave up. I cried.

I spent the next day, Sunday, at a metaphysical fair. The meditating and reading other people should have helped with letting go of all that had happened the night before, but I kept rewinding the events over and over. I wanted to be held. There could be no substitute.

When I returned home, Jason had called and left a message about getting together.

I called him. His voice was eerily high, and he laughed, or pretended to, a lot. I never got around to answering him about getting together and he didn't ask. Strange. It felt like some middle school game where there is an unspoken code and if one of you misses your cue, you lose.

On Monday, I called him from school in between classes. He was stony and abrupt. I had classes back to back until 11:30 a.m. When I checked my email before my 2:30 p.m. class, he had sent me a message saying he wasn't happy and could go no further in our relationship. That was it. No explanation.

Since Jason gave me no forum to discuss what had happened, I stacked all of his idiosyncrasies together into one big red flag and listed for myself all of the reasons why I should be happy we would no longer be seeing each other: When he'd come over to dinner and I was unloading the dishwasher, he'd told me that I should load each kind of utensil together to save myself time in unloading. He farted a lot and they smelled awful; he would not admit that the gas had anything to do with his intolerance to dairy and the fact that he kept on drinking milk anyway.

And then there was Cassie. I had hoped she could be a friend. I was sure lacking in that department. Most of my friends from graduate school had moved back to their home states. I still talked with many of them, but it wasn't the same as having someone right there to call and get together with.

Between the two, I felt worse about losing Cassie. Boyfriends, husbands, fiancés may come and go, but a girlfriend can be like gold. Treat her well and she'll never let you down.

Sometime within the week, Andy called me, or I called him. We had spoken of attending a Halloween party together dressed as two cartoon characters from a Paul McCartney movie. I had never heard of it and wasn't convinced it had ever even seen the light of day. But regardless, photos of the characters and the preparation for dressing up like the characters had made their way into a book Andy owned, and they had given him the idea. We had already shopped at thrift stores for the clothing; all we needed was the makeup.

Assembled, we didn't end up looking much like the characters in his book, but we did look startling. We were two of a kind: Our faces and skull caps were white. None of our hair showed. We both wore suits and turtlenecks. We embellished our faces with red lines. Andy said I looked better than he did. My sobriety radiated forth.

The party itself wasn't great. It was loud, and no one knew what we were. Though it had long been a trademark of mine to go to Halloween parties dressed in unique costumes, it felt doubly insulting to be with someone else and not be known.

We spent the next couple of weeks together, when I wasn't busy teaching, grading papers, and being a mother.

One Saturday night I called to find out what he was doing, and he said that he was thinking of going to a guitar concert. "You can come if you want," he said.

I thought his hesitance meant that he didn't want to be with me, but decided to listen to his words and the invitation instead.

I made sure not to under-dress as I had on our very first date. I wanted him to want me too. I put on thigh-high hose, black, with a seam mid-leg, a black skirt, a flashy violet blouse, and a long pinstripe black jacket. My shoes were a low pump that clacked against the sidewalk. I loved the cross-back lace that went across the top.

Since I didn't wear skirts or hose very often, getting in and out of the car proved to be a gymnastic feat. There was no pretense about it, I was as undignified as I appeared. And right on cue, my hose began unrolling as soon as I took ten steps. I clutched and tugged at them upward, trying to keep pace with Andy.

He held my hand and put his arm around me during the concert. We sat in a small church; it was drafty and cold. No more than forty people faced the stage.

At the intermission, Andy reunited with a few people from the master's guitar studio he'd been part of a few years earlier. I nibbled at the cookies and cheese and debated whether I could eat more without appearing piggish. I didn't know anyone there, so I forgave myself and ate what I wanted.

I watched Andy. He introduced me to one couple; the man still played guitar in the master's studio and told Andy that he shouldn't have given up on it.

Andy said he had spent hours trying to get a certain touch or stroke down. "It took too much time, man."

He critiqued the guitarist by saying that he was a virtuoso but not pleasant to listen to. I agreed. I had never heard or seen some of the sounds or moves the musician had performed, but did I want to listen to a guitar be played like a drum?

We walked downtown to a bar he was familiar with. We ate and drank. I was tipsy in a half hour.

We walked some more and meandered back to my car, where I dumped myself in and drove us back to his apartment.

The hours moved into morning. My eyes lay closed as I listened to his voice ramble in and out of stories with the music he chose as a backdrop.

At about 3:00 a.m., he asked me what I thought of our relationship.

I opened my eyes. "Well. I like you. I enjoy spending time with you."

"Yeah. Yeah. I like you, too. But I have to tell you, girl, I'm not in love with you. I want to have that feeling like Baudolino in Umberto Eco's book, where the guy is looking at the woman and he feels so in love with her." He paused. "But I like you. No one laughs at my stories the way you do."

I rolled away from him, so he wouldn't see or hear me cry. It was three in the morning. He couldn't have waited until breakfast? Or told me after the concert so I could have driven home at a reasonable hour?

I lay there unzipped, all of my innards prickled and wounded. I had to sleep, or at least try.

He had no trouble.

I dreamt all night about arguing with him and defending myself. I awoke and wrote about the dreams while he slept. Somehow, I got back in bed and allowed myself to have sex with him when he woke up. I felt defenseless about stopping it.

I dressed and told him I would go home.

He talked me into letting him take me out for breakfast.

At the diner, I couldn't look at him. I left the table and did not take my purse or jacket with me. I sat outside on the curb for several minutes.

When I came back in, Andy was gone but my purse and jacket remained.

I felt stupid and weak.

He emerged from the bathroom a minute later.

Over breakfast, he told me that I had a lot of silver in my hair.

"I do not."

"You do, girl."

"You have some too."

Horrified, he said, "I do not. You're only three years younger than me and look. That's why I couldn't stay with my wife. I was too afraid of walking down the street and having people wonder, why is this young guy with this old woman? Very immature of me." He shrugged.

"If you care about someone, you don't care about how old they are," I said. "There was a man I dated who was in his mid-fifties and I loved him more than anyone else."

"Are you over him?" Andy asked.

"I don't know."

As we walked back to his apartment, he put his arm around me and asked me what I was going to do that day. I said I didn't know and asked him what he would do.

"I'm going to masturbate over my sorrow."

"Oh no you're not," I sniped, delighted that for once I didn't hesitate.

"Ha. Hmm. You're smarter than I thought."

At my car, he hugged me and said, "I call you, you call me. We see, okay?"

After he had walked away, I tore up the sign he had given me to put in my windshield that allowed me free parking near his building.

I spent the afternoon crying until my head hurt and my eyes were the size of fried eggs. I was so sick of rejection and not being good enough for someone to see and love me.

Later that week, Andy left a message and invited me to go to an IMAX movie with him that Saturday.

I was furious.

I didn't call him back. I wrote him a letter, a bold-faced but believable lie. I thanked him for the invitation and said a funny thing had just happened: I was waiting by the elevator when one of the other teachers in the English Department asked me to go to a movie with him. I padded the lie by saying I had liked this teacher for a long time and I was glad to tell him I was available. Things worked out like they were supposed to, I wrote. Take care!

For the first time in two months, I felt good. I wasn't confused.

I ached plenty, but would this slow me down? I was beginning to get addicted to how quickly I could recover. It wouldn't be long before I got up and put myself out there again.

CHAPTER SEVEN

M & M

When Andy asked me if I was over Steve and I said I didn't know, I was lying. I couldn't put away my attraction to him. I couldn't let it or him back in either, however. I was looking for him in other men; I knew that much now. I was hoping he would shine through, but without all of his hemming and hawing and pushing and pulling. I wanted that crystalline reflection of myself that he was so good at revealing, with all of its contours and pits, rounded corners and thorny edges. I wanted to be seen and therefore known as he saw me. I missed him. I told myself I couldn't have him. I told myself I shouldn't want him. I pushed all of it down with a gulp.

I took a break from dating for three weeks, and then my friend Ron called and told me about a dance that was coming up. I had been to enough of these dances to know that they drew the fifty-five-and-older crowd. I had some dread about that—but then again, younger men just didn't seem to suit me. I put it in my calendar, and I went.

I spotted Mike right away. He wasn't as old as most of the men there. He looked to be in his early forties. Maybe I was finally attracted to someone closer to my own age? He was youthful looking, boyish almost. He had wavy auburn hair, a slight frame, and a trimmed mustache. I approached him with my hands folded and couldn't look at him directly. He asserted himself, and we danced for much of the night. I liked his certainty as a dancer. I felt safe in his arms. He was not as artistic as Andy, but despite his slight frame, he directed and held on to me with ease. I loved that he kept choosing me as the night wore on.

When we sat down, I asked him how much he had dated, and he said, "More than I can count." He had just gotten out of a relationship not even a week ago. He spotted a good friend of the woman and shrank. His face was a gully of shame. I liked that he expressed remorse. It meant that he could invest and care. I didn't need to hear the details. It was enough to surmise that he wasn't sleeping around. It turned out that Ron was also a long-time friend of his, so I knew at least one person who could vouch for him.

He walked me to my car at the end of the night and gave me his card. I chose not to go out with him and the singles crowd from our church for pie or pancakes. This ritual was sometimes a little fun, but definitely distracting and often annoying. Crowded in with the group around the tables that were shoved together to accommodate all of us, I could not deny how young I was compared to the others. I was thirty-six, fifteen to twenty years younger than most of them.

I called him, though, of course. It was near Thanksgiving; my wrecked soul didn't want rest, it wanted comfort, in the arms of whoever would have me.

I hoped it might work with Mike. He had a full-time job, a career with the government. He had children he still kept in touch with, even though they were grown.

As had been my MO since my dating adventures began, I jumped into bed with Mike inside the first three dates. He came to my place, and we drank tea. I had never seen anyone slug a hot drink before. Each time he set his cup down on the piano bench, my makeshift coffee table, he did so for only for half a minute before lifting it to his mouth again.

We began kissing moments after I had cleared the cups. I lost myself in his excitement, so much so that when I came up for a breath to take us to the bedroom, I panicked and asked where my eyeglasses were.

He laughed and took them off my face to hold in front of me.

In that moment, I thought I could love him. He didn't humiliate me when he could have. I had left the door wide open.

I asked about condoms, and he said that he didn't have any. I didn't either. I wasn't worried about birth control so much as I was about STDs.

"I trust you and you can trust me," Mike said. "I give blood regularly and get it checked as part of my job."

I was appeased.

I was glad I had turned off the lights. His penis was the size of a baby gherkin. I was afraid of biting it off and swallowing it. It couldn't have been any longer than three inches. He had to bang against my pubic bone as he pumped in and out of me to get enough friction to come.

Mike and I got together a few times before he traveled back to Wyoming to spend the holiday with his mother and sisters. He was the only son of seven children. His dad was gone; his mother remarried. He had confided to me over dinner one night that his dad had shot himself. "Please don't say anything to Ron about it," he said.

I didn't. I catalogued it as yet another secret that a man had told me within a very brief period of knowing him. Were all women receptacles for men's confessions so soon after initial introductions?

Someone in his hometown must have fixed the insurance papers, Mike continued, because his mother wouldn't have been able to receive the life insurance they got if the company had known it was a suicide. He made note of the fact, too, that he was older now than his dad was when he died. "I guess that's something." He shrugged in disgust and anger, shame. He was haunted.

The same night, he told me that shortly after his divorce, he had been visited by an impish figure after he'd gone to sleep. Frightened, he had curled up in a fetal position and called upon his Lord, Jesus Christ, to get him through the ordeal.

I wondered why he was telling me these things. Was it to

elicit sympathy? I wasn't sure, but I was more bothered by the fact that he had shown me the deer and elk heads he had mounted on the walls inside his house. The one that bothered me the most was a rabbit with antlers.

When I told my sister about the trophies, she said she would have walked straight out, with nothing more said. She loves animals more than people. Though I didn't care for these displays, I didn't see the need to voice any objection. It wasn't going to bring those deer and elk back to life. I could ignore them so long as I didn't look them in the eye.

Mike and I talked once while he was in Wyoming. I wanted to make sure he had made it there okay, so I asked him to call me when he arrived. The conversation was short; I could tell he didn't want to make much of talking with me. I imagined him shrugging as his mother asked who had called. Who was I to him two weeks into it? Could I be someone he might love?

$\mathcal{I}$ spent Thanksgiving with my sister and drove to Steve's to deliver a piece of pie that evening. I hadn't called ahead; I just showed up. Steve was depressed because the holiday reminded him of family time, and he wasn't with his sons. I was afraid he would close the door on me, but he let me in and we shared in our mutual misery. Shane, now five, was with his dad in Chicago.

I didn't tell Steve about Mike. There wasn't any point, and it was way too soon to be projecting anything about the relationship's longevity.

$\mathcal{The}$ days rushed toward Christmas. Mike and I hadn't talked about exchanging gifts, but I thought the polite thing to do would be to get him something. I had painted a watercolor of flowers when visiting my friend Joan in California during the previous summer and was particularly proud of it. I had discovered that Kinko's made color copies and was delighted at the idea of reproducing the piece. My intention was to make a copy for Steve and Joan; why not make one for Mike too?

I found a frame for his copy and put it in a shirt box.

Mike picked me up one night to go to dinner, and I handed the box to him. He immediately tossed it in the backseat. It bounced up a little, and I winced but forgave him as a child who knows no better. He probably thought it was a tie with poinsettias on it.

He opened it later that night and was flummoxed that I had given him a painting I'd made. He set it up on one of the tables in his bedroom. I felt happy. I teased myself with thoughts about whether he had gotten me anything or what he might get me now that I'd given him a gift, and then played the game of telling myself that it didn't matter when indeed it felt like the entire relationship hinged on it.

I met him for lunch downtown a few afternoons later. It was one of those bright December days with a crisp blue sky that Denver tends to see a lot of in winter, though it always feels unexpected.

We walked to a deli not far from his office building, and I asked if he was getting anything. He shook his head no. I ordered and expected that he would offer to pay. He did not. I filed this away, along with his obsessive talk about needing to sell his house so he wouldn't get whacked with capital gains tax. He had already bought another house but hadn't moved into it yet. He owned and rented out a condo as well. I told him that he and I differed in our sense of financial security: he was a lot more worried about it than I was.

"Well," he replied, "it's not a bad thing to be concerned about money."

I supposed not. But he could have sprung for lunch since I'd made the effort to come down and meet him and deal with parking in a congested metropolis. Stingy didn't look good on anyone.

When I was done eating and listening to him talk about work, Mike parked me in a chair downstairs from where he worked and told me to wait.

"I have something for you," he said.

He came back a few minutes later with a nice paper bag

that advertised a specialty chocolate. Now this was more like it!

"Wait until Christmas to open it," he said.

I didn't. I got into it as soon as I got home.

It was not a large, round, elegantly wrapped chocolate, as I had fantasized. It was a bag full of trail mix in a snowman cellophane bag sealed with a twist-tie, a tiny tote bag of Burt's Bees products, a few candy canes, and some Halloween suckers. The only chocolate was a Hershey's nugget. I opened the Burt's Bees bag. The cuticle balm had a dab missing but everything else looked fresh.

I rationalized to my sister that maybe he had had the Burt's Bees bag at an angle and the balm had melted inside the tin.

She was disgusted.

I couldn't sidestep it for longer than two minutes. I felt demoralized. Was this the sum total of office Christmas party goods and unwanted Halloween candy, or should I expect another helping at Valentine's Day?

The thought of rejection loomed mountainous next to acknowledging how crappily Mike was treating me. I didn't want to feel rejected, so I blamed his bad behavior on things I didn't know about—things that didn't have to matter.

I called him within the next couple of days about getting together. When after a day or two he didn't return my call, I called again—light and easy, no pressure. I was cool. He didn't need to call me back. I didn't need him. But my sister had to yell at me before I allowed myself to believe it.

"You call him back and tell him not to bother calling you again," she demanded. "God. You deserve better than that."

I did as I was told. She was right.

I heard from Ron later that Mike told him he had been tired and just didn't feel like doing anything that weekend.

He could have told me that himself.

But that wasn't the last of Mike. He invited me to dinner with his coworker Aileen and her husband for New Year's, and we had a great time. I liked Aileen a lot. Strong woman; mother of two daughters; had her own mind and didn't hesitate to express it. I believed we could be friends. She liked to write and was curious about clairvoyance.

On New Year's Day, Mike rose early to attend church and told me to leave when I wanted, and to lock the door on my way out. He didn't cook for me or make me a cup of tea. He left without offering a hug or kiss.

That was it. I broke it off.

I tried to build a friendship with Aileen, but within weeks of my dissociation from Mike, she told me that it was awkward for her to hang out with me and be his coworker and friend too. He asked about me, I guessed, or she couldn't help but tell him when we got together. I didn't press for details. I laughed when she told me she needed to choose Mike over me. Why not tell Mike where to stick it if he was curious about me or say he had blown it with me and if he had any balls at all, he would call and apologize for being a putz? Maybe she wasn't so strong after all.

Another potential female friend flushed.

If I needed any person in my life, it was a girlfriend who was not living in another state. I kept in touch with three whom I had known from various periods in my life, but it was not the same as having someone whose house I could go to, or whom I could call and invite out to a movie to get over feeling bluesy. I made a mental note to attend to this vacancy.

It was a few weeks before I ventured out again.

I attended a singles Valentine's dinner at a restaurant with members of my church. A man named Matthew—*another Matthew*—sat across the table from me.

I remembered him from church. I had liked him from a distance. His curly blond hair had drawn me in. I couldn't believe my good luck. I didn't have to pine for him from the sidewalk as I left church or wonder any longer what his name was. He was sitting across the table from me!

Matthew looked at me for a bit too long throughout dinner. As our group milled around after eating, he commented on my black jockey hat. He said he had quite a collection of hats and described a few of them. He was nervous, but we laughed a little and made arrangements to meet at the dance hall, where we were all headed.

I half expected Mike to be there because he liked to dance, and I didn't believe he would be quick enough to get so involved with someone new that he would skip a dance. He would probably be there, trolling for his next bed buddy. I had left a message on his answering machine to break things off. Not classy. Would he snub me if I saw him? Would I care? My indecisiveness made me antsy.

Sure enough, my angst did not have long to brew. As soon as I walked into the room, I saw him carrying a plastic cup of wine. We were among the early arrivals; the dance floor was about as empty as it would be that night, with approximately 400 expected.

We said hello, and he moved along. *Easy*, I told myself, *he's an acquaintance now*. I would dance with him a little while later and tell him that my self-published book was finished. I would also watch him dance repeatedly with a roundish woman in her late forties, early fifties. She had dark hair, like mine, but curled. Mike had sworn he'd never date a blonde because it reminded him of his ex-wife. He moved in on the chubby woman in the blue dress just like he had with me: several dances and only a few with others. It was clear that he loved to dance but to devote many to one person, well, that meant she was something. I wondered how long they would last. (My answer came in April when I went to a sock hop at our church. I saw Mike on the prowl that evening with yet another brunette who looked a lot like me.)

Matthew and I found each other and sat down at a table. We exchanged howdy-dos and what-do-you-dos and were quite rapt with one another, enough to draw the attention of a few women who knew him. One in particular swiped her fingertips on his shoulder in a playful nudge and told him to stop talking and ask me to dance.

"Geez. I want to talk to someone and get to know them," he said, peeved, after she had left.

He cleaned and polished cars for a living; he detailed

them. He'd had his own business since the '70s. He talked sideways about it, defending himself as "not a grease monkey" but seemingly feeling unsure of being proud. I nodded as his words circled me in incongruous ribbons. I couldn't hear everything that he said because it was so loud with the music and bustle of many bodies, but I could see he was interested in me and I liked that he was a bit sarcastic.

We danced a couple of times, and he brought me in closer to him. I could feel his erection, and I believed he wanted me to. His eyes focused intently on mine and turned watery with longing when we pulled apart. He held my hand and followed me to the drink table. I liked him—or rather, I liked that he was paying attention to me.

After forty-five minutes or so of this, I told Matthew I didn't feel well. That was the truth. I had been taking an antibiotic for a sinus infection and was subpar. I asked if he ever went to the singles brunch on Sundays. He said he sometimes did. I told him I would be there that Sunday and excused myself for the night. He had a forlorn look as he watched me go.

When I got home, even though I felt yucky and tired, I called Steve and asked if he wanted to meet for a while. I couldn't admit to myself right then why I called him. It seemed dishonest and foolhardy. I told myself I just needed to remember what it felt like to be near someone I felt comfortable with. Then I would know if I really liked Matthew or not. But as we sat across the booth from one another, I realized I also wanted to see if Steve was still interested in me.

He did all the right things: he complimented me on my dress and how pretty I looked; he was chivalrous when he told the waiter I didn't care for the food. I wasn't up to saying anything about it, but he thought it important to mention. I appreciated how he could be a hero like that at times. We wandered easily in and out of conversation and staring at one another.

He dropped me off after and I felt mixed, like I always

did when I was near him: full of regret that he was so caught up in his own pain he couldn't ever be consistently available to me, and happy that he saw me so clearly. Why did I love him?

9 attended the singles brunch on Sunday and saw Matthew there.

I looked sexy and sharp in my tightly meshed periwinkle sweater and dainty jewelry. We sat at adjacent tables and had to twist around in our chairs to talk with each other. I caught him looking closely at the V-neck and my boobs. I liked that he desired me.

I stayed after to talk with him. He went on and on about his friend who was a nutritionist and how I should see her. I was supposed to meet Joan, who was visiting from out of town, and I was making myself late because I didn't feel I could leave. I didn't want to make a poor first impression. I wanted him to want me; I wanted him to want to call me. At the same time, I did let it register that his talking on and on and on was grating. I made note, too, that he deliberately left his wallet open to his driver's license. He kept bending it backward and pushing it upward while I stood next to him, trying to exit. Not so subtle. Did he want me to know how old he was? That he was fifty-two?

He called me soon after. We got together, and after that started seeing each other regularly. I felt relieved that I was wanted and not alone, again.

He had just moved into a place adjacent to his detail business, and it smelled like cars, car cleaners, oil, and grease. The stench permeated everything. I imagined my lungs blackening with each breath. I couldn't believe he couldn't smell it; I knew I would never get used to it.

What he lacked in detecting odors, however, Matthew more than made up for in organization. All of his shirts, pants, and shorts were hung up by length and color, with a quarter-inch space between each hanger. The color scheme went from light to dark, each hue in its own group, every piece straight and wrinkle-free. The only things that were folded were his boxers and socks. I had never seen anything like it.

He solicited my input about where to put his furniture and paintings. We shopped at Pier 1 Imports to look for accessories. He wanted to change out the blinds. I didn't understand that since he was renting the place, but he said he wanted it to look nice.

After he had been to my place a few times, he wanted to make changes there as well. He thought my kitchen cupboards should be painted. They were industrial brown, the original color from when the place was built in the 1970s. He dreamt out loud about making them a light shade of green. Then he wanted to make cupboards underneath my counter for storage. In the bedroom, he said I should remove my single shelf and bar and install one of those shelving units that economize the space. He offered to do this for me.

I bought it, and he came over one night to assemble it for me. I didn't have Shane, but it was a school night, and I warned him that I had loads of grading to do. He was very enthusiastic and said it wouldn't take that long. I was a novice at home improvement but knew enough that any estimates about a project were inherently faulty. But Matthew insisted, and soon he set about the process of measuring and marking, taking the racks and shelves out of the box.

I checked on him a couple of times. Things were progressing steadily, and he seemed happy. I immersed myself in grading and felt happy that we could be together but doing different things.

An hour eventually turned into six over a missing screw, not to mention three trips to the hardware store. The evening edged into night.

Finally, when I was nearly on the brink of exhaustion, Matthew was done. He showed me the finished product, proud of himself.

"It looks great," I said. "Thank you."

"I could have used your help on one part," he said, his face splotched with disappointment.

"You could have come got me," I offered, but as soon as I

said it, I knew he was not capable of playing fair. The way he shrugged told me a lot: he didn't feel as though he should have had to come get me; he thought I should have known to come in again. He was a victim, a martyr, and needed to stay that way so he had leverage. I would owe him. Not good.

$\mathcal{I}$ soon discovered Matthew had been living beyond his means, and he'd had to move into his friend's garage. His business had been located a few miles away for several years, but with the economy just keeping its head above water, not many people were coming in to have their cars detailed, and the rent at the other shop had been too high. He tried to keep his prices fair, and he had no employees but himself, but he was eking by.

Once I had factored in all of these things, I really didn't understand his need to be extravagant—about the blinds or anything else. His financial circumstances did not make me generous when it came time to pay for dinner out, however. Previously, I had been in the habit of asking if we should go Dutch or even offering to treat a companion to a meal, but all of that went out the window with Matthew. I let him pay. I sat across the table and waited for him to ask me, "Do you want to go Dutch?"

He never did. But he did look miffed a few times, expectant and confused. I had saturated myself with men who were stingy or who couldn't pay. I was tired of it. If he didn't have the balls to ask me to chip in and if he had the money to pay for interior decorating for a place he was renting, he could pay for dinner.

On one of my first visits to his place, I had brought him a copy of my recently self-published book, *Pocket Change*. He propped it up on his coffee table. He told me that he had read the first few sentences and would read more later. I knew he didn't read. His bookshelves were full of knick-knacks. He didn't need to read it, however; in fact, I thought things would probably be better between us if he didn't, because the book was all about other men. I didn't need him reading anything into who I was or wasn't. Besides, I was quite happy with the book and didn't need anyone mucking it up by being critical. It would be more than enough if he could accept me as I was.

I slept with him right away, somewhere in between the second and fifth outing. There was no argument about wearing condoms, but we got lazy about that pretty quickly. Once again, I allowed myself to be vulnerable to a pregnancy, and once again, I knew right away when it happened. My body changed in an instant. I felt bloated and my boobs were a cup size larger within days.

"I'm pregnant." I said it quietly, my head tilted to one side. I smiled. I waited.

We stood in the church parking lot, and he drew one finger along my jaw and chin before giving me a gentle kiss. He teared up.

"Everything will be okay," he said.

"I know it will."

"I'll call you a little later."

I felt like a pet, though I knew he meant to be kind. He didn't freak out and that was a relief. Though I had a proven escape route with Rutin, I knew I needed to quit cutting it so close. I started to wonder if taking that much Rutin would have detrimental effects on my body.

Matthew's favorite pastime was riding his bike. He was serious about it, and his career as a car detailer often infringed upon his ability to get out and ride. One evening we attended a game night for the singles group at our church, and as we were milling in the kitchen, grazing on the hors d'oeuvres and happily chatting about nothing in particular, he took a quick breath and asked me if I liked to ride.

"Sure," I said. "Yeah. I don't have a bike now, but I miss it. I used to ride my bike to work all the time."

"Good. Yeah." He nodded and smiled.

I learned later that his ex-wife didn't like to ride, and this had come between them. She couldn't understand his obsession with it, and he couldn't understand why she couldn't understand. He needed to be with someone who loved to bike as much as he did.

I raised an eyebrow at this. While I was not fazed by anyone's interest in a sport or passion—my dad had trained for marathons when I was younger—I wondered at the need for one's partner to share the same passion. Sure, you would always have something to do together, but why did it need to be a requirement? Loving to do it might mean different things for each person, and it certainly didn't guarantee commitment or intimacy. I decided his aspiration was too simple.

One evening as we were on our way to dinner, I told Matthew that I was entertaining the idea of returning to graduate school for a PhD.

He was driving and distracted by traffic and where to turn but still laughed and said, "What is it? BS for bullshit, MS, more shit, and PhD, full of shit."

I let him drive. No point in making things unsafe. But after we were seated in the restaurant, I said, "You know, when I said I was considering going back to school for my PhD, you hurt my feelings. I felt completely not supported. You made it into a joke."

His eyes fell back, sad. And then he began to tell me that I could do anything I wanted and if this was a dream of mine, I should pursue it. Somewhere in there was an "I'm sorry."

I continued by explaining that I hadn't felt supported in my marriage, and I couldn't be with anyone who didn't support my dreams.

When we returned to his place and were in the bathroom brushing our teeth, he reached his hand down my underwear and roved over my clitoris with one finger. "What else did your ex-husband not support you in doing?" he asked with a grin.

I couldn't help but smile because he was making me feel good, but I hated the vapid sloth that looked me in the eyes. He was this manipulative, this insecure?

❧

I ended things not much longer afterward.

I had flown out to California to visit Joan for a long weekend. I called to tell Matthew that I had arrived, and he talked to me as though he was a chatty clerk at a drive-thru. I hung up hating myself for having chosen him.

When I returned, he wouldn't respond to my phone calls.

I drove to his shop and arrived at the same time he was pulling in. He apologized for not returning my calls and invited me in.

I used the bathroom and saw that my shampoo and soap had been taken out of the shower. He said this didn't mean anything. He had just taken them out, that's all.

I put them in my car and told him I was shopping for a bicycle. Would he like to help me? He turned happy but then retracted it by retreating the next moment. "You're doing it because you want to, right?"

I laughed a little and reminded him that I used to ride my bike to work. Would he question my motive at every turn? I told him I would call him, and I did, but again, my calls were not returned.

I wrote a brief note. "I'm going to make this easy on both of us and end things here. Best wishes."

I drove to his garage and dropped the note through the mail slot. I then drove to the grocery store and called him from a pay phone to see if he was there. He picked up, "Klassic Kars, may I help you?"

He sniffed, his voice was garbled. My note had rendered tears. I had meant something to him after all.

CHAPTER EIGHT

At the Door

I attended a Memorial Day singles picnic to window shop for a new man. It had been several weeks since I'd ended things with Matthew. I had been in four brief entanglements in less than six months. Depending on my mood, I bemoaned my bad luck or mused to my friends that I was cursed with the six-week plan, as none of these courtships had lasted longer than two months. I was on the prowl and hell-bent on finding someone worthy of longevity.

Throughout the day, I engaged in conversation with three men. Rob was much older than I—sixty-four, making him twenty-eight years older. He was lively and funny, very likable. He and I talked intermittently in the food line and while surveying volleyball. He handed me his card, and I put it in my back pocket, along with the assumption that he was simply trying to drum up a client for his handy-man business.

Louis was closer to my age, only six years older, and reminded me of an Aztec warrior. His jawline and nose seemed chiseled out of stone. His jet-black hair fell to his shoulders at one length. His arms and legs were muscular, his waist trim. He laughed easily. I sat next to him on the grass and half-heartedly watched volleyball. I didn't know how closely to sit. Should I lean in? Fold my legs, leave them outstretched, lean on him, lean on a tree or pole? I watched to see if he was interested in anyone else there, or if he had come with anyone. I had never felt permitted to sit so close to someone this gorgeous. I thought if I blinked he might disappear in a bubble of my imagination.

Harry was a forty-eight-year-old virgin. He confided that he'd had six dates with one woman in the last two years, and without mincing words said that he knew nothing at all about sex. He traveled all over the world as an engineer. I believed him. He looked the part. Between his black-framed glasses, which he constantly had to push up, and his pudgy body, he reminded me of a young boy who would be fascinated for hours at the edge of a pond. He talked fast, using an expanded vocabulary. His father had died recently, and Harry now found himself spending a lot of time with his mother when he was in town. He didn't strike me as wanting to be rescued or taught anything. He was innocent. I found it hard to fathom how someone could go through life excising himself from the trials and joys of coupling; by evening's end, I decided that his learning curve in the land of relating would probably be so steep that I would lose patience.

Of the three, I felt the most drawn to Louis that day. He was intelligent. He had a couple of degrees under his belt, but he also had an interest in the arts, and in particular, music. I could talk piano with him, as this was his instrument too. And the clincher: he seemed to like me. I kept winding my way near him that afternoon.

Before I left, I asked Louis for his card, but he had none with him. Ron—once again the mutual friend—was there and I coolly said that I would call him and the three of us could have breakfast sometime. Louis encouraged me to do this soon. I walked away from him and rounded the volleyball court.

As I got closer to the guy who was serving, he extended his hand.

"You're such a pretty girl," he said. "Where have you been all of my life?" His steps crossed one another, his face was rosy drunk.

I smiled. "I think you need to serve the ball."

He told me to wait, he needed me, but I kept walking. The belle of the ball, I was leaving with the world in the palm of my hands.

A day or two later, Ron called to find out if it would be okay to give my number to Louis. Delighted, I said yes. The formality of this tickled me; it felt like a gesture from another age, something between Victorian England and middle school.

Louis called within hours of my saying yes to Ron.

We talked on the phone several times before arranging a time to meet. He wanted to see *Shrek* and Ron loved that movie, so we made a plan to rent it the following weekend and watch it together at Ron's place.

Ron fell asleep long before the credits rolled, which gave me and Louis a lot of time to tease and flirt. We ended the evening by agreeing to make another date soon.

Louis called me frequently throughout the coming days. I had given him my office number, which was an archaic instrument and had no voicemail or answering machine— which meant that when someone called, it would not stop ringing. Louis called during three separate intervals while I was teaching one day and let it ring twenty times. My office-mate got so annoyed with listening to the nagging *brrring* that she picked up and gave him a piece of her mind.

I felt flattered that someone would be so persistent. I had finally birthed myself into a new land of man, where they remembered my name and didn't hesitate to use the communication tools of the modern age. Indeed, my six-week plan genus had been steeped in the schema of "unavailable" or "busy."

Louis and I made arrangements to watch another movie together—at his place this time, not chaperoned by Ron. The movie was horrible, forgettable, but we sat through it like good children.

Afterwards, we talked and talked as we slumped and slouched but never quite lay down on his floor. Finally, he said he wanted to know what it would feel like if he kissed me. He reflected that one girlfriend he'd had wouldn't let him kiss her for three months, and it was six months before they slept together. Then it was over. And then there were some he had slept with right away and things had gone on for months. Who knew what might happen?

He closed his eyes and pressed his full lips against mine. Soft, a promise for the next moment.

Then he became unglued, his eyes furtively searched for answers, a way out. I felt a too-certain cramp of disappointment form in my stomach as I watched him.

"You make me want to change my life," he said.

I wasn't expecting that; it alarmed me. I waited but before he could get it out, I knew. No one ever wants to change his life when he's happy. There was someone else.

He ineloquently explained that she had been his girlfriend before, but it didn't mean anything now. They had gone back to each other repeatedly. "You can always go back to your exes," he said. "And she wants to get things going again, but she means nothing to me. She doesn't understand music and anyone who sets foot in my house has got to know this guy loves music! I'm going to be a conductor, Jane. One day, you'll know this to be true about me. But you! I can talk to you. You're intelligent and pretty, and you play piano! You make me want to change my life. I mean it."

I stared at him incredulously, and then I laughed heartily.

"This is not funny, girl," he said with a frown. "I've got a real dilemma here."

"No," I said. "This is hilarious. I've got no business trying to be in another relationship, and here I've found someone who is unavailable! It's perfect. You mirror where I am. I'm not ready and neither are you!" I laughed some more as I stood up.

"But I want to be with you," he said.

I shook my head. "I'm not getting involved with someone who has got someone else."

"It's just casual sex."

"It's really late. I need to go home. And I'm very tired."

"You could sleep here," he persisted. "We could share my bed. Nothing has to happen. You shouldn't drive when you're tired. It's not safe. It's close to three. Stay. You can go home in the morning."

It is *morning*, I pouted silently to myself.

Maybe I wanted to believe that everything could work out. I didn't have a long drive home, fifteen minutes tops. It would have been easy to leave. Maybe I wanted to share a bed with someone. Maybe I needed to find out what would happen if I did stay. How would I feel? Maybe I was too tired to think anything more about it. I was tired in general. Tired of choosing men who didn't want to call me, tired of excuses, tired of searching, tired of hoping. Minutes before, when I'd told Louis that his unavailability was reflecting my lack of readiness, was the first time I'd started to accept that fact. I had been circling and dodging my denial of this reality during all of my recent six-week rendezvous.

It was one thing to look at someone and say, "No. Not you." It was another to realize that I was a magnet for the very characteristic that I found so discombobulating. I didn't want to let anyone in, and until I did I wasn't going to attract anyone who was ready or willing to unveil themselves to me either. This realization made me even more tired.

I stayed.

I climbed into Louis's bed with my underwear and shirt on and tried to fall asleep. He held me and asked me to imagine that he was Frederic Chopin and I was George Sand and we only had one night together. What would happen? I rolled away from him and said that we were Louis and Jane.

"No, no," he whispered. "Think about it. Two passionate people. A writer and a musician. Think about if they had this one night together. Do you think they would pass it by? Wouldn't they want to know?"

I tried hard to remember if Chopin and Sand were even alive during the same century. Historical figures and dates were not my forte, no matter how close they were to the heart and soul of my interests. I'd come up with all sorts of mnemonic devices to devise recalling these details when I was studying music history during my undergrad days, but none of them had taken root in my long-term memory. And I was definitely in no mood to dig around as the hours crept deeper into the night and edged ever more quickly into a sleep-deprived new day.

I made a feeble attempt to postulate that they hadn't even lived during the same era or in physical proximity to each other. It was a stab in the dark.

Louis argued that this was not the point.

We caught snatches of sleep between rebuttals, hugs, and kisses on the forehead and neck. Occasionally, too, his fingers would venture down the inside of my underwear. Each time I pulled his hand out or pushed it to one side, fearful of what allowing him to continue would bring. I had brief flashes of horror at trying to remember what kind of underwear I had on, too, and whether or not he might laugh at them.

I felt around the edge of my underwear, trying to remember if they were one of the too many I owned whose elastic had worn through unevenly but which hadn't quite shredded enough to graduate into the rag pile. Relieved, I relaxed. This was an older pair, but they had only a tiny, barely perceptible hole in the front.

I hadn't planned on spending the night in Louis's bed. I hadn't planned on removing my clothes down to my underwear and a T-shirt. Therefore, I was wearing my crappy but more comfortable undies. And maybe for that brief, bleary-eyed moment I was panicking about which pair of underwear I had on because that was within my control. I could reassure myself with this insignificant detail, despite the fact that I could do nothing to change it right then. It was simple to think about, an easy situation to resolve if I wanted to. What I didn't want to acknowledge or take any responsibility for was that Louis wasn't interested in my underwear but rather what was inside of it.

I had said "no" to him and yet there I was in his bed, letting him hold me and kiss my neck, listening to him whisper arguments about "what if," and loving the chiseled strength in his face and his lean body.

After his fingers had traveled the length of my torso and between my legs for the umpteenth time, I gave in.

I insisted that he wear a condom and felt briefly empowered. Since he had been teasing me for hours, I was more than aroused. Our embrace was compassionate but furious. Fantastic.

Finally, we slept.

Louis and I had told Ron separately that we would meet him and others for a weekly singles breakfast gathering, but we slept through it and Ron's phone call to rouse Louis.

When I did finally amble out of bed, I was groggy and felt an unmistakable dread set in.

We went out to eat. On the way there, Louis held my hand as he drove. It was reassuring, but I felt confused and impatient. I wanted him to choose me or reject me. I wanted an announcement of what would happen next. Was he going to talk to her, his casual sex partner/ex-girlfriend?

I watched him read the newspaper during breakfast. I didn't want to confront him. I wanted to be held. I wanted to run away. I looked to him to take all of my discomfort away, but I knew somewhere deep down that he wouldn't and couldn't. I had no words to share with him for what I felt. I was only feeling it and knowing that being consumed by it was stifling me at that moment. What had I gotten myself into? Had I gotten myself into anything? I could walk away. This didn't have to be anything at all.

The rest of the day was a blur. I called Ron to apologize for missing breakfast. I knew he knew what had happened. I felt exposed and embarrassed. He didn't say anything to let on that he knew; I was grateful.

I emailed Louis to say that I felt as though I had no respect for myself. I had let myself down. He argued with me that we had taken advantage of an opportunity. The next few days entwined and disassembled themselves, a series of meetings at restaurants and phone calls with him arguing that everything was okay and me wading through what felt so wrong.

I told him a few times that I was a strong woman and was clear about this. He said he could see right through it and that he didn't care because he could see I was vulnerable and sensitive too.

He talked a lot about being friends and getting to know one another gradually, but then he always circled back to how great it had been to be intimate with me. Looming between us was his ex-girlfriend. I had been party to triangles before, and that chapter of my life was closed.

Finally, I wrote him a letter and hand-delivered it to his house. When we talked on the phone, I told him, "Call me when you make up your mind. I'm not going to be part of this."

He insisted that we could be friends. He called several times, refusing to hear my "no."

I told him that I would contact the authorities if he called me again. This scared him enough to stop for a while.

The next time he contacted me was two months later, on my birthday. He emailed me and invited me to play piano at a soiree he planned on having in December. The date he suggested did not work for my schedule; I suggested another, believing that by then, I would not feel threatened again by being near him. He never wrote back.

$\mathcal{I}n$ the pits of self-loathing, I cleaned out my purse, found Rob's business card, and called him. It had been two weeks since I'd told Louis I would contact the authorities if he called me again.

Rob charmed the socks off of me, and I didn't resist it. We talked easily and shared the stage deftly. He was genuine, curious, and inquisitive. It felt like a salve on my battered heart. I didn't care that he was sixty-four, and I opted to turn off my alarm about other shards of his persona.

Somewhere between the laughter and fragmentary reminiscence of personal histories, Rob unraveled a yarn about how he had attended domestic violence classes for two years. He had not hit anyone but had been charged with harassment. His sentence had included a day in jail and two years of group therapy classes.

He shook his head in shame, recalling how he had to call his "little old mother," who was eighty-eight at the time, to come bail him out of jail.

"I just wanted to finish an argument," he said. "Gladys took off in her car, and I followed her. I had to have the last word. She drove all over town and then drove into the Castle Rock Police Department parking lot. She got out and told an officer I was harassing her. That was it."

I shook my head, which appeared like empathy, but I was quietly marveling at how quickly he had exposed himself to me. I had recently stopped feeling proud about people entrusting me with their confessions, but I had yet to piece together what exactly it was about me that seemed to impel people to unload their deepest and darkest confidences in the first few moments after meeting me.

I tucked away my red flag, believing Rob had learned something from his time in group therapy. And I thanked God I was meeting him now, years after the fact.

He wanted to know, however, if I had a story of equal (shaming) value. This I resisted. The worst thing I'd ever done was cheat on my husband at the end of our marriage, and I was not going to tell this to Rob or anyone else unless it was a matter of life or death. People like to draw conclusions about morality; they never forget the indiscretion and quietly watch for signs that you're executing your malfeasant ways. I had felt plenty guilty about having generated that much pain for both Matt and me. Rob didn't need to know all that.

I must have provided Rob with some embarrassing anecdote. It might have been from childhood—the time I stole the silver dollars from my friend's house across the street, for example. My dad made me return them that night after I told him I had taken them. I might also have recalled the time I farted at the grocery store and my son called out, "Mom! Will you stop farting?!"

He commented at the end of our lunch that he was surprised how much he liked me; he assumed that since I taught English I would be boring and no fun at all.

I called Rob that Saturday night and asked if he was going to the dance at our church. He hemmed and hawed. He'd been having trouble with his knees since his replacement surgery and dancing bothered them.

I went anyway.

Harry was there. He told me again that he didn't know anything about sex while we danced too closely.

I met another man that night who told me about "worry" stones. He explained that the color of the stone turned to white the more it was rubbed. He pulled out one stone from his pocket. It had been peach before, he said, and now it was all white. He'd been rubbing it for two weeks.

His eyes pooled and his sallow cheeks made me want to go to the chip bowl. I saw him pull the stone out again for another woman's viewing later on.

I left feeling defeated and ridiculous. Wasn't I worth more than a confessional?

I felt a little happy that I could call Rob again too.

Over the coming weeks, Rob and I met for a movie and a few meals, and I was amazed by how easy it was for me to talk to him. He was clever and witty and could follow any idea of mine effortlessly. He created analogies for himself, so he could better understand my world. It was endearing. I steeled myself against going to bed with him too quickly, though. Regret was fresh in my mind because of my experience with Louis; I didn't want to go further with something that would make the wound bleed anew.

I knew our age difference bothered Rob more than it bothered me. He brought it up in a variety of ways: he had kids older than I was and grandchildren that could be my siblings. He covered my ears at the movie theater when the clerk asked him if he was a senior.

But Rob's libido got the better of him, and it spawned a charismatic and devilish blend that I had difficulty recognizing at first. He was also acutely intuitive; his sixth sense was never off. Having been around only one other man (Steve) who was similarly sensitive, I was enamored and fascinated by Rob's untrained ability to read me. It had been a year and a half since he'd had sex, and I was soon to discover how important this was to him.

We were in his truck in the parking lot one evening, saying good night to each other. He said over and over again how a woman's body was the most sensuous thing on earth—how there was nothing finer. He told me many times that I was beautiful. His fingers touched my jaw line and cheek; he kissed my neck, mumbled a request to touch me, and then dipped his fingers inside my blouse and underneath my breast.

My "no" alarm went off. I lifted his hand and gave it back to him. He laughed and admitted to being "forward."

"I just love the touch and feel of a woman so much," he said. "So soft and lovely."

Bombarded, I couldn't keep up with what I felt. Angry that he wasn't listening to my "no"; fear that I was heading into bed with him and would regret it later; flattered that he kept calling me beautiful; squishy because I was still wounded over Louis; amazed and appalled that Rob (along with many other men) would just step in and take what he wanted; and aroused. Not in that order, though, and the percentages kept shifting. I couldn't catalogue all of this as it was happening; I was confused and simply wanted to follow the loudest feeling.

"We can just end the night right here and that will be okay. I don't want you feeling like you have to do anything . . . oh, that feels nice though," he said as he reached inside my blouse again.

It's your choice, he said with words. *Do what I want*, he said with his fingers. The contradiction was amusing and annoying. I couldn't hold those two ideas in my head simultaneously. It was going to have to be one or the other. I wanted the noise of all of my feelings to quiet and stop.

It took us less than five minutes to reach his mobile home. The minimum age to live there was fifty-five. Kids and young adults were visitors. I remembered my mother's mobile home park as I pulled into his driveway and asked myself what the hell I was doing. I squashed it with, "I'm going to have sex." This didn't have to be anything that lasted longer than a night.

It wasn't great, but it was satisfying.

When it was over, he rolled over and put his arm on top of me. He kissed me several times throughout the night. I wondered if he thought I was going to leave. I got no sleep.

I told him in the morning that I didn't like how he'd acted the night before.

He explained that he couldn't help it; he wanted to be close to me.

I decided to give him another chance.

$\mathcal{W}\!e$ resumed this conversation the next time I stayed over. Rob said then that he would try to keep to his side of the bed, but it would be hard to do so.

"I'll go home if you can't," I said.

He did try. It had been a year and a half since anyone had shared the bed with him.

The woman he'd dated right before me was a young, single mother of two sons. I heard a lot about her and about many of the women before me—more than I wanted to know, but I didn't stop him from gushing forth with it either. He seemed to need to get it out, and I was used to people telling all. Besides, I didn't really want him to stop; I was learning about him. This was intimacy, or at least what I had always believed it to be.

What bothered me most was Rob's repetition of the same stories and feelings, some of which were thirty or more years old.

He had been madly in love with the neighbor's wife, with whom he had had a seven-year affair while he was married to his first wife. The husband was a doctor and was gone frequently; Rob was a handy-man and was around a lot, did work for them around the house. They had talked at length about leaving their spouses for each other. They had talked and laughed and had lots and lots of sex. He'd been devastated when she divorced her husband and married another man—and when he discovered after his own divorce that his wife had been having an affair as well. She ended up marrying the guy and was still with him thirty years later.

He shook his head and looked at the floor when he said, "It doesn't make you feel very good about yourself when you find out news like that."

I thought it laughable that he could feel sorry for himself over this when he had been doing the same thing to her. He had even described playing footsie with the neighbor's wife when the four of them got together to play cards, right underneath the table they were all sitting at together.

I stuffed my urge to guffaw at this blatant contradiction and tried to stay focused on the question of whether he had changed. A friend once told me that it doesn't matter what anybody's done in their life that counts; it's where they are now as a result of those choices. Have they come through it and made peace with themselves, or has the sum total risen above the neckline so they're nearly drowning in it?

Rob had been married five years to his second wife. She'd told him on the stairwell of their mansion, after he had just finished the last home improvement project in a series of several, that she wanted a divorce. She ended up marrying an old boyfriend—husband number four for her—within a few months. That had lasted only a couple of years, he had heard.

Rob had felt so angry over this marriage's dissolution that he'd packed up all of the lingerie he had ever bought her and brought it with him when he moved into his trailer. He asked me a couple of times if I wanted any of it. I felt a little sick at the thought of wearing someone else's lingerie, never worn or not, and politely said, "No." What was he thinking?

I stored all of these stories in the back of my mind, along with the one I had heard first about his serving a day in jail and attendance at domestic violence classes.

I learned that the most recent girlfriend, the single mom, was a lawyer. Her ex-husband was abusive. "It was quite a sight to see her shrink whenever she said his name," Rob said. "I just wanted to save her."

After two weeks, though, she ended it. She told him that she could see where things were going, and she just didn't have room in her life for him. They could be friends but that was all. And they were. He still did things for her and they emailed back and forth a bit, but that was it. He had written her about me, and she was happy for him.

It seemed Rob had made peace with himself, and that things had calmed down for him. I could forgive old grief. Who was I to be judge and jury about what he felt then, or even now? Besides, he was very willing and eager to learn about me and "do for" me. There were many home improvement projects he wanted to take on.

I told him early on that I could not pay him for any of it. I would pay for supplies, of course, but not labor. He said he didn't mind; I was paying him in other ways—nudge, nudge, wink, wink. It made me queasy to think of sex as payment, but it wasn't as if I wasn't getting anything out of that too.

He wanted to paint my kitchen cupboards first.

We went to the paint store to pick out a color I liked. I chose a faint sea-foam green. We picked up a five-gallon bucket, paint screen, rollers and naps, masking tape and paper for Rob's masking machine, sand paper, tarps, and a stick to stir the paint. It wasn't that expensive, around $70.00. I paid for it.

He removed the cupboard doors with his electric drill and stacked them in his truck to be painted at his place, where he had a driveway and sawhorses. We were about two weeks into knowing each other. Things were fun and light. We joked, laughed, and talked a lot and were having a lot of sex.

He taught me how to paint using the roller and a sprayer. I was impressed with how he had devised a way to spray the doors. He tapped nails into the backside of the cupboard doors so that they jutted out at a forty-five-degree angle, and then used the nail as leverage to attach each door from a hook that hung from a clothesline. It made things much easier, as we were able to spray the doors thoroughly without having to contend with propping them up in precarious angles.

We also replaced the bathroom door and front door of my condo. Nothing had been updated since the place had been built in 1973, but I tended to ignore things like out-dated chocolate brown doors. It didn't occur to me that a dark color on a door could make a room gloomy.

Rob finished the doors first. The cupboard doors he held on to longer than I had hoped or wanted, but I felt helpless to demand that these be finished and returned. Tension was mounting between us; I felt uncomfortable about his re-peated moaning about the lost love in his life, and with the fact that he was beginning to accuse me of having affairs with other men. (This began at about week three.) There was tension, too, around his wanting to spend more time with Shane and my refusal to allow this.

Shane and I did go to Rob's mobile home park to go swimming one night, but that was the only time they had interacted with one another. The co-parenting schedule I had with Matt was fifty-fifty, so there was plenty of time to see Rob that didn't have to include Shane—and besides, I had reservations about introducing my son to any new friends. As experience was teaching me, I never knew how long anything was going to last, and I didn't want my son becoming need-lessly attached to anyone who might be gone in a few weeks. I also didn't need any additional encumbrances; breaking up with someone was proving to be difficult enough all by itself.

One afternoon, my friend and piano student, Lance, came over to help out with painting my bedroom ceiling. It had water stains and a spray of holes across it that appeared to be the result of a random b-b gunshot. I hated the sight of it, and since I had caught the fever for improving my home, I decided this, too, should be taken care of. Lance agreed to paint it in exchange for a couple of lessons.

The night before, Rob and I had hung and taped tarp around my bedroom walls to shield them, the carpet, and furniture from speckled paint. He did most of it while I watched and assisted him as needed. He had made it about halfway around my room and was near my computer desk when I tightened up and held my breath.

The ceiling was blanketed with tiny balls, the size of rabbit pellets—to conceal the panels of plaster, Rob had explained earlier—and as he aligned the tape where the wall and ceiling met the balls were falling off and sprinkling the carpet all around my room.

Rob turned around in the middle of leaning over my computer desk and said, "What, what? What's wrong?"

I felt startled that he picked up on my angst. If he could tell that I felt tense without looking at me, what else was he capable of noticing about me that I didn't want him to see?

"Nothing," I said. I knew I wasn't going to get away with that with him, so I added, "The little balls; they're falling on my computer. I'm afraid they'll get into the keyboard."

"Oh. We'll just cover them up like this, then. Okay?" He draped the tarp over the desk and computer. "Happy?" He smiled. "You scared me, I thought something was really wrong."

My fear shriveled me. I continued to watch him work. If he could sense me tightening up over fallen pellets, could he smell the doubt I felt about the two of us? I imagined myself in the presence of a predator, stealthily watching its prey. He was clever, smart, and highly attuned.

Rob let me use the remains of a large bucket of white paint he already had for the ceiling. Lance spackled the holes and put the first coat on easily and quickly. It looked good, but the stains bled through. He put another coat on. I played the piano while he worked.

Rob called to see how things were going. Lance's girlfriend called to see how things were going. Before lunch, each of them called us at least twice. While we took a lunch break together, the girlfriend called again. They were worried, though those were not the words they spoke.

Lance and I shook our heads as we sat down to lunch.

"What are they thinking?" I asked.

We laughed. It was safe to do so there, between the two of us.

One morning I went home from Rob's place to meet my teacher, Patrick, for a one-on-one clairvoyant course. Rob called right after I arrived at home and wanted to know what happened to the two bottles of lavender oil he had purchased. I told him I had them.

"Why?" he demanded. "What are you going to do with them?"

"The one half full is mine," I said. "I took it home to keep it here. I thought you had given me the other one. I didn't know if we might use it here or not anyway."

"But why do you need the other one? You're not seeing someone else, are you?" His voice was craggy, shrill. "Is Patrick there?"

Deflated, I became still inside. "No. Patrick is not here. He is my teacher. I am not seeing anyone else. Why would I, and when would I have time?"

"Why did you take them? I bought that new one. It stays here."

"I'll bring it back, but not now. I have my class in fifteen minutes. I wasn't thinking when I picked it up; I was just putting stuff in a bag."

Somehow, we got off the phone. He wasn't satisfied with my answers, and I knew we would go another round with this later on. I tried to push these thoughts out of my head and got ready for my session with Patrick.

I was doing a fourteen-month spiritual practice with him. He was guiding me through certain principles and releasing old wounds. It was powerful and was helping me begin to identify who in my life had a process for letting go of the past and who resisted doing this. I had decided not to look too closely at Rob. I hadn't made up my mind about whether or not I could be around someone who didn't have a process for letting go. What was clear to me, however, was that I didn't feel responsible for other people's unresolved issues.

I had spent much of my marriage feeling like I had to teach or guide Matt toward understanding me and building bridges that would allow us to connect with one another. When I left, I'd decided I would never go to those same lengths with anyone else. And each relationship I'd had since then represented another step away from feeling as though I needed to monitor the pulse of the emotional well-being of my partner. That habit had stripped my imaginative energy and worn me down. I wanted to devote my creativity to other aspects of my life, like my career and writing, and things that were not subject to the volatility of a relationship.

Still, I felt guilty for abandoning a post I had nurtured and guarded for so long. I had formed an identity around tracking the emotional weather of my partner. Who was I if I wasn't in a relationship? Would I be okay if I wasn't in one? I would talk about taking time off between men, but I could never rest for longer than a few weeks—on rare occasions, six weeks. Instead of allowing myself to receive an answer by leaving well enough alone and being alone, I would instead ask myself if I could be okay with the man I was with and still find my way with my other goals. I knew that I needed my partner to be supportive of me, to show an interest in me, and to share my interests. These were things I had over-looked when I decided to marry my husband but were now my minimum requirements.

Rob tried. He bought books about spirituality. He gave me a volume of Emerson's essays. We discussed a few of them. We could talk for long stretches in depth. We fed off each other's ideas and conclusions. It was dazzling and fasci-nating. But his angst about my abandoning him for another man played on and on like a talking toy whose battery could recharge at will. His constant score-keeping of who said "I love you" more and his need for me to account for all of my activities outside of our interactions drained me. I wanted sparkly, intellectual Rob who cared about my feelings to be around full time, and wished this insecure, squirming worm would burrow into the dirt and disappear for good.

One night at Rob's place, I baked pies. One large pie was for paramedics at a local fire department who were going to give me a free EKG. I needed one that showed I no longer had a heart murmur and therefore was no longer in need of a preventative prescription of antibiotics prior to dental appointments. The dose was dense, caused me great nausea, and always instigated a yeast infection. I believed the regimen was overkill, resented it, and had stopped seeing a dentist for several years as a result. I wasn't having any trouble with my teeth, but I did want to have them checked out.

Steve was the one who'd made the arrangements for me. He had been a paramedic and still had connections with his former cohorts. I'd asked him what a good repayment would be for the paramedics, and he'd said that they would love a pie. I did not tell Rob that an old boyfriend had made the arrangement; I'd stayed mum about the details, and fortunately, Rob hadn't pressed for them. I made a second, smaller pie just for him.

It had been a long day, full of painting and running errands. I needed to get the pies baked, however, because my appointment at the fire department was the next morning.

Rob had rented movies, and we watched one while the pies were baking. We sat on his couch, and I stretched my legs out into his lap. His fingers crawled like a spider up and down my arms and legs. I kept stopping the ticklish nuisance by holding his hand, but he never got the message for long; each time, he desisted for only a minute and then began again. He looked at me while I watched the movie. I was having a hard time keeping my eyes open.

The pies finished baking and the movie ended at about the same time. Finally, it was time to go to sleep. All I could think about was dropping into bed.

Rob, of course, had other ideas. When he made his advances, I asked if we could please make love in the morning.

"Ookay," he said, which meant that nothing was going to be okay. But I wanted it to be okay, so I took his word at face value and rolled over to go to sleep.

He got up within a few minutes and went out to his living room. I reluctantly got up and followed him.

"What's going on, Rob?"

"I'm just thinking," he said. "I got a lot on my mind."

"About what?"

Things escalated from there. I remember saying a few times that I was exhausted and asking, "Do we have to do this now?" He shouted back, "Where is my love?" He said that I had spent my time and energy baking pies for people I didn't even know, and now I was too tired to have sex.

I sat on his couch and listened to his rant, horrified by how insecure he was. My request to sleep and then have sex in the morning felt to him like abandonment. I knew right then that we would not last. He was making me crazy and wrung out. There was no safe place with him.

I felt trapped. Rob had my damned cupboard doors. I needed them back. But I knew enough about him to understand that he could be vindictive, manipulative, and nasty. Here was a man who was capable of boxing up and driving off with all of his wife's lingerie. A man who would follow a woman around town, even into a police parking lot, just to have the last word.

I could think of nothing else but the enormous inconvenience of not having cupboard doors in my kitchen and how I would replace them if I didn't get them back. When he had removed the cupboard doors, he had also taken out my filthy, thirty-year-old stove vent. This, too, had not been repurchased or replaced yet.

I knew which side of me Rob wanted, so for the next couple of weeks, I showcased her. I had sex when he wanted to. I told him I loved him often. I spent as much time as possible with him. I listened to him through repeat renditions of lost love and heartbreak. I masked my angst so he wouldn't sense I had one foot pointing out the door. I hinted at having the cupboards reinstalled by the time school started again. He was eager, happy, willing.

Thank God.

Within a few days of my kitchen looking normal again, I told Rob on the phone that I wanted to take a break from talking to each other. I was overwhelmed with classes having started up again for the fall semester, and I needed some time to myself. He resisted, saying that time off was going to lead to a breakup. "Not necessarily," I told him—and in my heart of hearts, I believed that was true. I didn't really know how I was going to feel after a couple of days. Would I miss him? Miss our conversations, the sex?

In a subsequent conversation, he said he'd told his younger son that I wanted time off, and his son had said, "Let her have it. If it's real and true, she will come back and then you'll know. Let her have a week if she needs it." To this Rob said, "I don't know. I don't know." But he capitulated.

After a day of not talking to Rob at all, I felt lighter than I had in weeks. The color of possibility was returning to my imagination. I believed talking with him could go well.

I called him, and we agreed to meet at the mall where we first had lunch eight weeks before.

I had written him a letter that called things off. I had decided the safest route out was to say I was too busy to be in a relationship with him, especially in contrast to the amount of time he had available. I had just begun a fall semester; I was on tap to teach seven classes and they were all English classes, which meant a lot of reading. I thought even through his paranoia and insecurities, Rob would be capable of seeing what busy looked like. Besides, it was true. It just wasn't the full truth.

I acknowledged that our intimate life was fun and said I appreciated everything he had done for me as far as home improvement projects went. I also reiterated that I felt uncomfortable that I could not pay him in a conventional manner. I didn't want to take advantage of him. I didn't want him to grow to be resentful of doing so much for me while I wasn't able to spend much time with him.

I was convinced being too busy would be my safe escape. It had seemed to work for the woman he last dated, who was smarter than I was and had ended things after two weeks.

I handed the letter to Rob as soon as we sat down for lunch. After he read it, the talking began. He fought me on all of the points I had made. I cried because I was so frustrated. He wasn't going to let me go. And because I wasn't relenting, he made it personal and ugly. We talked for hours—at the mall, in his car, on our way to the hardware store after he agreed to purchase and install my overhead stove vent.

At the hardware store, he extended one arm and bowed his head as he leaned forward. He said, "This is so hard, just so hard." He wiped a tear from his eye.

I thought he was kidding at first and wanted to laugh but deferred to being observant and cautious in case he was serious. I wanted comic relief. I wanted it to be over. I wanted him to go home and leave me alone forever.

While he installed my vent, he repeated to himself that he shouldn't be doing this. "She said, 'I want a divorce' after I put the last nail in the railing. She stood at the top of the stairs and ripped my heart out. Stupid. Stupid. I didn't learn, did I? I do for you, for nothing. I had sex every day of my marriage to her except the last two or three months when things were falling apart."

He stood in my kitchen and told me all he had done wrong was love me. That I was the one who couldn't love. I couldn't give it back to him, or anyone, maybe.

After he left, I laughed a little at my stove vent. He had done it; he'd put it in for me. And then I cried hard. Uncontrollably, I shook. I had held so much in for too long. I boiled over, and it all needed to come out in order for me to make my way back to a self that didn't lie or mask or leap or dodge in a pretense to please Rob or anyone else. I felt liberated, relieved. I didn't have to feel afraid anymore.

၇

Two days later, Rob emailed me.

The subject line was "last contact."

Been thinking about us tonight, putting a time frame on our time together and your letter on not being in a relationship; it doesn't seem that you've been out of one for very long, I believe you were still in one, or just out, when you met me, and Louis didn't work out, so that's when you contacted me. We hadn't been together too long before it got sexual between us and it was great, for me, but I've been thinking that might be the kind of relationship you want, that was the first thing in your notes Monday, was sleeping together and good sex, so when I cared so much and wanted more time with you is when you started backing off. I really feel like a stupid fool feeling that you will probably be in bed with someone before this month is out, I'm having doubts on how much you really cared, guess if someone can't return another's feelings, they must not be there, I will never know will I.

I'm hurt and angry, feeling like the fool knowing you will be in bed with someone soon.

I was furious. I wanted to call him and scream, "How dare you question my love for you!?"

But I had to get on with the business of preparing for my classes and getting Shane ready for school. I was exhausted from the drama and didn't want to invite more of it into my life. I did reply to the email by saying that what I needed most was a friend. It was not lover first, friend second. It was friend first, then we'll see what happens.

I also wrote that I did really care for him, and it didn't matter what I did or said because he always managed to question it. He'd been accusing me of seeing someone else since our second week of dating.

On the phone, I would have reminded him that I was the one hesitating the night we first slept together. I was the one saying that we should get to know each other longer, while he was the one putting his hand inside my shirt. I didn't bother saying this in my email.

᥎

A week later, I let my night class out early—at 9:00 p.m. instead of the usual 9:45 p.m. end time—and headed home.

I felt a dark heaviness around the stairwell as I walked up the steps to my condo. It reminded me of Rob, but I decided my feelings were simply leftover reverberations from the letdown and anger.

I let myself in and picked up the phone to call Steve. Before I started dialing, I heard a knock at the door.

I looked through the peephole Rob had installed in my new front door and saw him standing there, dressed to the nines in a sports coat, sweater, and slacks.

I opened the door and stepped outside with the phone in my hand.

"What are you doing here?" I asked.

He arched past me to look in. "Have you finished the kitchen?"

"No," I said shortly. "I haven't had any time. I'm busy."

"I went to the school, but you'd already left. I came to see you. I've missed you, and I hope you've missed me too." He looked me in the eye before leaning in to hug and kiss me a few times on my cheek and neck.

I didn't budge. "You're dressed up, Rob. You going out somewhere?"

"Hee-hee. I got dressed up to see you. I was thinking about what you said. I didn't understand that you needed time to yourself, like you said, but I understand it now. And I can give you that. I can try. 'Cause we had something great and I miss you."

I felt the number pads of the phone underneath my thumb. It occurred to me that he had been waiting for me at school and then followed me home from a distance. Either that or he'd circled back and forth between them a couple of times before I got home.

I thought of who I could call.

I stood with my hip against the door. I looked at Rob

and wondered if we could stand there together without saying anything and feel comfortable. I wanted that; then, maybe, I could believe in being with him again. But I also didn't want to struggle with weighing the pros and cons of this. I just wanted him to leave.

"Well, I came by to see how you were. It's been a week and all, and I sure do miss you. Call me. You know. I love you." He pivoted to walk away. "Don't watch me go," he said as he headed down the steps. "This is hard enough as it is."

I closed and locked the door and watched him through my peephole. I felt disgusted. My heart raced, and I was furious and afraid. Would this be the end?

I called Steve and vented to him. He feared for my safety.

I wrote Rob an email saying that if he ever came by unannounced like that again, I would contact the authorities. I needed to feel safe in my own home.

He wrote back that he'd only come by to see the look in my eyes, and they had told him everything he needed to know.

I quipped to friends that he must have seen a black hole of no future.

After about a month, just when I had begun to breathe easier, a package arrived via Certified Mail. Rob's handwriting. I knew what it was immediately: a book I had left at his place and had resolved was not worth my time or energy to retrieve. I realized that he had held on to it as a lure to get me to contact him. He had pulled a similar stunt the night we exchanged goods; he'd told me he had forgotten that shampoo I liked. I knew he was lying. Rob didn't forget anything, ever.

The book arrived a couple of days after his birthday. I knew he had expected me to contact him on his birthday as a friendly gesture, but whatever impulse I had had to nurture a friendship had washed out with the six hours we had spent breaking up at the mall and the hardware store.

Along with the book came a bill for everything he had

ever done for me, which he'd decided to charge at $40/hour. The grand total neared $1,200.

I was appalled and horrified. I wondered if he could take me to court over this.

I called my father, then my mother. Neither of them knew what to suggest. They tried to comfort me but could do little to assuage my panic.

I called my neighbors who worked for the police department. Patty wasn't home, but David was. He told me the police station got cases like this all the time. Rob didn't have a leg to stand on; anything given while dating would be considered a gift. He could try and take me to court, but they would laugh him out of there. David said to do nothing. Ignore it.

I breathed, relieved. Nothing. I could do that. That was the advice I always gave my friends when they didn't want to hear from an old boyfriend.

I put the book away, stored the bill in case I heard from him again, and thought surely now, that was the end. But no, I heard from him again six weeks later.

This time he emailed me. He wasn't contacting me to try and communicate, he insisted; he just needed to know if he had left his masking machine at my place. He couldn't find it anywhere, and it would cost him $50 to replace.

I wanted to tell him to add it to my bill, but I wanted nothing more than to never hear from him again, so I didn't reply.

A week later, I began writing a story about a woman who gets invited to a party and doesn't want to go. The story was about Rob and Louis and a few other men, all rolled into one antagonist. I wanted to forgive Rob, and I did while writing it. It was called, "Just Before She Left."

I sent it off to a contest and the journal wanted to publish it. For the first time since I'd started writing, I felt like an author: a journal that was issued by someone I didn't know wanted to publish my work. I also felt brilliant for having transformed those two months of power struggles, fear, and insecurity into a story about what I really wanted, which was the tenderness of love.

CHAPTER NINE

Post-It Note Affair

*J*arrod's bathroom was revolting but I told myself I could get past it. Musty urine assaulted the back of my nose and throat and made me gag. I papered the toilet seat and stuck my legs out away from the bowl so as to not get any of it on my pants. I couldn't help but look: the inside of the toilet had not been scrubbed in what I guessed was years.

One morning, I was so disgusted that I took a cleaning brush that was sitting on a ledge in the shower and scrubbed the outer edge. The urine stains at the north and south ends of the rim were so encrusted that even the most feverish effort lifted only a layer of it. I was using his cheap shampoo as a cleanser, as there was nothing else immediately in view. Off-brand shampoo does not clean well (and you thought Heloise had all the cleaning hints).

It helped, even if just a little.

I felt encouraged when he told me one night on the phone about a week later that he had gone through his house and thoroughly cleaned it. His mother, after all, had raised him to be as fastidious as Martha Stewart, he had said.

Much to my dismay, at my next visit, the bathroom still appeared and smelled as though it had been forgotten. Beard clippings speckled the sink and the top of the toilet paper. The baseboards, whose cobwebs were now absent, still had a gray layer of dust. The toilet not only appeared unscrubbed, it also contained a gift from the last time someone had stood over it.

So why didn't I say anything? No one is perfect, and this was an easily fixable thing. But what woman should have to tell a forty-seven-year-old man to scrub his toilet and to flush?

I decided I could tell him, or I could learn to ignore it. If this was the worst of his flaws, well, I might come out ahead. Too, there was no transference to his appearance: his clothes were clean and neat. *He* did not smell.

Jarrod had contacted me over email after viewing my profile on one of the singles sites I belonged to. He came in as an answer to my prayers. I had made a request that someone would please recognize me for what I had to offer, understand me, and be available to share time with me. After the menace of Louis and Stalker Rob, an unkempt bathroom could be blinked away.

His profile was perfect: he was a classical guitarist; he taught and performed; he was spiritual; and he was a competent writer. Furthermore, he had chosen me despite the fact that I had a child and did not have a photo posted. He wrote that he'd decided to give me a chance because my profile was so eloquently written. He referred to us as kindred spirits. I sighed, relieved and also charmed; my prince had arrived, the universe had delivered.

I learned over the course of a few email exchanges that he had been married for a little over a year and had divorced long before. His wife had a young son whom Jarrod had never stopped missing. He looked at the floor when he told me his wife had said she didn't think she'd ever loved him. He'd sworn he would never get involved with someone who had a child again.

The gravity of his taking this risk in getting to know me was not lost on me. I wondered whether he was sensitive or stuck. What was it that had convinced his wife to leave him barely two years into marriage, and whatever it was, was it still hanging around?

Jarrod had spent a great deal of his adult life without a

companion. I saw this as a plus at first; there wouldn't be so much baggage to wade through from the bitter rivalry of a messy divorce. By the second week in, however, I discovered that having been alone so much made him perhaps too comfortable with his own standard of living.

I would encourage him to spend the night at my place, I decided. I would take us into my bathroom and comment on what I had done to improve its appearance, and how I tried to keep up on the cleaning of the toilet bowl because my five-year-old son was wanting to stand more and more now.

"Those stains sure are a bugger if you let them sit too long, aren't they?" I would say. "What do you use to scrub your toilet? Do you use different brushes for the bowl and the rim?"

The toilet was not the only problem; it was just an easy target for those who had aim.

Jarrod told me that the minute he felt anyone leaning on him, he was out the door. He had cared for his baby sister when he was ten and enjoyed it but didn't want to spend any more of his life caring for someone else.

I was independent; he didn't need to worry about me. I was so good at taking care of myself he would hardly know I was there. But I did want to talk to him. I did want to find out more about what he felt made us kindred spirits. I wanted to know how he could say this without really knowing me. Was it because we both had music backgrounds, that we could write well, liked to read? I imagined he would simply tell me, that it would unravel deftly in the course of those early conversations of getting to know one another. It didn't occur to me to ask him.

Isn't being a kindred spirit special and rare? And if you found that in someone and declared it to be true, wouldn't you want to talk about it and defend it? But he didn't return to it again. It never occurred to me that perhaps he didn't need to talk about it, felt no need to expound on it or declare anything at all. That perhaps it didn't mean the same thing to him as it did to me.

I delivered the goings on of my life to Jarrod in a brief, clipped fashion, statements that would fit on a Post-it note: "I went running today"; "I played with my son"; "I worked more on my novel"; "My classes went well"; "It was cold today." No details or nuances; the rise and fall of day-to-day drama were voided out, null.

He was busy. I understood that. It was December, and he had gigs. He relied on them. Musicians were a hot commodity during holidays and weddings. He had to put himself out there. I attended a couple of gigs to show my support and spend time with him. I graded papers at a coffee shop and schmoozed with his friends while he provided the night's entertainment at a dinner party. I was walking the road of being the good girlfriend.

When we talked on the phone and he answered the door to let a friend in, I wanted him to tell me that he'd call me later instead of saying, "Gotta go. Al's here." I wanted him to call me on Christmas day to tell me he'd gotten to the hotel in Breckenridge okay. That the roads weren't too bad or that he had made good time or that he was well rested or that there were more people than he expected, and the manager offered him a bigger tip or that he would bring back any kind of dessert I wanted.

I wanted him to ask about my students, my son, my thoughts. I wanted to be asked about a time when I felt frightened and get more than three words out before he charged in with his own story. I wanted to feel as though I was more than a fixture. I wanted him to act like he felt something for me. I wanted to grow on him like vine, not mold.

I got very ill two weeks before Christmas and never called Jarrod through the worst of it, mostly because I was too weak to talk on the phone. When we did talk, I was on my way to being on the other side of it. He recommended getting a spicy chicken dish at a Chinese restaurant located not too far from me. It would be good for my immune system, he said. He didn't offer to bring it to me. He didn't call in the next day or two to check on me or ask how I was doing.

∂

A few days after Christmas, I was awakened by Jarrod's clock radio blaring in my ear at 5:00 a.m. and then the watch on top of his dresser beeping incessantly fifteen minutes later. He asked if I was awake and then climbed on top of me to hump me until my legs wanted to break. His heavy, muscular body went up and down up and down up and down, then finally, nothing. He didn't even come. He was out of bed a few minutes later and had the kitchen radio shouting NPR. He prepared breakfast and told me he'd talk to me later.

I was out of there, only to be greeted by rush-hour traffic.

The night before, he had lit two tall candles atop a bookcase in his bedroom. As I walked in after having brushed my teeth, smiling inside at a sure sign of imminent affection, he blew them out. Poof. Gone, just like that. Twenty-seven seconds of romance. I wanted more than that but said nothing. The message was too long for a tiny sticky note whose gumminess had already begun to dry out.

CHAPTER TEN

Remainders

$\mathcal{H}$is voice sounded vaguely familiar, but I wanted to get rid of him.

"Who are you?" I asked, deadpan.

"Max. Uh, we met at a picnic a while back. Dot Sero was playing at Hudson Gardens?"

"A few months ago?"

"Yes. Yes, during the summer. Well, I, uh, called to see how you were doing?"

"I'm fine."

"I didn't know if you knew, but there are a lot of dances and social events going on at the church. I haven't seen you in a while, and it would be nice to see you again sometime."

"Yeah."

"There is a dance next weekend and then another the following weekend at St. Thomas Moore. Those are always big dances."

"Thanks. Maybe I'll show up."

It dawned on me after we hung up that Max was fishing to see if I was interested in him. My memory was fuzzy. I remembered his son, Sean, better than I did him.

I had met Max and Sean months earlier, when Louis was still trying to talk me into being with him while he figured out whether or not he still wanted to be with Lisa. Louis had encouraged me to go to the concert at Hudson Gardens. I was looking for him when Max stopped me. I had Shane, who was five then, with me. We were on our way to the port-o-john.

Sean stood five inches taller than Max. Their faces were nearly identical, but Max's salt-and-pepper crew cut contrasted with his son's fawn-worthy red waves and goatee. I wondered what the age difference would be between his son and me.

Max looked as though he'd just returned from a short walk after a big picnic lunch in his summer hat and striped button-down shirt, which did little to conceal his protruding belly.

"Have you heard this band before?" he asked.

"No, I don't even like jazz." I almost included that I was supposed to be meeting someone.

He sneered as he shook his head. "I don't either!" He laughed.

"It's not Bach!"

"You like Bach?" His face lit up. "I am from Germany, by the way. I love Bach!"

"I could hear it in your voice," I said with a nod. "I studied German in high school. I played piano for a long time, and Bach was my favorite."

We laughed.

I smiled at his son, who smiled back. Peaceful, casual, solitary, and of course, beautiful. What could I say to get him to talk? Too young, too young. He would want to have his own baby, and at thirty-seven, I had just started breathing the good air of having a child who could eat and pee by himself. Looking and longing to run my fingers through that red hair would have to be enough.

"You must have been pretty good then," Max offered.

"Okay. Yes. Bach made sense to me."

He tilted his head. "I haven't seen you at anything before, have I?"

"No." Shane jumped off and on a big rock in my periphery. "We have to go," I said. "I forgot what we set out to do. See you later!"

Shane and I headed toward a tiny bridge. On the other

side were footpaths to various floral gardens and the port-o-johns.

"Haha. Nature calls! If you're not sitting with anyone, you can sit with us!" Max said to my back.

After our visit to the toilets, Shane and I sat on a grassy hill about a hundred feet from the jazz band. Families lounged in low cloth chairs or stretched out on blankets all around us. It was not packed, but Dot Sero had nothing to be ashamed of either. I recognized a few people from the church Max and I belonged but no friends.

Shane and I grew cold and damp as the light slipped from the day. In my haste and anticipation to meet up with Louis, I had neglected to bring a blanket for us to sit on. I'd expected him to find and sit with the others from church, but I never saw him. Shane and I did sit close to Max and Sean, but we didn't talk much the rest of the evening. He asked for my phone number, and I gave it to him, but I didn't think he was interested. He was in his late forties, or early- to mid-fifties, and I had decided already that men who had grown children were not interested in a woman with a young child. They had done it, seen it, and whether they'd hated it or liked it, they were sure they didn't want to ever go through it again, and especially not with someone else's kid. I decided he must be on a social committee at the church and wanted my number to call about upcoming events.

Max didn't call me again for several months after that first time. I saw him at church occasionally and we exchanged the same easy banter each time, but it was always brief.

I saw him one Sunday in December, over a year later, and we talked about the Christmas Eve services coming up. He told me that he would be coming with his son to the 4:00 p.m. service.

I made a mental note to be there at the same time. Max had always been at church when I attended; I laughed with him, and maybe I had judged too quickly. I had become jaded and disgusted with the men in my life. Could something with Max be better? I convinced a friend to attend the service with me.

When I arrived, I walked around the circumference of the church twice: once to find Max and a second time to see if he was watching me. My friend Kim and I had agreed to come separately, and I was looking for her too. But I really didn't expect to find her, not with 800 people standing in line. Too, she was always late.

I found out what I needed to: Max was waiting for me, smiling, as I rounded the bend for the second time.

"You look like a character out of a Charles Dickens novel!" he said as I walked up.

I laughed and tapped my black top hat. The rest of the ensemble consisted of black low-heeled shoes that laced over the top of the foot, black slacks, a long black jacket, a cream blouse, and a long silk magenta scarf.

"Did you know there are two New Year's Eve dances coming up?" Max asked. "One is at the lodge at Wadsworth and Hampden and the other is at Parker Road and Havana. I haven't decided which one I'll go to yet."

"I've been to the lodge," I said, smiling.

He pinched his lower lip and scratched his chin while looking me up and down. "Hmm. That's the one I'll go to probably." He smiled back.

I hoped he would. I felt as though I had been popping disappointment pills like multi-vitamins: they had become too much a part of the regular diet, without the fun of glow-in-the-dark urine.

I had just ended things with Jarrod. I had had really high hopes for him. We were kindred spirits, after all—on paper, anyway: creative, well read, poor muses. He was the only kind of man I believed could understand me. But he was busy, too busy, a musician always on a quest for the next gig. He didn't say thank you enough, and there was no landing spot if I felt raw or weepy. All of his emotions went into his music.

I considered myself to be very independent, but I also needed someone to tell my stories to. I needed to feel as though he was in my life, I wrote in an email.

I kicked myself right after sending the email for not leaving the door open for him to rectify things, but I also felt as though I had earned the right to make a quick decision. I had learned some things from my dating experiences since my divorce, and one of them was that it didn't take years or months to call a lemon a lemon. Choosing quickly also showed me why I had been slower and more discerning with some of the others: to be sure, to convince myself beyond a doubt.

I was way overdue for laughing, and Max knew how to flip that switch. More importantly, I expected him to.

Kim came with me to the New Year's Eve dance. She didn't get out much because she was a full-time single mom of a teenage girl. She had asked her parents to take her daughter for the night.

"It's going to be a bunch of balding men in their fifties!" I said, laughing.

"I don't care," she said, smiling. "It's just great to get out." She looked out the windshield. No one would ever accuse her of being out of control. I knew her well enough to read her excitement, however shielded.

Kim wore a traditional V-neck black dress. She had been a stylist for years and knew how to make her hair flip and fall softly around her cheeks. Her face reminded me of a doll's, with her big, deep-set brown eyes, perfect oval face, and even lips. She didn't have to do much to look pretty and this dress alone would wave a man in, if she would give him half a chance. Attending a dance was practice in dipping her big toe into the pool of dating. So far, she had never gotten as far as getting anyone's phone number or giving hers out. Her ex-husband's alcoholism had depleted her emotionally and financially and sent her back to living with her parents.

My experience with men hadn't been *that* bad. I was still willing to barrel through and try one after the other until . . . what? I would wither from woe, romp on happily into the sunset with the perfect one, or, or? The conclusion would have to reach itself. But I wasn't going to not date; that was simply not an option.

I wore a bra that pinched and pushed underneath a translucent lavender floral blouse with a black skirt, fish net stockings (of course), and the same cute flat black shoes with cross lacing over the top that I'd worn with my Charles Dickens get-up. My hair was clipped up; the curls boinged out, aimless.

We spotted Max immediately, and he told me that I looked quite sexy in my outfit. Relieved, I felt the thrill of being wanted. The crowd at the dance that night was a cast of homely, paunchy middle-aged men and thickly made up, scantily clad women who teetered in stilettos. I was the youngest one there. It didn't have to matter, but it was notable. I told myself not to stare at the guy whose hairpiece had slid to one side.

Our entrance fee covered a pasta dinner and salad. We served ourselves cafeteria style in the most dimly lit room of the lodge. The ambiance concealed the soggy, overdone spaghetti and the mixed greens that were nothing more than iceberg lettuce with carrot shavings. No doubt, the hosts were counting on all of us hanging our hats on wine and the promise of love—or at least a night of hope.

Max sat next to me at our table, which Kim had snagged in an alcove. We talked for a half hour or more and then I began to get bored. It was chitchat and I floated along, drifting into the timbre of their voices. Max's syllables curled as he labored to enunciate English through his thick German accent. This lullaby threatened to send me off, so I got up. He quickly followed suit. Good. He did want to be with me.

We headed to the dance floor. He knew what he was doing, and I was both relieved and ashamed because I did not.

"It'll be better if I close my eyes," I offered.

"Watch me," he said. "Now follow, like this."

I stepped toward him when I should have gone back.

He laughed. "Try again. Close, close."

"Let me get my drink," I said. "Then I won't care, and you can spin me any way you like."

"Yes, I will . . . you'll get it."

We danced a few more steps.

"There," he said. "Great!"

I felt encouraged that he believed I was teachable. Even through my hazy, alcohol-induced blur, I could tell he loved to dance. I worried that this could present a problem if he stopped laughing at my insistence on leading.

He leaned in and held me at the small of my back with one hand and behind my shoulder with his other hand. He was only a few inches taller than I. He spoke into my ear with a mellifluous tenor that aroused me. We talked about music, and he told me he had played the clarinet in high school. I asked if he was any good and he laughed and said he had broken hearts all over Europe.

He danced with other women here and there but danced the most with me.

Kim asked if I was ready to go at 10:30 p.m. I had seen her talk with one man. She didn't need rescuing, but between blinks I could see she was bored and getting plaintive. She announced that she wasn't going to be able to make it to midnight, so I said my good-byes and asked if Max was going to be at church the next morning. He said yes. I left him sitting at a table with a few people I knew and a few I didn't. I wondered if he would sidle up to another woman, but the wine had done me in as well, and I cared more about getting home to sleep than what he might do with someone else.

The next day, during our first real date, Max and I sat for a long time in his car, parked in the church parking lot. It was New Year's Day. He caressed the arm of my sweater and asked me what it was made of.

"Angora. Rabbit's fur. Part of it, anyway."

"Hmm. Nice. Soft. These are rabbit fur too." He circled the inside of his glove with one finger. "Your rabbits must have lived in the penthouse. Mine were the laborers in the basement."

I laughed and knew I was happy.

His uncanny sense of humor unbridled me. I had never

shared the stage with anyone like I could with him. We had an ear for each other's wit and played off of it effortlessly.

Once, while we sat together during church, an announcement was made about a workshop called "First Thing's First." Max leaned over and said they ought to have a workshop called "Last Thing's Last" for the procrastinators who missed "First Thing's First." I said, "Yeah. They could register late and not miss anything."

Those first few weeks were a dream. I was as happy as I could ever remember having been. We laughed, attended concerts and movies, and went out to dinner. He was a passionate lover, and he wanted to be with me. My fears that he would not be interested in me because I had a young child had turned to a pile of ashes.

One night, we were watching TV at Max's place and though we sat right next to each other, his arms were folded, and he seemed far away.

We had been dating for six weeks.

He turned to me. "You're young and you'll want to be married again someday. You'll want to have someone there for Shane. I don't know, Jane. This is really hard for me because I enjoy being with you. You're funny, I laugh with you. We have a good time together. My boys . . . they gave me such a hard time when they were teenagers."

Capsized, I began to argue with him. "You're not even giving this a chance. We hardly know each other. I don't know that I do want to get married again. If it didn't mean living with someone, then I might like that. Shane has a father. I'm not asking you to be a father to my son."

"Maybe we need to take a break, Jane, so I can be clear about this thing here."

A break? I knew what that meant. I did my best to convince him to hang in there with me, even though I knew this was not over. The issue of raising Shane would rear up again.

I left his house crushed but hopeful. I wasn't ready to let go of laughing like that with someone.

Just after our conversation, Max left town for a retreat at a hot spring. He didn't call me while he was there, and it gave me time to think. I wrote him a letter and broke things off. I couldn't stand the thought of waiting for him to tell me that I should want to be married and it couldn't be to him because he didn't want to raise another boy.

He had gone shopping for me while he was away and brought back a handmade mug. He shoved it at me and said, "Oh well. I go away, and then I get your letter. Crap."

He didn't argue with me, though. He didn't say, "We should try. Let's give it some more time. Yes. I am willing to work this out." So, I didn't think I was wrong. If he couldn't get past this, what was the point?

I felt void. Sadness sprawled as vastly as it had after my divorce. I couldn't rest, though I was exhausted. My thoughts wrestled with my heart: I hadn't known him that long; I shouldn't feel this way; it shouldn't be that hard. But at a glance, it had cumulatively been hard. I'd been separated from Matt for three years, divorced for two. I had been dating non-stop since six weeks after the divorce papers were signed.

I devoted my time to talking to friends and going to church. I wanted to be around people, a lot of people I didn't know, and church offered this idyllic biosphere.

I went to church for the Wednesday night service and ran into Max on the way out.

I had been crying at something said during the service that triggered the dam I was trying to hold back. It had been too easy to let it out. I had been crying at commercials and stoplights those days and nights, too.

My red face announced everything, but I looked down and away from Max. He said my name, and I grabbed his arm for a long moment. His eyes were wet and full of concern.

I knew he assumed I was sad about him, and he wasn't

wrong, but that wasn't everything. It was too much disappointment and too many men who were not right.

A couple weeks later, he sent me a letter that listed everything he liked about me. The list included how I put up my hair, that I "tenderly and lovingly" cared for my son, the way I laughed at life and "funny stuff," and my easy-going, warm energy. "The way you hold your hand when making a point" and "the way you dress in adventurous ways." My heart prickled here. He had seen things that made me, me.

He wrote that he wished wonderful things for me, that I would remain forever young, and included hand-copied lyrics of Bob Dylan's "Forever Young." On the last page was a sketch of a rose.

I called him and thanked him for the lovely letter and the sketch.

"You should draw and paint, Max. You're good at it."

"Another girlfriend gave me paints a few years ago, and I have the bag of stuff you gave me," he said. "I need a book. Sometimes, I watch a show and the guy makes it look so easy and I tell myself I could do that. I need a few more things but I don't want to spend the money."

Defeated, I said nothing. It was one thing to be with someone who had never risked and didn't know their artistic muse or creative alleys. It was another to be with someone who was so enamored with his endeavors that he had little time or space for anyone else. But it was altogether something else when someone knew he had talent and interest and yet collapsed under apathy, or worse, laziness. How was he going to support me in my creativity if he didn't believe in it enough for himself?

He would need to do it on his own because he wanted to. I knew that practicing the science of encouragement could easily bleed into being a pushy nag. Could he learn from my example? If he saw me devoting time to writing, would he become alight with his own inspiration? *Would* I need him to be creative to better understand me? Would it hurt? Would it help? Would it settle us into a ratchet of being comfortably committed?

He said he missed me and asked if we could see each other again. I had missed him too. I missed our banter and laughing and passion. It was worth another shot.

Max and I got back together and picked up where we left off. Things resumed feeling comfortable and easy. We talked on the phone every night and got together once or twice during the week and on the weekends I didn't have Shane. When I did have Shane, I managed several times to arrange sleepovers for him at a friend's house, so I could be with Max.

For the most part, Max and Shane did not interact. Shane definitely did not need the looming uncertainty, and I didn't want to compound my burden by determining what male friend of mine might be right for him. Until things truly felt safe, I was not going to entrust either one to the other's company.

It was early spring, and I was suffering from a virus. I had felt feverish for a couple of days and was hoping it would break before Max and I were to get together Saturday night. It didn't, but I was taking a regimen of herbal aides that thwarted the effects and curbed the fever, so I felt up for our date.

I showed up to his place saddled with a humidifier, pillow, and an overnight bag with a change of clothes. We were going to a concert, and I didn't want to have to wear evening clothes the next morning. I set everything down carefully. Max kept a very neat house, and I didn't want to tromp snow or mud on his white carpet.

We went to dinner and then the concert I had suggested: the Colorado Symphony Orchestra was playing Bach.

My head throbbed as the music whirled around us. All I could think about was how much I wanted to put my head down and sleep. I thought about leaning over and resting on Max's shoulder but thought he would shrug me off or feel anxious that I would get sweat or snot on his suit. I did my best to hold my head upright.

On the ride back, I asked if we could stop off for some Epsom salts. Max finished a story about how he had broken up with a woman on the way back from a singles ski trip while two other people listened in the backseat of his car just as we pulled into the store's parking lot. She had asked him what he thought of their relationship, and he'd said that he didn't see a future in it. She'd wept the whole trip home.

A few minutes earlier, Max had asked me about the worst breakup I had ever been through. I was surprised and befuddled by his interest in this but told myself he was branching out and trying to build intimacy. I didn't want to tell war stories, so I summed it up in about three sentences. Rob had won the gold medal in this event, between our six-hour argument the day we broke up, stalking me a week later, and sending me a bill for the work he had done at my place.

When Max finished his story, dread set in. Why was he telling me about the weeping woman from the ski trip? I reassured myself that we were here at the store getting Epsom salts, so I could take a bath and feel better. I did lean into him at the check-out line, and he didn't pull away.

We arrived at his condo, and I pulled the Epsom salts out of the bag. He put in the CD I had given him for Christmas: again, Bach.

As I walked down the hall, I said, "Why don't you join me, Max?"

"Jane?"

I turned back and met him halfway.

He put his hands around my triceps. "Jane. I want us to just be friends." His voice quivered a little.

He continued talking but I stopped listening. The words were nearly the same as they'd been three weeks before.

We sat on the couch. I told him, "Why now? Why make plans for this weekend? Why not tell me before the dinner and the concert? I feel like shit, Max. I brought all of this crap here."

I got up and rammed my feet into my shoes and stuffed my arms into my coat.

"Here. Take this." He handed me the Epsom salts.

"No. It's yours."

"What am I going to do with it? I won't use it!"

"I've got a ton of that shit at home. I don't need it."

"Let me help you with your things, Jane."

"No. I got it up here by myself. I got it. See you around."

I gingerly made my way downstairs saddled with all of my wares, careful not to slip on the new snow.

$\mathcal{I}$ called Steve, though I hadn't talked to him since the debacle with Rob. If nothing else, he and I were friends. I was still holding out hope that we could be more than that one day but dealing with one disappointment was plenty.

I met him over at Lyon's Park in Golden and we walked the Clear Creek path back to the dam. The leaves were tight, lima bean–green fists waiting to unfurl. Sunshine streaked in broad rays through the branches. It was warm for a day in March. I felt grateful and safe.

We walked in silence for several minutes before Steve asked if I was heartbroken.

Tears stung, and I hoped they wouldn't let loose. I didn't want to show him. Even if he could be there for me, I wouldn't trust it. I couldn't commit to what that might mean or hope that he could be there consistently.

"Yes," I said softly.

I didn't know what I wanted. I hadn't taken any time to calibrate my compass. All of my decisions were reactions. Others spun my dials, and I let them. I didn't know how to stop it. I didn't know if I wanted to. Was I ready for that kind of responsibility? Who would I be if I designed my life around what I genuinely wanted?

He folded my hand in his and rubbed his thumb between my thumb and index finger. We walked this way until we reached the dam, where we sat and watched the water rush and engulf ice chunks from the holds of winter.

The familiarity of him put me at ease. I didn't expect anything. He didn't ask questions. It was okay to be quiet. I felt as though he knew what I needed in that moment, and I loved him for it.

෨

𝒜 letter from Max came in May with another sketch and a handmade certificate inviting me to dinner. Expiration date: 2018. I had twelve years to cash it in. He wrote that he felt terrible about how he had ended things between us and would I reconsider seeing him again?

I was bored and wanted to have sex, so I agreed to it. I knew that even if it didn't last for very long, I would be okay. This neutrality lightened the inevitable: it wasn't but a few weeks before Max called it quits again. I felt triumphant at gliding out of it more easily this time. He was leaving for Germany to go visit his family for two weeks, and I believed this time apart would mark the line in the sand between us for good.

I met a man in the grocery store a few days later and was going to start seeing him, but he didn't end up calling me for over a week. By that time, I had started seeing Evan, a man I'd met online.

I had stopped attending church with any regularity to avoid running into Max but happened to attend one Sunday later in the summer. He was there, of course. We talked with mutual friends for a while. He shared stories about his trip to Germany; I laughed. He told me privately that when his plane went over my home state of Michigan, he had sighed and known that he missed me.

I nodded and thought, *Oh well.*

As our group was breaking up, Max asked if he could call me.

I said, "Sure." I could always use a good laugh.

That evening, he called and left a message.

I didn't call back.

𝒪𝓃 early July, the mailboxes at my complex were switched out and all of our mail was held at the post office. It was quite a jaunt to get there, so I wasn't picking it up very often.

I retrieved it one Monday and found a letter that Max had sent a few days prior. He started it by writing, "You probably wonder, 'What does this guy want now?'" He went on to explain that he had missed me a great deal and had resolved that he could give me what I wanted—time and space to write—and that he could be a role model for Shane. He realized that he didn't have to be a father figure to my son and this relieved the pressure.

I wrote him a note explaining that I hadn't known of his letter when I saw him on Sunday and that when he asked if he could call me I assumed it was to have lunch sometime. I also informed him that I was already seeing someone new. I wished him well and couldn't help feeling smug. *You see? You waited too long. Why couldn't you see things sooner? I wasn't lying to you about not wanting you to be a father figure to Shane.* Poor Max.

I couldn't help but wonder if I should have waited a little longer but swatted that thought quickly out of my mind. I had a new guy, a younger guy, someone who wouldn't be waffling on the fact that I had a young child, since he had a son the same age as Shane. I had struck gold and I didn't need to look back.

I didn't see Max for the rest of the summer but did run into him at church in the fall. He asked me how things were going and told me there was a Halloween dance at the end of October.

I invited him to lunch, and he said he would call me.

Our visit turned into a bitch session about unmet needs.

"I don't know," Max griped. "Linda likes a man who is still married. I like her, but she likes him. Why should I bother? What's a guy to do?"

I looked at him and thought, *You're getting what you deserve. Of course she's unavailable; it's because you were unavailable to me. Karma, buddy.* I also thought that perhaps this foolhardy pursuit would make him want me and appreciate me.

I alluded to things not going well with Evan without speaking about any of the details. The luster of dating a younger man with a son my son's age had tarnished quickly.

〰

One Saturday morning, Evan and I spent forty-five minutes on the phone arguing about when we might get together because he wanted to have the oil changed in his car that day. I didn't understand why he couldn't get the oil changed another day; he only worked three nights a week and had other days free. Our time together was pinched enough as it was because we lived an hour apart. Boxed in by this appointment, our day, which we had planned as a family outing—we both had our boys, an infrequent event—felt too cramped. I wanted to have a leisurely time together.

"I'm trying to be responsible here by taking care of my car!" he cried out.

I hung up, exasperated.

The boys were different and our approach to parenting them was *very* different. Drew played with the boy who lived next door to his mother's house on occasion, while Shane had several friends at his day care and at school. Drew was overweight and pensive; Shane, athletic and gregarious.

One day, we all got together halfway between our homes, in Boulder. It was mid-October and had snowed the night before. We went to a park and the boys ran around and started throwing snowballs at each other. Shane pelted Drew in the head, and Evan made them stop so Drew could express his feelings to Shane and make Shane apologize. I didn't object but I knew that Shane was more accustomed to the schoolyard method of resolution: getting pelted back, and then doing something else.

Evan and I busied ourselves with discussing our trip to visit his parents in Connecticut over Thanksgiving.

"It's a month away," I said.

"Actually, we'll be there in four weeks," he said. "A month would have been Thursday but today is Saturday. There's a difference."

I rolled my eyes while he kicked at the snow.

"We're going to have to get to the airport early because

my dad transposed a letter in your first name with a letter in your last: you're now Jabe Ninns."

I tensed. "It's going to cost $100 for them to change the ticket. I shouldn't have to pay for that."

"I know. I'll ask my dad to pay for that." Evan sighed.

Shane and Drew chased each other around the jungle gym.

"Come get me, fatso!" Shane called.

"Hey, hey, hey. There will be no name-calling. Shane, what do you say?" Evan said.

"Sorry," Shane said.

Drew cried a little as he looked at the snow.

That night on the phone, Evan told me he thought Shane was maladjusted to the separation between his dad and me. Lisa, Drew's mother, had suggested this as the reason why Shane had been "aggressive" toward Drew.

"Shane apologized. What more would you like me to do? I can't put him on the phone to talk to Drew; he's at a sleepover at his cousin's. I wish this had come up sooner. I thought we had resolved things before we left."

"I'm stuck in the middle here, defending Shane to Lisa," Evan said. "How do you think I feel?"

Get your kid involved in team sports, I thought. *Have him do something other than going to Tai Chi and watch TV. You're not doing him any favors by not giving him opportunities to make friends.* I didn't say any of this. Evan worked very hard at engaging Drew in physical activity by riding bikes and going on hikes with him. It wasn't my business to tell him to sign Drew up for soccer, and it wasn't his to tell me that Shane was maladjusted. The fact that Drew's mother felt entitled to offer an opinion was more than I could tolerate.

I called my mother and she asked when I might be coming back to Michigan for a visit. I decided right then and there that now was as good as any other time. I called Max to see if I could park at his workplace garage and if he would drop me off at the airport. He was glad to do these things.

I could hear the sound of Evan's nasally whine in my ear the entire five days I was away. I felt suffocated and didn't call him. I vented to everyone in Michigan and each of them told me that I knew what to do.

I broke things off with Evan a couple of days after I returned.

Just hours after breaking up with Evan, I met Max at the Halloween dance.

I had been dreaming up a costume that could win first place. Max had always complimented me on my creativity at the Halloween dances of years past, even before we started dating. I was always hell-bent on spending as little as possible on my costumes, so I'd constructed all of them with items available at home. One year I had gone as an eggplant. I wore a plum turtleneck dress, purple tights, and purple felt hat, and I cut the green stem and leaves from construction paper and pinned them to the hat. I painted my face purple as well. One man thought I was sick and wind-burned, and a woman thought I was a palm tree. Max thought I was a grape.

This time I decided to go as a rose. I had a floral dress in mauve and olive, green tights, and satin red material for the rose petals. I painted my face red and attached a stuffed ladybug and caterpillar to my head and shoulder, respectively.

Max wore an ensemble he'd worn in years past: a felt hat with a feather sticking out of one side and a satin jacket imprinted with playing card symbols.

"Jane! I would have known you anywhere!" He squeezed the ladybug.

I adjusted the caterpillar, which was slipping from my shoulder.

Max stood next to a thin woman in blue jeans and a long-sleeve white T-shirt. An 'n' of creases branched from her nose to her chin, and a fan of lines spread out from her eyes. Her tight auburn curls were cut close. She held a black eyemask up to her face. She nodded and laughed and just as quickly looked around the room.

"Linda, that is Jane in there," Max said. "She is always so creative with her costume. I can never think of a thing, so I do the same thing year after year. Jane, Linda. She's your competition for the night!"

Max jumped liked a boy excited over a new toy. Linda and I smiled on cue.

This was who he had been chasing all summer? I had nothing to fear. No costume? Short hair? Max once confided that he found short hair on women "butchy." I couldn't understand why he was forgiving a lack of ingenuity and hair in her, especially when he had made a point of complimenting these things about me.

Still, he spent a good deal of time with her that evening, and I spotted him pecking her on the cheek after a slow dance. She didn't push him away, but she did hold him at arm's length and looked startled that he was in front of her.

I stood off to one side as much as I danced. My thoroughly red face seemed to cause people to step back from me; few men asked me to dance. I was also distracted by the constant shoving and reattaching of my stuffed appendages. They were fastened well enough to stay on but staying in one place was out of the question. I couldn't move without the caterpillar sliding off my shoulder and drooping over a boob or around my hip.

I did not even place in the costume contest, though a few people said I had the most original costume there. A witch said I looked like a character out of *Alice in Wonderland*. I was not ashamed or ornery after that.

Max and I did dance closely for one song, and as we swayed I took a leap and said, "I've missed you."

He said he had missed me, too, and that he had thought of me on an "odd Friday." I laughed.

At the end of the night, he walked me to my car.

"You've probably been having more sex than me all summer, Jane!" he said. "I would go to these picnics and meet women, have a nice conversation all afternoon, ask her for her phone number, and she would say no! And Linda. I like her, but she's only been over to my place once, and we never really kissed, just really quickly. I am getting nowhere with her. I think she likes that other guy she was standing with tonight. I don't think she wants anything serious." He sighed. "Jane. I will let you know. We always had a good time. I need some time, but I will call you."

Max and I went out a week later, and he said he had ended things with Linda and wanted to begin again with me. I hopped up from the bar stool where we sat and kissed him on the cheek. I was happy to be wanted and to laugh again with him.

I believed now that his fears would flit away and take their rightful place as fingernail dust. After we had been together consistently for a while, I hoped, his doubts would be filed down, allayed. But what would reassure me that he wouldn't abruptly want to break things off again? Would he offer to take Shane to the movies for an afternoon so that I could have a little time to myself? Would he send me cards, just because? Or give me roses instead of carnations on Valentine's Day?

Max's schedule of card-giving had so far been limited to my birthday, Christmas, and petitions to reinstate the relationship. So, when he showed up at my house one day with a rose, I froze, fearful of what would happen next.

His eyes were wide and vacant. I let him in and we sat down on my couch.

"Eric has Crohn's disease."

"Oh, Max. I'm sorry." I moved closer and put my arms around him. I rubbed his back.

"Just like me. I wouldn't wish that on anyone, least of all one of my kids."

"Will he go in for treatments?"

"He doesn't have any insurance, and he doesn't have much money either. I'll help him, of course." He wiped his face with a handkerchief.

A shingle of his armor had fallen away. Was it a risk for him to show me sadness? Had we graduated to a new level of intimacy? I had become so accustomed to his jig of caution and ambivalence, I didn't trust this display of emotion. I wanted to. It was genuine; I knew that. But would it grow into a taproot of commitment? Would this be a seed that might sprout into a belief that I was worth the gamble, even with my young son? I hoped so.

One of Max's pluses was that he always insisted upon paying for dinner, though we never went anywhere too bourgeois. I would offer to pay or split it, but he would decline. He also liked to pick up a meal under $20 at the deli counter and leave no tip. I understood frugality. I didn't aspire to eat in places where it was sport to return the food or ask to speak to the chef. But did his thriftiness mean that his heart was cheap, too? Was there a correlation between what he gave materially and his willingness to show me the divots of his soul?

I wasn't looking for it or expecting it, but Max's stinginess erected itself crisply one afternoon. We were at a lodge enjoying a hot drink after spending the day cross-country skiing. He fingered his mug as he leaned across the table and gestured for me to come closer. His eyelashes were long and flush against his ruddy, doughy cheeks—he looked like a boy with salt and pepper sideburns. He laughed and whispered that he never donated anything to the love offering basket for coffee during community time at church.

I sat still. The words dropped between us, inert. The confidence had not been innocent but rather crude; it fell like rusty tin in my lap. Why was he telling me this? I sagged inside. It had been such a lovely day. I had learned how to balance myself while skiing and watched the regal evergreens quake in the fractured wind, sneezing whirls of snow around us. I didn't want this truant confession to spoil it.

I could put it away, then, for the moment, drink my tea, not worry about getting home from Frisco because I hadn't pissed him off by challenging him, and let the day continue on with a bath and languid love-making after our achy cold bodies had finally arrived home and disrobed. So I did.

❧

After we had been back together for about four months, Max and I attended a Valentine's Day dance. He loved going out to dance, and if I'd had enough to drink I wasn't bothered by stepping all over his feet.

Max knew most of the women there, and each time we walked away from someone I had just been introduced to, he would murmur that he could never date a tall woman, or that he had dated that one only a few times, or this one he had seen many times but never dated. I felt like the default answer on a multiple-choice exam, where you'd have to be a moron not to select it: not a, c, d, e, or f; the correct choice shouted b! The only one left. Was he still trying to find the princess whose foot would fit perfectly into his glass slipper? I felt young and invisible, sultry but unwanted.

On the dance floor, Max introduced me to a man whose voice and name I immediately recognized, as he had called Max that day during breakfast.

"Oh," I said, "you called this morning!"

Max was mortified. His complexion blanched, and he shook his head quickly.

Oh. It was not supposed to be obvious that Max and I were seeing each other or that I had spent the night, though we had known each other off and on now for over a year. How had I misstepped? Why did I feel accused? My dear old reflex of becoming frozen in the midst of abandonment held me still. I was not accustomed to noticing rage blistering underneath. I could not speak.

Max was adept at keeping his thoughts and feelings regarding relationships mysterious, opaque. What I meant to him had become plain, however. He held all the cards, and I let him. I hated myself for that. If I said anything about his mixed messages, he would likely deliver more of the same. Saying nothing, however, I felt suffocated and wanted to run, to fill my lungs with the cleaner air of being alone. I didn't mean enough to him, and I wasn't willing to pretend anymore.

ᐁ

Max met me at the car dealership in late February while I was waiting for an oil change. He handed me a decorative gift bag with an Easter Bunny on it. The card stuck out above the tissue paper. I opened and read it while he stood in front of me. He said, "There's something else in there for you at the bottom."

A small box. Earrings.

"You seemed like you always liked the dangly ones."

They were lovely. The series of progressively larger sterling circles with various shades of green stones glinted. He hadn't given me anything this nice when we were dating.

"Here are your pans back. That was way too much banana bread, by the way."

"Thank you." The heart-shaped pans clanged as I set them on the floor.

He asked how I was, and I blubbered about my older brother writing me to leave him alone. He had left his wife and family. I had written and called him, inviting him to talk to me if he wanted. "He doesn't want to talk to anybody."

"God. Jeeza. I couldn't stop talking to anyone when I divorced."

"I know. Me too. It's hard right now. I felt close to him, like we got along the best of all my siblings."

"It's hard for him, poor guy. And Shane? How's he?"

"He's fine. He's a good boy."

I got up to hug him. I was failing at not crying.

He pointed himself back the way he came in and slumped away slowly enough for me to say, "Hey, wait!"

I didn't.

He took me out to dinner for my birthday several months later.

I wondered whether he was seeing anyone but didn't ask.

"You know, Jane, I realized the other day that every

woman I have ever dated has been fine," he said. "We always had a good time together and there was an even flow to it, but I have not felt really excited about anyone except right after my divorce. I never fought with these women. Everything was always fine. Maybe I've been dating too much. It has me worn out." He tore a bread stick and bit into it. "Phyllis is nice. I like her. She's the right age, too. We broke up a few weeks ago but are back together now. She gave me a book on unconditional love. I have read only a little of it but it's good. I probably won't read the whole thing."

I held my tongue.

"I want to feel that something special," he said. "It's great in the beginning and then it goes away."

"Well, Max," I said, "as long as you never allow things to go any deeper, they will always just be fine. A relationship is up and down and if you realize that you can go through the down periods with someone, then you've got someone worth hanging on to. It was really frustrating to be with you because you'd get scared and break up."

He nodded and laughed a little but wouldn't look directly at me.

I was relieved I wasn't the one who was supposed to care about him anymore.

"And you? Are you seeing anyone?" Max asked.

"I met someone on the train out to California. He was going home, and I was going there to visit my friend Joan."

"Ya? How long is that train ride?"

"Thirty-six hours. There is no sleeping comfortably, either. I didn't get a sleeper car and neither did he. We met during dinner. They group you all together to fill the tables, so you get to meet a lot of people. He is a professor at San Jose State. We had a lot in common, and we laughed. It was a great way to pass the time, but I don't know. The distance, for one thing: 1,500 miles is too much. I've done that long-distance thing and it's too hard. You work harder just to stay in touch than you would if they were fifteen minutes away, and then there's always that shadow of trusting him."

Max nodded.

"But this guy calls and we have a good time on the phone," I continued. "I was supposed to go out there this summer. He offered to pay for the plane ticket. We had this really long phone conversation, and he was talking about how his thyroid was off and he was sleeping way too much and then that he was going to donate a kidney to a friend of his. And I'm thinking, this guy is not thinking. You can't donate a kidney if you're sick, yourself. And then he started talking about his cats and how they had pissed on the bed the last time he went away for a few days."

Max laughed. "Did you ask him if the cats would be upset with a visitor? Would they be happy cats or pissed off cats?"

I laughed and slapped my knee. "Oh God, Max. That was it. I couldn't do it. You know you can't ever get that smell out. Gross. He called me again, but I never picked up. That's all he had to say. Yuck."

"And Shane? How is he?"

"He's great, such a sweet boy, so much fun . . ." I smiled. "Are you painting or drawing?"

"Well. Glad you mentioned that. I bought a book, and I opened that one you gave me for sketching. I am going to dedicate it to you, Jane. I drew a ball. Once you master a sphere, you can draw anything. It's a good ball, too."

"That's good, Max," I said like a mother who has three kids waving artwork in her face while she is busy thinking of what to cook for dinner. I repeated silently: *He dedicated his book of drawings to me.* I dared not ruin any of it and ask him why. His saying "I love you" wouldn't have been as kind.

"Happy Birthday, Jane."

"Hmm," I said. "Fourteen years between you and me."

"It will always be that . . . we cannot change that," he said like a scientist. "Are you coming to church on Sunday?"

"I don't know."

"Your friend, what's her name?"

"She can never remember your name either. Kim."

"Haha. I see her all the time. We talk about you. I ask if she's talked to you. It's a bit extreme, don't you think? You shouldn't have quit going to church."

"That place is too big, and I hate the seats. I feel like I'm at the Pepsi Center with that stadium seating. They ought to put in cup holders. It was much more intimate with the pews. The parking is still a mess, too." *And I don't want to see you all the time anymore, either.* "I can really only handle it every once in a while. I'd rather stay home and meditate."

I never told Max that I loved him, not once during all of our in and out and back and forth. I was always convinced it wouldn't make a difference—that, in fact, it would actually make him run farther, faster, sooner. I subtract the variables upheld as irrevocable reasons for things not working out and reconfigure Shane being older, me being older, and Max sheltering a more flexible, generous heart and longer, broader view, but the equation will not balance. There is always a remainder that continues, ad infinitum. There is no calculating the sum of lost love.

CHAPTER ELEVEN

The Exception

$\mathscr{I}$ talked to Steve only a handful of times while I was dating Max, and I saw him only once. That was the longest period we had ever gone without communicating or seeing one another regularly since I'd known him. I never forgot about him, of course, and frequently longed to talk with him.

I called him shortly after Max ended things for good.

We met for dinner at a buffet. We sat down. Steve got up to get us drinks. "Water with lemon, right?"

I nodded, feeling special that he had remembered.

When he came back to the table, I told him the story of Max and Evan. He nodded empathically and laughed on cue. Effortless.

It felt as though no time had passed. We fell into ease and familiarity. Old friends. Maybe enough time had passed now that he wouldn't be so inclined to pull away. And maybe I had learned how to navigate his choppy waters, so it wouldn't feel personal and deliberate.

The past year and a half away from Steve had allowed me to see what I couldn't in our previous dalliances together. Vignettes etched from when we were together were clouded with worry about that time and those moments ending and were book-ended with our separations—which, whether they lasted days, weeks, or months, always felt permanent. My relationship with him was less about time and chronology and more about making the most of when we were together and the ever-present fence I rode between questioning whether or not I could feel safe with him and actually feeling that way. Was there ever love without struggle? Which struggles were worth it, and which were better left alone?

Even though Steve had told me how much he hated unannounced visitors, I dropped in on him on my way back from Idaho Springs after spending the day with Joan, who was visiting from California.

He opened the door with a dulled grimace but invited me in. *I shouldn't have come*, I thought. This wouldn't be good.

I sat across from him on the rocking chair, the coffee table between us. I cut my losses by not assuming familiarity and sitting next to him on the futon. He leaned back and looked out the window, disconsolate.

"What have you been up to?" he asked.

I laughed. "Managed to get a ticket in Idaho Springs. Was up there with Joan. We were only gone an hour. I had to get soap at that shop, you know?"

He smiled. "What happened?"

"I parked facing the wrong way. I didn't know you couldn't do that. People do that all the time on my street because they never plow. I guess I should've figured, though, since everyone else was facing the other way. The cop was such an asshole, and Joan was so scared. She offered to pay for half, and I told her no way." I shook my head. "He was this big barrel-chested dude, biceps out to here. God." I got up from the rocking chair and thrust my chest out. "'Ma'am, do you mind telling me why you parked the wrong way three feet out from my curb?' He got out and measured, too. I wanted to say, 'Seemed like a good idea at the time,' but I didn't want to piss him off, so I decided to go meek and said, 'I don't know.'" I laughed.

Steve laughed along with me. "You're damn lucky he didn't see you dive in from the opposite side of the street. Those cops up there have nothing better to do, Janer . . .

You're something, you know that? I don't know another person like you. You don't like anyone in charge and we wouldn't get along if you did. Jesus Jones." He chuckled again. "How much did they get you for? Do you have to go to court?"

"No court if I pay the forty bucks. It's not that bad. Oh well. My curb, my curb??" I laughed.

He smiled and thanked me for coming. I squirreled away this vindication, telling myself all the while not to be hopeful. I couldn't help it, though. I was.

There was less hemming and hawing and our time together went more smoothly if what we did was Steve's idea, so I lapsed into a habit of deference. I was being practical: the objective was to spend time with him. I didn't care what we did together, and I didn't want to give him any reasons to reject me. I wanted to see him. I wanted to tell him my stories. If he wasn't going to declare a hiatus on intimacy, I wanted that, too. And he never suggested anything dangerous, illegal, or life-threatening, so it was easy to go along. I was content to rent a movie and go for hikes on mountain trails, or go to a bookstore to putter, or sit at his kitchen table over a cup of tea. If he wanted to fix the drip in my faucet, it would happen sooner rather than later. I wasn't the type to enlist anyone in honey-do projects, anyway. I might say that I noticed the occurrence of something amiss but would be nonchalant and indifferent to rectifying the situation. Honestly, I would rather watch a thin river and its attendant tear-drop rust stain evolve in my sink than change a worn-out washer.

Steve's birthdays were usually desolate landscapes with only a few tufts of spry growth springing forward. In his fifty-five-plus years on the planet, only a smattering of cards had been sent. A sister and an aunt usually acknowledged him; his teenage children were wont to forget, which aggravated him greatly. A former coworker might or might not remember. His mother usually offered to make a cake.

The terrain of uncertainty and disappointment that attended each of his birthdays prompted spewing of vitriolic complaints. I listened. I would prove him wrong. He had ignited purpose and ebullience inside of me. It was my mission to show him he was worthy.

I knew Steve loved the Sonoran Desert, but other than this, he was not forthcoming about his likes and dislikes. I embraced the challenge and turned my observation skills on high. He sometimes talked about bird watching, so one Christmas I bought him a stone carving of a bird made out of quartz and agate that stood about three inches high. He marveled at the craftsmanship as he pivoted it in his palm. We combed through his bird watching book but could not find an exact match to the tiny sculpture. He placed it proudly on top of one of his bookcases.

I noticed stones and crystals on end tables. I bought him a seven-by-five-inch hunk of amethyst. He put this on top of his windowsill.

He considered me to be a talented watercolor artist. On occasion, I would paint him birthday or Christmas cards. He framed one and hung it in his kitchen.

"No one else has ever been so attuned when gifting me, Janer," he said one day. "The gifts were always generic. These are so personal, extensions of me. One year for my birthday, my ex-wife told me to go buy myself a pair of jeans. The money all came from the same place, she said. I had a big smile on my face when I let those things sail out the window cruising down C-470 after I left. CDs are more fun, though. They break."

Happy that I had made an inroad, I mistakenly assumed that his sensitivity to disappointment on his birthday would translate into a guarantee that he would always remember and acknowledge mine.

I asked him to call me on my birthday during a summer when we were "just friends." He didn't. I drove over to his place and knocked on the door, but he wasn't home. I had brought a book with me that he had loaned me and left it at the door. I didn't want any reminder of him in my house. But

I couldn't wait for him to acknowledge that I had returned the book, either, so I called him. He apologized for forgetting my birthday. I told him it was okay. If I forgave this, I thought, maybe he would come back and stay longer with me.

I dreaded the birthday that took place a few months after Max had ended things and Steve and I had resumed being a couple. A couple of weeks before, I sensed Steve's discomfort and retreat. I didn't take it personally, but I did want him to acknowledge me happily and without ambivalence. I believed if he could do that, we would have arrived at a new level of union.

Steve's discomfort with my birthday came from the fact that he had no control over its arrival. It was my day, and this implicitly meant that I expected him, my friend and lover, to make some effort at doing pleasant things for me.

In the end, he did the right things. He gave me gifts; we ate at a nice restaurant; we made love. The tension I felt over wanting him to be able to do these things without squirming made all of it almost unbearable, however.

Steve leaned out the passenger-side window, smiled ear to ear, and yelled, "I've been smiling at you for the last two lights!"

The month before, he had mailed back his copy of my house key. There had been no note included, but the key had been wrapped in heavy paper and sandwiched in between two thin pieces of cardboard. I cried until my forehead hurt. It really felt like the end. I questioned myself: What was the problem? Had I not learned how to go on without him? Hadn't there been several events in my life that I'd had to handle on my own, without him? Hadn't I shown myself that I had grown up and away from the need to lean on him to carry me through?

I called my mother. I called my best friend. I blubbered what had happened. Empathic, sympathetic, accustomed to my grief over this man, they comforted me as much as they could. I had to laugh minutes into my moaning. I had a date. My mother told me to pull myself together, and go have a good time. Fortunately, it was a bright, sunny, typical Colorado summer afternoon that required sunglasses, and my eyes were concealed until nightfall.

When my old love's truck pulled away from me in the next lane, it took my brain a second to register that it was his. I raced to catch up to him and at the next light, I rolled down my window.

"Are your teeth clean?" He laughed.

Self-conscious about the toothpick in between my teeth, I laughed and nodded. "Where you headed?"

He put his fingers up to his lips in the shape of holding a joint.

I nodded. I had forgotten that his pot dealer lived near my side of town. Fluttering, a little panicked, I held my hand up to my ear in the shape of a phone, and mouthed, "Call me?"

He nodded.

I pulled ahead of him and went a short distance before realizing he had turned down a different street, out of view.

He looked the same. Baseball cap, frumpy Fu Manchu mustache. A guy on his way to buy pot for the month.

Sleep was always difficult for him. Rarely would he spend the whole night in bed with me. He would be up and out in the living room usually an hour after I had gone to sleep. I would awaken to use the bathroom and find him out in the living room either reading or asleep on the futon. Occasionally, I would persuade him to come join me in his queen-size bed. I would offer to sleep out on the futon, saying he could have the bed if he didn't want to sleep together.

Sometimes he would stonewall me by shaking his head and saying nothing. Other times, during normal waking hours, he would explain that he was afraid he would wake me with his twitching and murmurings. When he was a paramedic, the guys at the firehouse had often poked fun at him for the sounds he made during sleep.

Neither one of them were that bad, I told him. And they weren't, though the twitching was more noticeable than the high-pitched mumbling. Sometimes I would watch him while this went on and believed my presence diminished its intensity because he could sense my care for him.

Pot helped him sleep, but he never told me this as an explanation or defense. It dimmed the flashbacks and quieted the explosions of Vietnam. He had served as a medic in the jungle for eight months and in a Vietnamese hospital for six. I learned of this through alleyways in our conversations. Nothing was ever linear or logical. It was tangential, fragmented. These mismatched fabric pieces gathered in my lap, and I began to darn them together, forming a tapestry of his story. I listened hard for how to stitch this quilt. Many times, I didn't know how to respond. He listened to me so well, and here I sat, mute in the face of his revelations and grief. Occasionally I felt successful when a pattern materialized, and the colors complemented one another. Maybe I was listening better than I believed.

I worried that Steve wanted me to exculpate his actions, but he never solicited this. He unraveled paragraph after paragraph about how he had never dealt with his issues and how he should, but the other and stronger half of him always said, "Fuck it!"

He never intentionally talked about his experiences in Vietnam with me, and at first, I took it personally. I had opened up so much to him; why couldn't he talk about this?

Steve said that he had talked about it with others in the past and they hadn't known how to react. It was too much for them, and it had made him feel worse that no one could understand. He'd decided long ago it was better to keep it to himself. I suggested that he read Tim O'Brien's *The Things They Carried*. He refused. He doubted it would help. He had read other accounts and it had done nothing to alleviate his own suffering.

Others had experienced far greater trauma than he had, he believed. He had not lost any limbs or sustained any internal damage as a result of bullets or shrapnel. He had attended group therapy at the Vet Center, hoping to elevate his sense of camaraderie, but hearing others' stories had only exacerbated his guilt. He could not feel validated for how he felt or what he thought.

In group therapy, he told me, he'd once shared that he

used to smell peaches right before a soldier died. The therapist commented that scenting roses was common among medics who cared for the nearly departed, but not peaches. He shrugged when he relayed this to me and said he couldn't stand the smell of peach tea because it reminded him of the doorway to the other world and the many times he'd been able to do nothing but watch spirits float through the veil. He kept a box of peach tea in his cupboard, however because a friend who visited often to play chess with him liked it.

He confided once that he never did get used to having a normal conversation with a guy one moment and watching him get blown to bits the next.

One afternoon, he paid me a rare visit (most of the time, I was traveling over to his apartment, twenty-five minutes away). He brought me roses because I had been feeling like a failure about my life and decision to divorce Matt, though I always came around to believing it was the right thing to do in the long run.

We sat on my living room floor so long that my butt grew numb. I talked myself through all of my sadness, and when I was done there were a few minutes of quiet between us. His face went grave, pensive; his eyes retreated back, far and distant. Before I knew it, a confession tumbled out. He said it was expected then and they were rewarded for killing, but how could he live with himself knowing that he had taken someone's son from them?

I watched him. I waited to hug him. I didn't know what to do. My grief seemed of little consequence then. But as quickly as it had bumbled out of his mouth, Steve retracted it all and apologized over and over again for having said any of it. He hadn't come here to tell me this, after all.

Steve called our sex life "spectacular," and I knew it was the best I had ever had.

Though we both expressed our joy over this, it often did not come easily. He always pleased me, but rarely came himself. Maintaining an erection was a problem. We remedied this with the market's finest: horny goat weed, various herbs, and of course Viagra. Contrary to popular opinion, however, an erection does not unequivocally correlate with reaching orgasm. So this became a mission of mine: to get him to share the wealth of the pleasures available to us. Many times, Steve said he enjoyed sex either way and this was enough, but when he didn't come I felt slighted and rebuffed. It seemed like he was holding out and deliberately not surrendering to the power of shared bodies.

We didn't discuss this very much. He did comment once about not coming, and I told him that I didn't feel as though it was up to me—that I was doing everything in my power to help this happen, but ultimately it was up to him to want it to happen.

"Hrumph," he said.

I didn't push to talk more about this. I remained optimistic despite feeling insecure.

A few times after we made love, Steve asked me if we were still friends. He felt afraid that we wouldn't be. He felt afraid of getting too close, too.

Each time I told him, "Yes. We are friends and lovers. It feels easy and right to me."

One afternoon, we had spent hours in his bedroom making love. He had not come yet and though I was nearly exhausted, I revved up to give him my best. Thirty minutes later, he was driving himself so hard inside of me I thought I would split down the middle, but I didn't care. He was making the sounds of pleasure; he was climbing so hard and fast, I was ecstatic for him. He let out a cry I'd never heard before and followed it with syncopated smaller, shorter cries. His fluid exploded inside of me. I was elated. If we could do it like this once, it could happen again.

After we had pulled apart and were lying shoulder to shoulder, I told him that what had just happened was beautiful.

He crossed his arms, averted his eyes from mine, and said, "You just wouldn't give up, would you? You kept coming after me."

I smiled, but he didn't. Something had been triggered deep within him, and I wasn't allowed in. I felt as though he thought what had just happened was offensive and unwelcome. I felt horrible, accused, defenseless. How could what seemed so powerful and wonderful to me instigate such fear and repulsion in him? Was I interpreting his body language incorrectly?

Doubt was becoming a regular feature for me, and as much as I stretched my ever-thinning good feelings over my uncertainty and ambiguity, I was beginning to reach a point of no return. But I muted my suffering with hope; doing that was easier than leaving.

CHAPTER TWELVE

Just Between Us

$\mathcal{I}$t was January. Steve and I were in the midst of another "off"/friend-only period. I called him up and asked if it would be okay if I came over to paint and would he like to accompany me? He suggested that I come at night; there would be a full moon next week.

The day of my date with Steve, I told Mike, whom I'd been seeing for two weeks, that I wouldn't be talking to him on the phone that night. I spit out that it was going to be a full moon; I needed one for the book I was self-publishing, and I had to do it that night. He didn't understand. An unspoken bubble hung between us. I didn't explain anything further. I also left out the part about getting together with my old love.

I wore my long coat that looked like a sleeping bag with a hood, circa 1989. I wrapped a large scarf around my neck and cheeks and put my thickest gloves on. Steve looked like the Michelin man in his thickly padded coat.

He set up a sawhorse and put a piece of wood on top of it for a table. I dipped my brush in and out of the paints and a cup half full of hot water. I had to do this repeatedly and quickly because the bristles kept freezing and forming tiny globs of paint. He had brought out a stool for me, too, but I preferred to stand. He held a flashlight and oscillated it between the moon and my paints.

The sky was black, the branches of the tree that we stood under pointed in craggy lines beneath the brilliance of the moon. The moon itself was a fiery white encircled by a thin layer of purple and orange that radiated in uneven peaks around its circumference.

Less than a half hour later, satisfied with my moon and tired of feeling our nose hairs prickle with each breath, we packed up and headed inside for tea.

Steve checked the thermometer at his window on the way in and called out, "9 degrees Fahrenheit! God, Janer, are we nuts?"

We laughed while he put the water on. I got out my painting to admire it. I set it on his table and he complimented me on the hint of purple and orange on the edges. "It really did look like that. I hate you," he said, laughing. "You're so good."

I left it on his kitchen table while we drank our tea. Watercolor paint remains frozen at nine degrees, but at seventy degrees, it travels. The tiny globs I had tried to thin while outside had begun to thin on their own from melting indoors. I leaned over my painting, horrified and incredulous.

"Oh my God! Shit! It's melting. God. I am so stupid! Of course it's melting! It's watercolor!" I started to laugh.

Steve laughed too. "Why didn't we think about that before?"

We watched it grow and bleed into a different life form. It held our fascination for several minutes. It didn't occur to me to pick up my brush and make it do what I wanted. What would it do untouched? We were like two chemists in the lab, observing the gurgling and gaseous release of substances never before combined.

"I guess I should have just stuck it in my car right after, to keep it frozen. But I still would have had to deal with the thaw eventually . . . Oh well."

"Hmm," he agreed as he continued to watch the paint drool into a new area of the paper.

The painting ended up retaining a moon-like appearance, but I painted a new one for the book anyway. I needed something smaller.

و

It was a white-bright, cottonmouth summer day. I met Steve at his apartment to go for a walk along the creek. As we ambled along, he casually mentioned that we should strip and dip in the icy creek farther down the path. I didn't think that he would follow through with this but before I knew it, we had come to the spot that he deemed "safe" and he said, "Okay."

In no time, he was splashing and fluttering in the creek, the water cascading over his back and legs as he lay propped upright, holding on to two rocks inches below the surface.

I took my clothes off. My turn. He held me as I lowered myself into the same spot. The cold chilled my skin instantaneously. It felt wonderful. We were together and had taken a risk; we were free.

We dressed without getting "caught" and headed back to his place. He said he was surprised I had done that. He didn't know any other woman who would skinny dip next to a well-traveled path. I smiled and felt triumphant.

Hereafter, that area—formally coined "Iceland" because of the ice formations during winter near the dam at the end of the path—was renamed "Naked Creek."

We reminisced several times about a watercolor moon turned asteroid and our bones turning blue in icy water amidst the still dearth of summer. I imagined him papering his grey matter with these tiny shards of rainbow. I hoped they helped to crowd out his endless nightmares.

Steve often described himself as having one foot in and one foot out of anything/anyone that he was involved with. I heard this with one ear and hoped I could pull him through to have both feet firmly planted in the here and now, to be ready. His behavior or response was not an anomaly when compared to many Vietnam veterans. But I didn't know this until I started reading about it, and I didn't want to start reading about it until the emotional pushing and pulling had the better of me and I *needed* an explanation. I needed someone else to tell me that his behavior was "normal" in the context of being a vet. I could accept that, I thought, and make this palatable with the knowledge that I loved him anyway.

He did stop smoking pot during our third interval of intimacy, which lasted one year. He told me he needed to be done with it—thirty years was long enough. He didn't like himself when he smoked it. He by no means believed this would be the end of his struggle with it, but it was the beginning. He stopped smoking to be with me. That was a condition of mine, stipulated after our second "breakup."

I was happy but wary. I knew this was just the beginning for him. Gary had taught me well. This was a process, and there would be a tendency to transfer the addictive behaviors toward the relationship. I would be leaned on and reached for like the pot or alcohol. I would be the object turned to for reassurance and comfort, and like any good substance, I would be expected to be reliable and to not have any reactions or feelings of my own. My job was to fill the void of worthlessness and fulfill his self-esteem.

I knew I could not do these things, of course. But this was a first step all the same, and I waited to see if there would be others to keep this one from backsliding. I would encourage him to join a twelve-step program or renew his interest in meditation. I could listen and bear witness to his process. I intended to do that fully. If this was what saving him looked like, I could do that.

We were very happy in those early days of renewing our intimacy. We had permission to melt into one another, and we did just that. No holds barred. Our intimate life was adventuresome and free; sleep was an afterthought. We were especially excited because we had already known each other for a couple of years, and after going in and out of each other's lives, we were back again. This was reassuring. Despite the pitfalls and grievances, there was forgiveness. We would last.

I noticed the difference not smoking pot anymore made

in his disposition, too. He was not as distracted or grumpy or maligned or peevish. He was still sarcastic but sweetness pervaded. He was attentive and concerned. I was beginning to believe I could depend on this.

Fairly soon after our reunion, however, the holidays—always a bad time for him for a plethora of reasons—arrived. The most recent of those reasons was that he had left his last marriage shortly after Christmas, and the anniversary of this event usually left him foul and inconsolable.

For this reason, I dreaded the holidays. That Christmas, though, he surprised me and said he felt happy to be with me and was not feeling any regret at all. I had a difficult time unwinding myself from bracing for the worst, which would have been an endless diatribe about the holidays, his guilt, and his regret, but eventually relaxed. We cooked a great meal together of scallops in cream sauce and pasta and ate the cherry pie I'd baked for dessert.

By March, things had resumed a familiar negative flavor because of Steve's need to find a job and failure to find one that would be both fulfilling and garner him a livable wage. He could no longer work in fire service because of rotator cuff injuries which had been operated on six times. His shoulders were too weak to carry water hoses, not to mention people. He had been let go at his job six months before we met in the meditation class.

In the interim of these couple of years, Steve had cashed in his pension, and spent it all, and gone on to rack up $9,000.00 in credit card debt. He lived in a tiny one-bedroom apartment; his expenditures were not large, but he wanted to treat himself to things he'd always wanted: a good telescope, a computer, a flat screen TV, a mountain bike—and he wanted to treat his kids to things they wanted, too. He was not good with money. To be fair, he'd told me this during that first Christmas dinner.

A few times I offered to help him out. After my divorce, I received a chunk from the sale of Matt's and my house and

offered to pay rent one month for Steve when he was struggling. He refused, as he did all other times when he was
without. I told him he didn't need to worry about it; he didn't
have to pay me back. But he refused. He didn't want money
to be part of our relationship. That was one thing I gave him
credit for.

He was depressed about his fruitless job search. It ate
away at him. He felt like a failure. He used to save lives. He
used to be a hero. He used to feel good because his life had
purpose. Now, he had nothing to show for it. It meant nothing to anyone, and he couldn't return to smoking pot because
nearly all the places he was applying to were doing drug
screens. Some even did hair samples, which could detect
drugs in the body up to one year.

He complained to me. I listened, and I hoped something
would come through for him. And eventually it did: he got a
job at a juvenile rehabilitation facility for boys.

Steve was really excited about this job. It met the criteria
he had wanted: decent pay and worthwhile work. Perfect. His
job entailed watching the teens during a study hall–like
situation. But he soon found that their bottled-up frustration
terrified him. He sensed the boys could smell his fear and
would attack. It created a trigger response for him that dated
back to his days in Vietnam. It was debilitating, and he could
not hide from it.

Steve began visiting the Veterans Center to meet with a
counselor he had seen a couple of years earlier. She advised
him to quit the job at the rehabilitation center, so he did. She
also suggested that he apply for post-traumatic stress disorder grant money from the government. He would have to tell
his story to a couple of doctors for an evaluation, but he
might see a check in as soon as a couple of months. He set
about putting this in motion.

A couple of months later, Steve got a letter in the mail
that said he would receive full compensation (100 percent)
from the government for his PTSD. It was not a lot of

money, but enough to live on. The stipulation with this compensation was that the recipient would not work.

The day he received the letter, he had picked me up to drive us around a park grounds to seek out a place to go camping. It was late May. He asked if the letter read the way he thought it read. I looked it over and assured him it did: within a month's time, he would begin receiving checks.

We were smiles and pats on the back for the rest of the day, though silently I wondered what would be next for us. With no reason, financially, for him to stay away from pot, would Steve persist in his commitment to being done with that part of his life? He had renewed his counseling at the Vet Center and this was bringing up old issues, unresolved pain and strife. For so long, pot had been his only savior.

9 requested more information from Steve's counselor about my role as his girlfriend, and she loaned me a book by Patience Mason entitled, *Recovering from the War: A Woman's Guide to Helping Your Vietnam Vet, Your Family, and Yourself.* I read part of the introduction and flipped around through some of the chapters. I did not want to read it but could not help picking it up, either. One night, I read a few passages and then I put it down, stilled by a plain truth. The author had written many conditional statements about being in a relationship with a Vietnam vet. She had allowed many indulgences to go on with her husband over the years, she said, because he had been so traumatized. She also explained why this group of vets was different than others (the lack of national support both while they were there and upon their return), and that she forgave her husband because he was dedicated to making a change for himself. He wanted to try.

I put the book down. I needed to talk to Steve. Fear welled up in me.

The next time we saw each other, I sat down across from him in his rocking chair. He sat on his futon.

My throat was dry. I quivered with anxiety. I forced myself to speak.

"I feel afraid about you and me. In the book I've been reading, the author writes about how much she supported her husband, and I'm afraid because I did that in my marriage and I waited and hoped for something to be different and it wasn't. I need reassurance that you'll be willing to work on this, because I can't do it all. I can't be the one to carry us. I couldn't even if I wanted to. It's not in me anymore."

"I can't offer you reassurance of anything," Steve said. "I don't even want to talk about this, with anyone. I wish no one knew about it. I wish I didn't know about it. At your earliest convenience, please return the book. I appreciate that you have stood by me through this. You have been rock solid. I don't want this to be part of our relationship. I don't want it to be part of my life. I'm sick of it, and it won't go away." He wouldn't look at me.

A quick breath rattled me. Everything collapsed. I wanted to die. I had failed. He did not love me enough to even try and love himself. We would fail. The wall of his resistance was larger and stronger than my patience and my love. I had believed I had been chipping away at it, but here it stood before me, so tall and broad I could not see over it or around it. I had only been fooling myself that I could.

We hugged and kissed and said we would talk soon.

I drove home furious that I had gone back in for a third time for this: rejection and refusal to grow. A "fuck you" attitude welled up in me. I was determined to delve into the book more. I refused to return the book to Steve and scanned a lot of it over the next week or so. Then I got tired of looking at it on my counter, where I left things that needed some sort of action, so I put it in my car.

We continued to see each other. Steve even rode with me in my car on various excursions, and whether or not he realized the book was close at hand, he never mentioned it. I never thought he was oblivious to it; I chose to believe he was being respectful of me and my decision about when to return it.

Six or seven weeks passed before I was able to hand it to him neutrally and with a cavalier, "Here."

We never said another word about it until a couple of months later, when I wrote him a letter about the current status of our relationship. I wrote that it was too hard for me to go on as we were. (We hadn't made love in nearly two months; our conversations were sporadic. I had dropped in on him a few times, but it was clear he had retreated again into the cave of his own suffering.) I reiterated that I needed reassurance from him that he was willing to work on himself and our relationship with me—that I couldn't do it alone. I also told him I had read quite a bit of the book and had even called the Vet Center to try and make an appointment, so I could talk to someone about our relationship. But they'd told me I needed permission from him to be granted access, which I did not ask for from him because I feared denial. I had gone online and joined a chat room to "talk" with other people about PTSD. I loved him, I said, but I needed more.

I did not think I would hear from him again, but he wrote me back a week later. He said he had misinterpreted what had transpired between the two of us that day entirely. He'd heard that I was not willing to go any further with him. He'd felt shocked and a bit put off and had talked on and on to try and cover his feelings of disappointment. He was surprised that I had gone to the lengths that I had to try and understand this process and his feelings but asked me to please not contact the Vet Center again. He said again that he appreciated how I'd stood by him through his re-entry back to counseling, that I had been "rock solid," and that he held me in the highest esteem. He treasured our experiences together and considered them unique in his life. He was tired, however, and did not want to continue to be lovers anymore; he was no good at relationships and was sick of "fucking up people's lives." Furthermore, he had returned to his pot addiction, which he knew was a deal breaker for me. He did not want to lose me as a friend, but he feared this would fall on deaf ears.

I wrote him back right away and said it was true: I could

not and would not compete with a drug for his attention, but I would still be his friend. I still enjoyed talking to him; he was one of my favorite listeners.

I recognized, however, that he had written the same words to me a few years earlier at the time of a different "ending": "I am tired of fucking up people's lives." Nothing had changed. Nothing had moved for him. It made me feel sad, and for the first time it was uncomplicated by denying myself that I felt just that. I didn't pretend or try to cover it up or tell myself he would be better next time.

We spent the holidays together again, and they were predictably melancholic for Steve. I spent both Thanksgiving and Christmas wishing I had done something else, but at the same time his naked grumpiness was familiar and therefore comfortable.

I continued to call him. Our conversations were brief and emotionless, nearly.

I tried not to focus on the fact that he had read my novel three times and had provided me with pages of detailed critique and corrections. Nor that he had driven to my place late one night to make sure that I was okay because I had a pain in my side and a fever. I tried not to remember that he had held me tightly and let me sob into his arms after I got off the phone with my younger brother, who had found out that day that he had Stage I Hodgkin's and would need six months of chemotherapy. Nor that he said to me once, "For the first time in my whole life, I feel like someone loves me for me. When you meet new people, they judge you immediately, but not you. What you offer is rare. You accept me. I haven't been this happy since I was a little boy. I think my sons can look at me and say, 'This is what Dad looks like when he's happy.'"

I needed to forget—temporarily, at least—how easy it was to talk and laugh with him, how familiar we seemed to one another the minute I met him.

What I focused on remembering was reading to him two

paragraphs by John Calvi from a piece entitled "True Love," published in *The Friends Journal* in 1992:

Surrender to love is the hardest damn work I have ever done in my life. Put me working in prisons to teach murderers how to give good massages or give me tortured women who haven't slept without nightmares in ten years, but don't ask me to be open and receive tender loving care of someone who is going to know all my dirty laundry and stick around anyway!

Why is it so hard? Well, I guess I've just been on the road so long I don't know the difference between my feet and my boots and here comes someone to offer a foot rub and I gotta feel how tired my feet are and how long I've been wanting some good touch and lay down all those other times of disappointment and confusion and let this in without overwhelming myself or anyone else with grief and longing. I didn't learn how to do this at home or school. Did you? It takes a combination of mercy and love we give ourselves.

It reminded me of Steve, and I thought it would make him feel okay, that he wasn't wrong or weird for feeling afraid. I also hoped it would inspire him to embrace what we had and to try.

After I finished reading it, he said he didn't want to hear it. He was flat-out not interested.

I felt hopeless.

I thought, too, about how after we ended things the second time I screamed in my car all the way home from his place. My throat had not felt that raw since Shane's birth, since I pushed my son out into this world.

I remembered how hard it had been to not call him after that second time. How angry I became at him for telling me after we had broken up that I had been his best lover, that nothing had ever felt so natural to him before. How could he say that to me? *Show me!* I thought. *Fight for me, then. Try.* I became mute and inconsolable. I was so depressed I could not write. I did not want to see my thoughts on the page. I turned to another outlet: that summer, I painted two watercolors. I spent a month on each. The first was a single rose in a broken vase with petals of another rose falling on it. The second was of a creek near my house. I sat on the rocks and painted the little waves that cascaded up and down, and the tree branches that hung lazily along the water's edge.

I remembered how, in those early days of getting to know him, I used to wait for him outside his apartment—for hours sometimes—just for the chance to see and talk to him, and how ridiculous I felt doing it but how I justified it because I needed to have him hear me.

I remembered the many times I called him, and he did not call me back. How I forgave this and how this forgiveness made me feel I did not respect myself.

With these memories, I started to see how each departure unveiled layers about me, and about Steve, too. I began growing a self separate from him, one that expanded her reach to new friends, new audiences. I began to trust and remember that I enjoyed my own company. Many times, I was all I needed. I could tell my stories to myself and not risk rejection. I was rather entertaining; my ever-increasing circle of new friends told me that often.

It became okay for me to see Steve for who he was; the rose-colored glasses of who I wanted him to be were fading. He was fickle about when he could be receptive and never communicated how long he would be "out." Though he appreciated me I never knew how long his ability to show that appreciation would last. My walnut pile of insecurities and seemingly innocuous withholdings was growing, not receding.

I was also beginning to suspect that he was using my ease at processing my feelings and thoughts with him to vicariously feel and think about his own issues, without ever really doing any of his own work. I felt manipulated when I thought of him like this. His occasional comments that he was all talk and no action validated my suspicion but did little to quell my icky sense of betrayal. And this, more than anything, made me feel cheated and furious. I had worked so hard to understand all that made me human, and he refused to try. It was hard to accept that I could do nothing about this and harder still to realize that his unwillingness had nothing to do with me. I never said anything to him about this, though. I chose to hope that my steadfast listening to him would eventually turn that key over in his mind, and he would be willing to start finding the right path out of the maze he was in.

With each separation, I was realizing what I could *not* tell him: the devastation his repeated desertions and retreats had caused me. I also developed wariness around the things I did tell him. What would trigger him into a retreat from me? I felt as though everything I did say had the potential to make him abandon me, and there would be nothing to explain it. I would not be able to calculate or anticipate it. And he could not help me understand what it was that took him there to begin with. It was as though I was standing in the midst of a bumper car ride and becoming dented and bruised by the repeated, erratic ricochet of the cars. I knew I needed to remove myself and I even knew how to do it, but if I did, could I still know him? Could I keep him in my life and keep myself safe?

What bothered me the most was his saying he wasn't himself in our relationship. "Some other guy stepped in and took over doing things for people and then the resentment," he told me. "I can't do the day to day of a relationship. It shuts me down."

I prided myself on unlocking the closets of people's stifled selves. Time and again, my students had thanked me for showing them that not only could they write, they liked to. And what of all the men who told me about their long-buried secrets or desires? Why couldn't Steve be himself with me? How could he say that? Nothing he could have said could have wounded more. But I could surrender, finally. There was nothing more for me to do or to say.

He didn't know who he was or what he wanted. Since he had retired, he didn't know how to spend his time. I had tried to convince him months earlier that finding a way to invest oneself in a meaningful way required support and that I could offer that.

"I am not going to crack open," he said one day. "I am not going to be any more available than I already am."

"Is there any way to work with this?" I pleaded. "I have the number for the counselor at Denver Family Institute."

"There are many people who know psychology better than I do, but no one is going to sit there and act like they know more about what is going on inside my head than I do," he said. "At least 51 percent of me doesn't like being intimate with someone. I can't handle it. I have to listen to that guy. There are probably ninety other things I should be saying about how much I love you, but it doesn't seem fair. I don't think my brain is working properly. I think there is something not quite right. You have offered me more than fertile ground to grow, and I can't."

"I feel as though I have failed," I said.

"No. No." He shook his head. "I always regret letting go, and I am sure I will here. I can't stand to see how poorly I have treated you. The counseling made me want to be more selfish. I have tried to think how what I want to do will fit into our relationship and I can't see how."

More selfish? He already oscillated back and forth at whim, agreeing to do things and backing out at the last minute. He spent a lot of time alone. He wanted more? What dreams did he have that he couldn't share with me?

"Is there anything else you would like to tell me?" I asked.

"No. I would only loop through it again. I wouldn't be ready to have this conversation in twenty years."

"Do you want me in your life?"

"I don't feel as though I have any say-so about that. You are welcome as a friend."

I could not do it. I could not end it. I knew how low and miserable I was. I knew how much my light was dimming. Countless friends had told me to leave him for my own good. I had become quite good at separating his wet paint of depression from my buoyancy, and I convinced myself I could live this way. He would have to do it. I could not give him the satisfaction of abandoning him just as everyone else had done in his life.

My return to him engendered a loyalty, he said more than once. I had penetrated him. He told me, "Everyone else would say, 'You're fucked up.' But you're the only one who ever asked why."

I struggled with the measurement of how much good this did. What of cracking the pea-size opening of his heart a micrometer more? My gaze was narrow. Of course it mattered; his heart had opened, period. But should this obligate me to persist?

We continued to wander back in and flirt with possibility. I suckled on the nectar of hope as it was pinched out of an eye-dropper. Caring for him gave my life a shape in which I could walk and breathe.

And I had reasons to hope: for one, he had taken me to one of his favorite places, Tucson, Arizona. We camped there in April 2007, a time when the bloom blinks open, blessing the desert with its silky pastels. I fell into a deep trance with that glory. He had shared it with me. I felt baptized in his forgiveness, his grace. I didn't trust that this was anything more than a dreamy interlude.

I began seeing Jack—another unavailable male, this time due to the fact that he lived in another state. That relationship disassembled within a few months, and Steve enticed me back in. I made clear my commitment to him. There wasn't anyone else I had felt as strongly about, nor for whom I would endure so much pain.

We sat on this pillow of familiarity and comfort for a few months.

I came over one day, let myself in, and sat down at Steve's kitchen table.

"Hey man, do you know if I'll be able to transfer this service in a month?" he asked the Dish Network installer who was packing up his tools.

"You'll have to call the customer service line about that," the guy said. "Don't think it should be a problem, though. Your contract goes with you regardless of address. But don't take my word for it."

A month? I waited, sitting on panic.

"I am moving to Arizona in a month," Steve blurted out when the installer left. "My boys are grown, I have always wanted to live there. I need to declare this, or I'll never do it. There's nothing here for me."

Nothing?! "I'm surprised," I said, trying to stay calm. "I thought things between us were going well. I want you to be happy. I know you love it down there. I don't want to keep you from that. But I love you and care for you, no matter where you live ..."

Crushed. How could he do this?

I swallowed. "Do you still want me in your life?"

"I hadn't considered that," he said. "I thought you'd never want to talk to me again. Okay, sure, we can stay in touch and visit."

After Steve's move, we started talking on the phone several times a day, and for the first time, I felt as though we were in the inside of a relationship. I felt needed and clear about my role. I felt as though this would secure us toward a path of mutual care. Physical distance was not a deficit; rather it intensified our desire to be with one another. It also didn't look like convention and we both liked that. There was freedom to make our relationship into what we needed it to be.

I flew down to see him every three weeks. He said that my presence made him feel safe. It gave him meaning, a reason for being there. It made the desert the beautiful place he had fallen in love with. Making him feel safe was part of the cost of caring for him, and I gladly paid it because he validated the parts of myself I held secret and dear. I felt okay about showing my raw, naked self to him.

After eight weeks, he broke his lease, packed up his things, and came back up to Denver.

Steve was despondent when he returned. His dream of living in his beloved Arizona had crushed him. It was 2008. We continued to see one another but our intimate life had no recognizable pattern. I talked him into couple's counseling offered through the VA. We attended three times. The route to the therapist's office took us past the Prosthetics Department, which made Steve distraught. He said he could taste blood in his mouth. But there was no other entry into the office; we were seeing the therapist after hours and the building was closed at several doorways.

That was the end of this round of therapy together.

I learned to accept him and to be content with what he could offer on his own timeline. It wasn't easy, but I didn't ask myself if I liked it. We persisted without much variation in our ups and downs, ins and outs for the next two years.

In 2010, Jack wove his way back into my life. When he asked me out again I didn't say, "No, I'm with someone," because I didn't feel as though I was. Steve wasn't offering anything more than an inconsistent ear. Torn, ambivalent, not wanting to dismiss what might be a second chance with Jack, I began seeing him again. He was no longer out of state. He had moved back to Denver.

As if on cue, Steve, sensing the threat of a more permanent departure, perked up and began communicating more regularly.

Over the course of that summer, I went back and forth between Jack and Steve. Neither one knew explicitly about the other; however, I received a sideways glance from Jack when I told him I'd gone to Ouray for my birthday (omitting the fact that I had gone with Steve), and after our return from that trip Steve yelled at me, suspecting that I had been seeing someone else.

I did not confess. I didn't feel I owed him that. After all of his inexplicable silences and retreats, I felt less guilty about going off with someone else.

Jack returned to college in the fall and became extremely busy, leaving me bored and wanting attention. Steve allowed me back in and we began again for a couple of months, but by February 2011, our relationship had dissolved.

CHAPTER THIRTEEN

Pierced

Y ou're going to take one look at—what's his name,
Ray?—turn around, and get a ticket back to Denver,"
my friend said. "I bet you don't leave the airport. I bet you see
him through the window as his car pulls up and you run before he sees you."

I laughed, glad he was worried for me. Someone needed
to be. But I didn't take his concerns seriously. Excitement
busted up through me like a geyser; worrying about what-ifs
was impractical and a nuisance, even if it was warranted.

"I don't know, Jane. Sounds pretty sketchy, flyin' halfway
across the country to hang out with a guy you've talked on
the phone with for two weeks. You know people out there,
right, in case it goes south?"

"Yeah," I said. "I've been to Boston, Maine, New Hamp-
shire. My family used to go there for summer vacation. I
went to grad school at Syracuse. I still know some people
there."

"What are you going to do if it works out? Would you
leave your job, would you leave Shane with his dad?"

"I don't know! It'll be an adventure. I'll be okay," I reassured him.

My escapade needed to be fun. I needed to laugh. I
needed to be someplace other than Colorado for the week of
my birthday. And if I fell in love, well, I would lap up my

good fortune. Memories from my last birthday had recently rolled in and threatened to capsize me. One year ago, Shane's father had announced his intent to marry his girlfriend, and the love of my life, Steve, had spiraled into a depression on the heels of our vacation in Ouray—a one-two punch.

I wasn't supposed to feel anything about my ex-husband getting married. We had been separated since Shane was two, and it felt wrong to feel abandoned by someone I had left, but I did. It was 2010. I was forty-three years old. The one thing Matt had always offered me, even in our separation, was security and stability. He did not falter—and now he was giving that to someone else. The untimely abandonment by Steve left me vanquished, crushed, and naked.

Six months after Matt's announcement, the last day of March, I sat in the parking lot outside my brother Richard's place on Pennsylvania and 14th in Denver, waiting for him to return with breakfast. We had just finished loading my car with his things. It was moving day. He was heading back to Michigan within the next few days to be near Dad and help with his care. Dad had been declining gradually for a few years because of neuropathy, his mobility compromised by atrophied muscles. Richard had just left his job as a barista and was ready to return to our home state with a higher purpose.

Bored, I played with my phone, roving back and forth over Steve's name in my list of contacts. It was his birthday. I told myself not to call him. I told myself it would be okay. This went on for a couple of minutes, and then my phone rang.

My gynecologist was on the other end. Not good. The doctor never calls with good news.

"The results of your latest pap smear show precancerous cells on the cervix," he told me. "Adenocarcinoma. The usual course of action for this is a hysterectomy. Call the main number and schedule an appointment for my office. We will do a LEEP first to see if this has spread."

"Okay," I whispered, tears spurting.

Richard opened the front passenger side door, sat down, and handed me a plastic cup of orange juice. He saw my tears and furrowed his eyebrows. "What's wrong?"

"Shit, dammit," I said, wiping my cheek. "The doctor called . . . I've got precancerous cells on the cervix."

"What? What do they do for that?" Richard asked as he rubbed my shoulder.

"It's fucking precancer, not cancer," I said. "He wants to do a hysterectomy. I've got to go in for another test first. I need to call right now."

$\mathcal{I}$ never called Steve. He swung unpredictably when it came to my needing him. I couldn't risk a disappearing act, compounding my nervous worry about what lay ahead. It was better to get support where it could be given easily and unencumbered, even if that meant feeling alone in this.

From April to June, I lived under the rule of what my doctor pronounced about test results. They had "gotten it all" with the latest LEEP; I was a new woman, or at least a healthier one with the abnormal cells now gone. I opted not to have a hysterectomy because the oncologist explained I was at Stage Zero, which meant there was a 3 to 40 percent chance of recurrence. I heard 60 to 97 percent chance of no recurrence and believed my odds were great since I generally took excellent care of myself.

Emerging triumphant from this trial, I felt the urgency to drink any trickle of love's nectar. I wanted someone else to worry for me. Awakened from the fear bred by uncertainty, I arose free enough to be crazy and crazy enough to turn the improbable into reality. Time had narrowed. I had a bruised heart, but I was alive and curious and aware again that I was young.

I spent hours upon days on the phone with Ray prior to my visit in August. We had met online and fit into one another like tailored gloves during our first phone call.

Open to the innocence of new love, we laughed, delighted

in our shared humor, the mirror of joy and recognition we found in one another. He called me the next morning to thank me for such an enjoyable phone call the night before. Radians of hope sparkled. He was vulnerable and could hear my heart. He felt within reach; the 1,800 miles between us seemed immaterial. We grew to talk two, three, sometimes five times a day.

He invited me to visit him within a few days of that first conversation. He didn't offer to pay for my plane ticket, not even part of it, and I didn't ask. I parted with the $600 to see what this would be, to discover its passion, and to experience the delight of being with him. Consumed by the haze of possibility, I ignored a lot.

When Ray arrived at the airport to pick me up, he was not svelte, and he stood an inch and a half shorter than the five foot seven he proclaimed to be. The long hair trailing behind at the nape of his neck seemed wrong against the sheen on top of his bald head. Though he had forewarned me about his chipped and missing teeth, it still startled me to see a serrated smile.

I forgave it all. His midriff paunch was due to his being fifty-four. He played tennis and hiked every day. He ate a balanced diet. The hair he did have was curly and soft, and the teeth were going to be fixed.

I ignored other things as well, like his phone service getting cut off because he hadn't paid the bill, and his failing to follow up with the innkeeper after we got lost en route to Vermont the first night we tried to make it there, and the fact that his car had been manufactured the same year I graduated high school and looked as though it hadn't been cleaned since then.

I also ignored the fact that he betrayed his best friend, James, a chiropractor, by taking me to see a different chiropractor—a guy named Schlemsky—when my back kinked from traveling. James was a friend loyal enough to loan Ray money to bail him out here and there and to serve as his banker since Ray didn't have a checking account. (Ray owed fines on the account he had once shared with his ex-wife and couldn't open a new one until the matter was resolved.)

The week I visited, Ray received a check from a client from his life-coaching business. He had it with him when we arrived at a restaurant for a late lunch. Ray tried to reach James. We waited. When James called back and said he could help right then, Ray left me at the restaurant, promising that the "Bank of James" transaction would take no longer than thirty minutes. Confident, he even ordered soup before leaving.

I finished my meal and watched the five people in the restaurant change faces and places. A filmy, gelatinous goo formed on the surface of the soup after it had sat there for an hour. I began to wonder if I could tell a cab driver Ray's address, and if I had enough money to hail a cab back to the airport. But in the spirit of my adventure, I let the story roll on and called him instead.

"I messed up, Jane," he said. "But I can't talk. I'll tell you when I get there in fifteen minutes."

I had his soup heated up. More people floated into the restaurant for the dinner hour.

When Ray finally arrived, he looked like a raccoon narrowly missed by an absent-minded driver. "I told him I took you to see Schlemsky," he said, looking down at his soup.

"You what? Why?" I demanded. "I told you not to do that, remember? When you asked me yesterday?" I shook my head. "How did it happen?"

"I don't know," he said, flustered. "We were in the middle of the aisle at Trader Joe's. I guess I thought he would be interested."

"How did you leave it? What did you say?"

"He wouldn't look at me. He said he didn't think I was slippery, or that I was trying to get away with something. I tried to tell him that he doesn't stay open that late like Schlemsky does. I told him I wanted to be private. That I, uh, wasn't ready to introduce you yet. He said he understood. I think it will be okay. You know, James never asked about your treatment or how your back feels now."

I also chose to ignore the dust bunnies drifting about, flitting in fits from underneath the bed at the slightest breeze, as well as the coins thrown asunder on the bedroom and bathroom floors of his house. I got used to the feel of a dime sticking to my heel as I stepped out of the shower. I didn't move a thing. I didn't sweep or collect the coins into a jar. I resisted the temptation. Ray had an expansive, creative mind—it was fluid, a racing river. I could excuse the flagrant mess as overflow of his creative prowess.

I did not ignore his wizardry when we did finally make it to the Inn at Ormsby Hill in Manchester, Vermont, an hour and a half after check-in time. We snickered, wondering whether or not the doorbell was working. "It turned green, didn't it? Try it again."

The innkeeper clomped down the stairs after Ray had rung the doorbell eight times. She looked a fright in her fluorescent white bathrobe and face slicked in cold cream. She told us she would not let us in. Ray implored her to re-consider, telling her that we had gotten lost (second night in a row) and that we had called her at 9:00 p.m., the latest hour for check-in.

She said she would check the voicemail messages and closed the door. A few tense minutes later, she reappeared and confirmed that we had called. She showed us to her finest room, complete with a "his" and "hers" bathroom, fireplace, hot tub and sauna, patio overlooking the green mountains of Vermont, and king-size bed with a canopy.

The next morning, Ray won her over with his charm, complimenting what she and her husband had done with the inn and lured her into regaling him with the history of the area, the inn, the people who visited them, and the seasonal festivities in Manchester—important, since he had made an arrangement with her previously to feature her inn in *SAAB* magazine in exchange for our one-night stay.

In addition to billing himself as a life coach, Ray identified as a journalist and travel writer, though he needed someone to do his actual writing for him because he was dyslexic and all thumbs when it came to making his way around a word processing program. (That was where I came in. He would throw out the ideas, and I would craft them into an article.)

The innkeeper giggled by the end of the interview, happy we had come. I silently applauded his ability to turn her around, wiling his way back into her graces. I felt privileged to glimpse this genius, a pristine glint of the diamond within. This was how he had done it. He had survived by shimmying his way in and out of the mini tsunamis he had stirred up. I laughed, believing I could learn from him.

I did not ignore his sexual ineptitude, but I did forgive it. I declared to myself that it took time to build intimacy. Our bodies were foreign to each other, our rhythms and patterns, habits and techniques, all to be unveiled. He told me he had attended Tantra workshops before I arrived, and I cheered— less to teach, yes! After being with him, however, I could not fathom what he had learned.

After I returned to Denver, I officially stamped that first week with Ray a success. We had gone blueberry picking and swimming in a watering hole on my birthday. I had gotten away from home and landed in the middle of an adventure. I wanted nothing more.

In the weeks after I returned, we maintained our lengthy, invigorating phone sessions. We discussed growing his life coach business and creating a new website, me leaving my job to become a writing coach, and the letters and articles we would write.

I told him more than once that Shane was my priority, and each time he said that a couple should put themselves ahead of their children because the children will eventually leave. I disagreed but there was no concession from him. His children were twenty-eight and twenty-one, supposedly old enough to be out on their own. They hovered still, however. Ray told me that his twenty-eight-year-old son often harangued Ray about all his failures as a parent. He didn't say "thank you" when Ray gave him a ride or brought him food, and he repeatedly told Ray that not everything was about him. This, I did not ignore. I listened. That anger hadn't grown in a vacuum. It had been fertilized by years of feeling invisible.

Ray would throw in side comments about me leaving my son with his father, so I could go out and be with him. He wanted me to get out of my job as soon as possible. He told me that my writing was self-indulgent and self-emergent and that journaling was a divisive tool between couples. He had designs on transforming my writing for his higher purpose of propagating the philosophy of eternal union and relationship miracles. I argued with him that not every union was sacred or worth fighting for, in particular if one person had an addiction to drugs or alcohol and was not willing to devote him/herself to the relationship. He would not budge. He could not see that individuals were responsible for their growth and that this wasn't implicitly the responsibility of the relationship.

"What's the other person supposed to do if the addict cares more about the drug than the other person?" I asked.

He did not have an answer but definitely believed the person should not leave.

Ten days before I was to visit Ray for the second time, James advised him to tell me he was still on the singles sites.

I was rational at first. "I don't have any control over what you do," I told him. "I have taken myself off because I can't divide my attention like that. It's too distracting to talk to you on the phone and be emailing someone else." I paused. "Why are you still on?"

He explained that it gave him information for his new website about coupling, and it was helping him figure out his own state of mind as he heard back from various women. He confided, "It made me uncomfortable to tell you, Jane. You are leagues ahead of anyone else I have met. I've lived a monk's life these last two years since my divorce."

He said this as though it should be enough. His revelation did little to rub out the insecurity and threat that was growing inside of me like mold. He did not offer to get off the sites. He said nothing more about it. So there it sat billowing up, clouding my trust and agitating my angst.

One week before my flight out of Denver, Ray started joking about my ability to tell a story. My stories had no point, he said, but he enjoyed the soothing sound of my voice and had become reliant on it to fall asleep at night.

I balked. "You don't accept me for who I am. There has to be space for me to be me."

"I told you I was a big energy, and I invited you to come play with me . . . but let's not divorce the relationship, let's divorce the pattern," he said. "Let's heal this together. I can see that I need to step back so that you can step forward."

The next day, I told him a story about Shane's friend who got caught trying to pee in the stairwell of our complex.

A yippy cotton-ball dog appeared first on the grass three floors below us, its long leash stretched into the entryway of our building.

"That's Jay's dog!" Shane said.

Shane called to Jay just as the neighbors pointed and shouted from their patio, "That boy is peeing down there!"

Jay ran up the stairs to our place with his hands down his pants. I waved him toward our bathroom. "I didn't do it, I didn't do it!" he cried.

"Why didn't you go before you left your house?" I asked.

"I didn't have to go then," he yelled back from the hallway.

Shane shoved his feet into his shoes as fast as he could and ran downstairs, calling back to me, "I'm going to see the puddle!"

When I relayed this to Ray, he was waiting for a guy who had bought a new battery for his car. The mechanic was bipolar, and Ray owed him some money. Anxious and distracted, he didn't really pay attention to what I said.

After the mechanic left, Ray said, "That story actually sounded worth listening to. Please tell me again."

"Forget about it," I said with a sigh.

ℒ

The day before my departure, I printed off the boarding passes, filled out a mail-stop request online, and packed two carry-on bags.

That night, an anvil settled onto my chest. I got up at 3:00 a.m., raked my hair away from my eyes and shook my head. Sudden and sharp, an iridescent clarity pierced my awareness. I couldn't go. I wouldn't go. Conjuring up Ray's hands on me for five irredeemable days curled my lips in revulsion.

What would I tell him? This question threatened idly, taunting me from above like a guillotine. I had a few hours. I would lie. Sick? Food poisoning? In the hospital? No. I could recover. I could still get on a flight later, even in a compromised, fragile state. I could still go there. No. Car. My car. It would break down on the highway. I would tell him the check engine light came on. That had happened to me before, in other people's cars—in fact, in Ray's car, when I was there to see him in August. My car remained reliable, a great car, never any trouble. Would it be believable? I needed to buy some time.

I sent him an email from my cell phone at 6:00 a.m. and told him I was waiting for the tow truck. The check engine light had come on; my car had died on the way to the airport.

At 10:30 a.m., I sent an email saying that the shuttle from the dealership would be here soon to pick me up. I would let him know when I knew more.

I called a mechanic and asked him to list off any reasons why a car might stop in the middle of a highway. He rattled off three, but I only caught one of them: throttle position sensor. That sounded interesting and I guessed that Ray wouldn't even know what this meant, since he was as ignorant about car problems as I was.

Concern laced the mechanic's voice as he asked me when I would like to bring the car in, that they wouldn't be able to make a full diagnosis unless the vehicle was there. I told him I would wait and see and call back later for an appointment. I turned the word, "diagnosis," around in my mind as though I were palming two billiard balls in my hand. Diagnosis could mean hours. More time.

I called my therapist, Thomas, and made an appointment. I needed a reality check before I made my next move. I texted my friend Barb and told her I'd decided not to go. She called me back and we talked for an hour. She had told me three days before to go as an observer, to bear witness to the dynamic between Ray and me and then decide if I wanted to stay in the relationship. I did not need to take in any more information. But I did need to tell him, and it was important to me that I do it well. The stubborn stain of affinity bled through despite the sheets of reasons about why I did not want to be with him anymore. I would explain when I had my bearings, later in the day. I would be calm and kind. I would send it to him in writing, so he could take it all in. I would listen but not respond to the ten voicemails he would leave in the next sixteen hours.

A younger Jane would have driven to the airport in a blind faith that it would all work out okay. But I was not twenty-five, I was forty-four. Not freshly divorced, I was no longer prey to the vulnerability that comes from being on one's own. I was young enough for an adventure but old enough to know that I didn't need to lose everything in order to start over.

CHAPTER FOURTEEN

Reemergence

The subject line of the email was "PLEASE READ." He wrote that he had made an egregious error by letting me go. He asked if I would forgive him. What we'd had together was far richer than anything he'd ever had with anyone else, and would I consider, please, being friends with him?

Tears stung as I re-read his email. I was at work and quickly grabbed a tissue to blot my eyes. Self-conscious, I turned my chair away from my office door and blew my nose.

It had been seven months since our last conversation. It was September of 2011. I didn't even remember exactly what we'd said during that argument. I did remember that it was intense and angry. He was upset that I was upset about Matt getting married; he didn't feel as though I was fully in our relationship.

Me, not fully in the relationship? Really. I didn't have words to say that this was a handy distortion, considering the fact that Steve expected to be excused from all of his retreats and missteps when he extricated himself unannounced.

I took in what he said. I considered it. I examined my attachment and reflected on whether or not it was exaggerated and unhealthy. I couldn't decide. I was worried about Shane. My control over what happened in his dad's presence was loosening. Who was I going to be in the midst of the addition of Jill and her four children?

There had not yet been any reassurance or invitation to continue with what Matt and I had lived by in regard to Shane in the nine years since our divorce. I was afraid of what I didn't know about the dynamics of this new way of being. I felt threatened. Each holiday and school or sporting event involving Shane would unravel the new pattern; nothing was certain. The last thing I wanted was for Steve to feel abandoned by my confusion. I needed him to be the stable, reassuring one this time, telling me that it would work itself out, that Matt and I always kept Shane in the forefront of our actions.

Of course, Matt had deviated from this course when he didn't tell me right away that he was getting married. Three weeks passed and then I found out. Shane had been moody and sullen, and I didn't know why. I assumed it was because he was a pre-teen.

I was angry with Matt about not telling me sooner, felt that I could have helped Shane with adjusting to this if I had known. I wrote all of this in an email. Matt excused his actions with the justification that he had moved around a lot as a child and this shouldn't be a big deal to Shane. I argued that Shane had not moved at all and now he was being asked to give up the friends he had known since he was three. They would be moving forty-five minutes across town, from Lakewood to Aurora.

What I most remembered from my argument with Steve in February was him declaring that he could no longer continue with me. I felt wrong about feeling vulnerable and confused about Matt's marriage and not knowing how it would impact Shane. I didn't feel as though I had a right to feel uncertain—or maybe I just felt that I didn't know how to be or where to step anymore. Maybe the control I had had wasn't right; maybe it was intrusive and boundaries should have been set around it. I only wanted Shane to be at the center of everything. I wanted him to grow up knowing he was loved and lovable, and that he was safe. I wanted to continue to work together with Matt on this. I believed this was possible.

And now here Steve was on my computer screen. I didn't

want to feel happy that he realized he was wrong to end things. I didn't want to feel excited about the possibility of reconnecting with him. I did feel vindicated. Maybe, maybe, maybe. This time it might work.

I wrote back, forgiving nothing, and telling him all that I felt about my frustration with him and the dynamics of our relationship, that I had wanted "to run screaming from the room" when I saw his email.

I told him about my health scare and how I had let a few friends drift away because they didn't ask how I was doing and didn't offer to help me when I had asked them to. I hoped the implication that I was also ready to let him go was transparent.

He wrote back immediately. He was happy and relieved that I was okay. He understood why I would want to run away from him, but he hoped he could make it up to me.

Curious, relieved, and hopeful, I agreed to meet him for lunch.

"*Have* you worked on any of your stuff?" I asked.

He shook his head. "Not really, no,"

I nodded, knowing full well the red flag that flapped in my face. His familiarity and our history assuaged me. We couldn't create more good times if we weren't together.

We spent time together as friends at first, but in a short time were back to talking on the phone a few times per day, and eventually went back to spending one or two nights per week together. At the first signs of backpedaling and retreating, I suggested counseling again.

He agreed to it, but he asked that I find the counselor. He said searching for anything on the internet frustrated him greatly.

I found a counselor who had worked at the VA for thirty years. He had retired from that job and now had a private practice. We began seeing him in the summer of 2012, and I felt lucky to have found him: he wasn't at the VA, so we wouldn't have to be in an environment that triggered memories for Steve, but he had had a lot of experience with veterans.

Steve didn't have a car, so he took the bus to meet me at work and I drove us to counseling from there.

We met with him weekly at first. We started by summarizing our history and dynamics. It took a couple of sessions to unwind all this for a newcomer.

Steve said that he believed I had a man in the wings for anything I ever needed or wanted when he wasn't available. I didn't protest that. But the implication was that I was supposed to wait for him to come out of wherever he had gone to each time he disappeared. Everything had to be on his timeline.

The counselor asked me how I felt when Steve retreated or broke up with me.

"Sad, angry, like I have failed," I said.

"I think you feel shame, and that's why you run out to be with a new man," the counselor said.

He was a stickler for not going over with our time, so we left without my having a chance to respond to this. I didn't agree with him at all.

I vented to Steve about this when we got back to his place, and he said I should bring it up at the next session. When we got into the counselor's office the following week, though, he beat me to it: "Jane would like to address something with you that was left unfinished from the last session," he said.

I marveled at Steve's need to create a landing strip for me. Given how much ambivalence and aversion to commitment he usually showed, I was surprised at his matter-of-fact announcement. I didn't immediately recognize that he was committing to following through with what I wanted to say to the counselor on *my* behalf, not on his own.

"You said I felt shame when Steve broke up with me," I began. "I have felt like a failure and rejected, lonely, but not ashamed." I felt ashamed sometimes after the fact—embarrassed that I had behaved inappropriately—but feeling shame was not the instigator for my pursuit of other men. Shame sometimes resulted from how I acted but it was never the cause. I didn't differentiate this out loud, however.

The counselor said nothing for over a minute. Then he stammered that perhaps shame wasn't the right word—that he'd meant to say I reacted in a way to fill a void.

A couple of weeks later, Steve read a letter that he had addressed to me. It was about seeing a man's watch on my desk. He had been at my house to caulk my bathtub and saw the watch in my bedroom. He wrote that he had felt crushed. He claimed to have seen it six months ago.

I searched my memory for when this could have taken place, because it hadn't been in the last six months. He hadn't been to my house to tweak or fix anything in a couple of years. Finally, it clicked; I knew what watch he was talking about. It had belonged to Shane, and I would show it to him.

As I was driving home from that session, Steve told me to pull over. He got out and stormed off down Broadway.

Later that evening, I went to Steve's apartment to see if he was home. I feared he would look out and see my car in the parking lot, so I parked two blocks over and walked. I didn't want to knock on the door out of fear of pissing him off. I checked to see if there was a light on and if I could see him moving around in there from the parking lot. He lived on the third floor, so it wasn't easy. I couldn't make up my mind about whether or not there was any activity.

When Steve wouldn't return my phone calls, I called the counselor.

"Are you concerned for his safety?" he asked. "Do you think he's suicidal?"

"No," I said. "But I don't know what to do."

"Do you want me to call him?"

"No. I think that would piss him off."

I called Steve once more, and he picked up. He had been doing laundry. He seemed okay. I went home, relieved.

$\mathcal{I}$ wrote a letter in response to Steve's revelation and shared it in counseling the following week, along with the watch I thought he had seen. It was not the one he remembered seeing.

In my letter, I set the record straight that Steve had seen Jack's watch during the brief period we had reconvened in the summer of 2010. That had been two years ago, not six months ago.

Steve yelled at me during the session. "Why are you here?"

"Because I care about you!" I shouted back. "Why would I go through all of this if I didn't care?"

After this session, he wouldn't let me drive him home. He got out at the corner of Belleview and S. Lowell and walked south.

When I got home, I called his friend Bob to see if he had come to pick him up. He said that he had.

Later, Steve wanted to know how I had Bob's phone number.

"Because he called one time when you were at my house, and it was saved on my caller ID."

The longer we talked, the angrier he became. He asked for everything back that he had ever given to me. The only thing I still owned was the book of his father's art, something his brother-in-law had self-published.

He wanted to know what I had done with the early-edition *Davy and the Goblin*, a book with screen-printed illustrations and gold-edged pages, he'd given to me and Shane as a Christmas present. He had found it online and had been delighted it was in such great condition. It had been his favorite story as a boy.

"I gave it to another little boy," I lied. I had packed it up and given it to Good Will. My heart had sunk every time I went into Shane's bedroom and I saw it on his bookcase. It reminded me of Steve—what was broken, and what felt leaden and irreparable. I hadn't believed we would ever talk again after he had ended things in February of the previous year.

"The sapphire and diamond earrings?"

"I gave them to Joan." Another lie.

"The fire-topaz ring?"

"I gave it to Rochelle." The truth was, I'd pawned the ring and the earrings. I'd hated remembering. When he gave me the ring, he'd said he had "saved a bundle" on it. I felt cheap to him, cheated. The earrings were one of the gifts I still had from that Valentine's Day extravaganza during our early days.

I returned the book of his father's paintings to him when we met at counseling the following week. Steve had taken a cab there.

Steve walked into the appointment with a challenge to the counselor: "We are going to break up, and we want you to talk us out of it."

The counselor listened to Steve's barrage of complaints about how he couldn't trust me, and my rebuttal: that I continued to love him and was willing to try anything to penetrate his wall of resistance.

At the end of our exchange, the counselor stated the obvious: "It is clear that you care very much for each other. The fact that this has gone on for years speaks for itself. It is not as though you have been married and then the PTSD appeared, and you are dealing with this change. You have been in a relationship since it began to appear, and you, Jane, are still here, and so are you, Steve." He looked at me. "Do you love him?"

"Yes," I said. "Very much."

"Do you love her?" he asked Steve.

"Yes." Steve nodded.

There wasn't another question to ask. It felt good to have someone else look through the window of who we were and sum it up roundly, with no remainder.

The counselor then announced he was going on vacation for three weeks. I wasn't confident about how the dynamics would play out between us in his absence, but I wasn't anxious anymore either. I hoped Steve could relax into what had just been reflected back to us.

It appeared he could. Within days, we were talking about getting married.

"Don't ask me on a holiday, and please not my birthday," I said with a laugh. "I want this to be separate, its own thing."

Steve nodded.

We shopped for rings at a jeweler in Golden.

Steve liked a rectangular tourmaline that was boxed in with small white gold posts propping it up on a white gold band. I didn't. That thing would do bodily harm to someone, either by accident or on purpose. I could see scratching myself easily with it and forget about getting dressed with it on. It would snag on everything.

I liked a rounded triangular spinel that had four tiny diamonds on both sides of it. The diamonds were inset on the yellow gold band. It was a ring I would have bought myself. The stone was not the purple of amethyst and not the blue of sapphire, but a translucent midnight purple. I looked it up online because I'd never seen or heard of it before. It turned out it was a stone used on the crowns of royalty long ago and was rarer than sapphires and rubies. I loved it.

Steve bought it and the accompanying band, which had perfect grooves to fit into the peak that framed the spinel. It had diamonds on both sides.

Several days later, I went over to Steve's apartment and we went for a walk along Clear Creek, which ran adjacent to his complex. We walked down to the creek's edge from a steep grade off of the trail. It was where we had joined others in swinging from a long rope tied to a tree into the rushing creek a few summers before—a fun memory for both of us.

He got down on one knee, took out the ring, and placed it on the fourth finger of my left hand. "Jane Camille Binns, will you marry me?"

"Yes, yes!" I said.

We hugged and kissed and then scaled our way back up the hill. When we got back to his apartment, I went swimming at the recreation center and he went for a bike ride.

He asked me later if I thought that was strange.

"No." I hadn't even thought of it until he asked. Each of us was comfortable enough with the other to go do our own thing. We had known each other so long, it felt natural to go let the reality of our engagement settle on our own for a little while.

Steve and I got engaged on October 14, 2012. We decided to get married on April 16, 2013.

"That's not a lot of time when you think about it," our counselor said after Steve announced what had happened while he was away.

I thought it was doable. I was happy to go to the Justice of the Peace and bring in one witness. I didn't want to go through the stress of planning anything too involved. Memories of dealing with all of the details for Matt's and my wedding choked me. I remembered resenting that most of the decisions seemed to fall on my shoulders.

Having gone through three weddings himself, Steve wasn't too keen on a full-on celebration, either. We did resolve to have a small ceremony at a metaphysical center in downtown Golden. We would invite our kids, my close friend Joan and her partner, and two of Steve's friends.

We met with one of the owners of the center a couple of times and talked through logistics of seating, where we would stand, the length of the ceremony, and who would perform it.

We went back and forth for a couple of weeks about invitations and expanding our guest list for a dinner after the wedding. I painted two calla lilies with snapdragons in between and entitled it, "Love Between Lilies." The painting was bright and didn't reproduce very well. Steve didn't like it very much, which hurt my feelings. We decided on a template pattern we had found online. It was a simple painting of a rose.

I bought a moss-green, sleeveless, low-cut gown and gold, sparkling high heels.

Everything was ready to go. We hadn't addressed or mailed out invitations yet, but reservations had been made for a restaurant after the ceremony, and we had informally invited our guests. We had a photographer lined up. The honeymoon was still being discussed; Shane was going to be in school, and Steve really wanted him to experience the Tucson desert in April, so we were considering waiting a while after the wedding to go.

I had decided to move to Lakewood so that Shane could go to Lakewood High School, one of the best high schools in the Denver Metro area. Matt and I had lived there when we were married, and I liked it. Lakewood was also much closer to Golden than Southwest Denver. I didn't need to live with Steve after we were married. I had always believed I would be happier with someone if I didn't live with him, and that the marriage would have a better shot of lasting if we lived separately. I had shared this sentiment with Steve many times and he agreed, but the conversation wasn't resolved either. I printed off a map of Lakewood and gave it to Steve, so we could have a visual of what we were looking for, should we decide to live together after all.

Shortly after 7:00 a.m. on Saturday, March 7, 2013, a nurse from St. Anthony's called and said that Steve was in the hospital.

He told her to tell me that he had not attempted suicide. He had had a heart attack. I felt alarmed, taking in "suicide" and "hospital." Did he assume that I knew he was suicidal? Why would he say that? Was he? Heart attack? What?

I drove over to be with him. He was still being assessed for next steps when I arrived.

The doctor had put in two stents. One artery had been 90 percent clogged. It wasn't clear yet if more surgery would be necessary. Steve's dad had died of a heart attack when he was sixty-one. Steve was going to be sixty-four in a couple of weeks.

I sat with him for a couple of hours while nurses and

specialists appeared. I left to run errands and then returned in the afternoon. It was decided that a few more stents would need to be put in in a couple of days. He would also need to start taking a beta blocker and statins.

"Oh no. No," Steve said when he heard this. He would not be able to take any Viagra if he were on these. The nurses gently argued that he would need to be willing to play with this and see how his body responded.

I remained quietly positive, believing we could overcome whatever medical challenge lay in wait, but a soft, pulsing dread also began to thud where I didn't want to listen.

Steve had surgery a few days later. Seven additional stents were put in. He had to stay in the hospital for another day. He told me over and over how much he appreciated my being there.

I brought him home to stay with me. It was during a week I didn't have Shane. I stayed with him the first couple of days, and then we agreed that I would go to work. He helped out with meals and dishes, and I saw a little glimmer of what it might be like to live together. It felt easy.

On the sixth day, his friend Bob picked him up and took him back to his apartment. When I got home, Steve had left the photo of the three of us—him, me, and Shane—on top of the wood frame of the couch. The photo had been taken after we had announced our engagement in the fall.

There was no note. I didn't want to believe he had left it behind deliberately, but I knew he had. I snatched it up and put it with other extra photos I had from that day.

"You left the photo here," I said when I talked to him on the phone later.

"I don't have a frame for it, and I didn't want it to get ruined," he said.

This sounded reasonable. I knew there was something he wasn't saying, but I didn't pursue it.

When I went to his apartment a couple of days later, I saw the map of Lakewood I had printed for him on his refrigerator with a large question written in red in the middle of it: "NOW WHAT?" The all caps in his unmistakable print were offensive. His question was as much an announcement that he did not intend to live with me as it was a reminder to himself that he didn't know what he wanted.

We sat in his kitchen, the map in my line of vision. Steve meandered into a monologue about his nephew—how he had had second thoughts before he got married and how Steve believed there was wisdom in that. I could tell he was building into justifying an impending retreat from me and our relationship.

I cut him off. "Tyler did get married, and he had an affair while Julie was pregnant with Eric."

"'Affair' wasn't the word he used," Steve said.

I shrugged. That's what it was. He slept with their therapist, and he and the therapist were still a couple. Julie had been making the details of co-parenting Eric, who was nine months old now, a living hell for all involved.

"Do you have any reservations about getting married, Jane?"

"I'm a little nervous, but I think that's to be expected. No, I'm okay." I didn't ask him if he had any reservations. If he was going to deliver that blow, he was going to have to summon the wherewithal to speak it.

"Have you dealt with everything in your past to be ready for our future?" he asked.

"I think so. I believe we can work out anything that comes our way." I knew he was posing these questions to himself as much as to me.

A few days later, I called, and he didn't answer. I called several hours later and still nothing. I hated it when he didn't return my phone calls. I called my therapist and made an appointment. I had started seeing him after my cervical cancer scare in 2011, and these days saw him intermittently, only when I felt overwhelmed. I had been considering Steve's comment about having dealt with my past and thought maybe I still had some things to sort out.

I called Steve again in the morning. It was Friday, March 22. He answered.

"I've been worried about you," I said.

I don't remember how he responded initially or what his exact words were. I remember the words "cancel the wedding" and "at least postpone it." He unwound himself through paragraphs of excuses and reasons, but all that was clear was rejection. He offered to call the officiant, the metaphysical center, the restaurant, and the bed and breakfast where we were going to spend our wedding night. He offered to pay for the invitations, "if you would please send me the receipt." He also offered to pay for Joan and her partner's airfare, since they had already booked a reservation.

All of the clichés of feeling sucker-punched, my heart being ripped out, and feeling frozen came to mind. Overused, but still definitive and exact. Hurt. I hurt. It was too familiar. But I knew what it was and this by itself was reassuring.

One friend suggested I act like nothing had happened, that I just go ahead with everything as planned and pretend that his rant was just another conversation. I didn't, and I couldn't. A rut had been made, one that wasn't going to be rinsed away with time. We would need a miracle.

I felt too angry to pick up the phone. I was prepared to sit on myself for the distance this time and fight the urge to ever speak to him again.

I drove to the mall the following morning in a white-out snow storm to return my dress. I kept the high heels, believing I might wear them someday, if I ever felt like impressing someone again.

I called friends and family. No one was surprised. My mother said, "But you were so happy." Dad said he was sorry. I felt humiliated. I thought of packing everything up that he'd given me, either to get rid of it or ship it back to him. But I had already done that so many times before. This time I would get rid of nothing. I would keep it all. In a superstitious inversion, I decided the act of getting rid of things actually fed an unconscious desire to communicate. I couldn't talk myself into it making sense.

He called four days later. He apologized and explained that he had eaten pot brownies the night before he called me. He'd eaten them to calm himself down—he could no longer smoke pot because of the heart attack, but he could consume edibles—but they were unpredictable, and their effect had been delayed by twelve hours. That, he said, was why he had talked on relentlessly, offensively.

Why would you do that? Why would you eat something you didn't trust? How could you do that to me, to us? How could you put your hands on something you knew wasn't a sure thing and risk ruining things between us? I didn't say this. I was tired. I didn't want to hear anything more he had to say.

I didn't know how we could move forward. I'd never known how we did that, really. It defied linear thought and reason. We kept talking. He said he'd be willing to try a different counselor. I found her. I summed up our situation and history to her over the phone, and she agreed to see us.

He didn't rebuff her. He was willing. He revealed that the idea of being a father figure to Shane frightened him and that was the main reason he didn't want to get married.

"Then why did you propose to me?" I yelled. "Shane has a father. He doesn't need you to be one to him! Or, why not wait to propose until after Shane graduated high school? What was the hurry? We've been in and out of each other's lives for years. Do you think a few more years were going to hurt?"

"I messed up with my own boys," Steve said. "I didn't want to mess up with yours."

It didn't take very many visits before he hit another wall and didn't want to continue.

I called her individually, breaking my promise to him that I would never again call a couple's therapist without his knowing.

She made things very plain to me: "He doesn't want help. Leave him alone. He is not willing to change."

I heard her words and held on to them, waiting for the moment when it felt okay to walk away.

CHAPTER FIFTEEN

Back Home

I told you about this back in April," I said. "I asked if I could have him a couple of days from the week he was supposed to be with you, so we could go to the Grand Canyon. You said that would be okay."

"I don't even remember that," Matt said.

"I emailed you, and you said there shouldn't be a problem."

"Well, things happen spur of the moment around here, and that's the week when Jill's kids are home."

"I'm already giving you three days for your road trip," I said. "I've been planning this for a couple of months."

"What about July eighteenth through the twenty-seventh?"

"That's my week, and we were planning on going to see Joan in California. Her birthday is that week, and I wanted to be there for it this year!"

Matt stayed calm. "You've got to meet us in the middle somehow with this."

"I've got to reserve my hotel in Utah now if Shane and I are going to go in June. I don't even know if we're going to be able to go, though, because my dad is at death's door . . . Let me see if Joan can have us early August. Can you be flexible at all?"

"I don't know. It's so hard to get everyone on the same schedule. Jill's sister is going to be here and then there's the four kids."

"I'm not the one being rigid here. I gave you plenty of notice," I said. "I'll get back to you about our trip to California. If this works, I want him back by August third for my birthday."

"I thought your birthday was the fourteenth of August."

"No. It's the fourth. Your brother Terry's is the fourteenth. Jill's is June fourteenth."

He paused. I knew he wondered how I knew when Jill's birthday was, but I wasn't going to give him the satisfaction of telling him. I'd found out through happenstance, like I did most things that were going on in their household. Shane had mentioned it once and I'd never forgotten it; I've never been able to forget anyone's birthday once she or he tells me when it is. The detail sifts into a crevice in my brain and settles there indelibly.

My intrusiveness about tracking what was going on in Matt and Jill's household was as much about curiosity and envy as it was about self-preservation and anticipating when I might be asked for a schedule shift for time with Shane. Matt and I had fifty-fifty custody. After he and Jill married in 2011, we'd gone from a three-days on/four-days off schedule to a week on/week off arrangement. This fit better when Jill's four older children were with her.

I had not contested the schedule change when Matt requested it. Shane was older by the time they married—eleven—and he seemed capable of handling being away from each of us for a longer period. When he was younger, I'd noticed he would get a bit depressed if he was away from either one of us for longer than three or four days. At that time, Matt listened to me and usually responded with, "Whatever you think is best." Now Jill hung like a specter, pulling his arms and legs like he was her puppet, funneling her desires into his every thought. But he was still the mouthpiece, and he worked at trying to accommodate both of us—me out of habit and her out of his new allegiance. I felt a bit sorry for him and would cave sometimes just because I couldn't stand to see him struggle like a pinned insect.

The first time I saw Jill was in the bleachers at one of

Shane's Little League baseball games. Matt wouldn't introduce me, and I stayed away from them, not knowing what to do with myself. One friend suggested I go up to her and introduce myself, but I never did. I alternately busied myself with watching how Matt was with her and cheering Shane on, which included a lot of pacing. I envied their picture of togetherness and commitment. Steve's attendance was always sporadic.

I finally met Jill at Shane's eleventh birthday party. Matt had reserved a table at Red Robin. I arrived a few minutes late. Matt met me at the entrance and announced, "We're up there," pointing upstairs.

"We?" He wasn't referring to himself and Shane, was he? The whole group of Shane's friends? I wasn't ready. I walked up the few steps and sat down across from her. I stuck out my hand and introduced myself, and over the next two hours made small talk with her about her job, living in Colorado, her home state of Nebraska, and her kids. Matt interjected not one word. He spent the party telling the parents of Shane's best friend, who had emigrated from Mexico shortly before their son was born, about the differences between various German dialects. Matt prattled on to Nick's father, a liquor store clerk who barely understood English, for hours.

No other adult ally showed up. I kept waiting for the mother of another one of Shane's good friends to arrive but found out later she had taken herself to the hospital because of appendicitis. I quietly wilted inside, doing my best to keep coming up with questions, encouraging Jill to talk more about herself. She was an accountant from Kearney, Nebraska, who worked for Oppenheimer Funds. She had four kids. Her youngest, the only daughter, was four years older than Shane. She had been an English major in college but did not write.

Jill didn't ask me one question about myself. She was not a threat to Matt, and I believed he felt some peace about that. She was vanilla, bland, but a good person, and for that alone I was willing to stay open to congeniality, for Shane's sake. It was obvious their relationship was heading toward cohabitation and marriage.

I watched Shane interact with his friends. He told me later he saw me talking to Jill. I said, "Yes, I was trying to be friendly." I brought the only kind of cake Shane ever requested: a vanilla/fudge swirl cake. At the end of the party, Matt packed up four large pieces to take home.

Later, I cursed Matt for not letting me know ahead of time that Jill was going to be there. I felt blindsided, and that he had done this deliberately. I stewed and vented to friends.

A few of the friends I complained to said Matt didn't have to tell me she was coming. It would have been respectful, polite, but there wasn't a script we were supposed to follow. We hadn't exactly excelled at respect and deference when we were married. It was unreasonable to expect it as a divorced couple. Still, a nod toward sensitivity would have been nice.

Once Matt and Jill were married, I simultaneously envied and cringed at their blended family. I wanted that stability and safety that family represents. I also recoiled at the thought of being around that many people all the time. I grew up with three siblings, both parents at home, and learned from that experience coming from the same DNA doesn't translate to connection. My parents were no model of marital bliss, with Dad's frequent bouts of being sullen and Mom's insistence on attention made manifest through little dramas and occasional outbursts of yelling and tears. They were consistent and stable, however. Dad had the same job for twenty-five years as a chemist, analyzing metals, in particular molybdenum. Mom received her bachelor's degree when I was seven years old and taught alternative high school for thirty years. We moved only once, and they stayed married until I was twenty-one, which was around the same time that I met Matt.

My parents' divorce impelled me to fill in the hole created by their imploding relationship and whatever illusion of security I had conjured from it. I did that by marrying Matt.

All of the explanations about my parents' dynamics and why they were the way they were didn't make my siblings and me feel heard, seen, or known as we were growing up. We did not reach toward one another; we didn't know how, and perhaps believed we weren't supposed to. Together but isolated. The idea of family was not comforting, but I still longed for it, and my relationship with Matt was the closest I had ever felt to having it. It was one thing I still missed about having been married to him.

But here he was, married again, and me, I was still on again/off again with Steve. It was 2014 now. I was forty-seven. I stopped trying to explain to anyone why I still called him, or why I still hoped. I accepted him and all of his push-pull craziness. I was his lighthouse. Deep where no one else could see, this counted; it was everything.

I hung up the phone with Matt, furious. I hated the back and forth and the endless negotiations to accomplish a small thing. I hated competing with him and Jill for time with Shane. It didn't matter if I planned. Jill would utter a whimsy and my carefully drawn blueprint would be smeared into incomprehensibility. I had to wait for her flight of fancy to settle. I resented that. I resented coming up with alternates in case what I wanted fell through. Matt and I didn't speak much anymore, except when there was a schedule change. I had learned to hate hearing from him. I was exhausted from having to be accommodating, having to be nice. When could I stop this façade?

My fury with Matt got me what I wanted: Shane and I left for the Grand Canyon in June. I didn't invite Steve. I wanted to remember this time as an adventure with my son; I didn't want to deal with Steve's hemming and hawing and possible last-minute cancelation. He said he'd never been there before. I heard him cry a little as he said this to me over the phone. I was not deterred. I remembered the handful of times he'd taken trips with his sons and failed to invite me. I remembered his pronouncement about moving to Arizona and how I'd fought with him to continue on with our relationship long distance. I was also still mad at him for telling me he didn't want to spend the rest of his life married and calling off our wedding. He could see how it felt to be left by me for a change.

Steve and I also hadn't been intimate in over a year at this point. I didn't want to deal with the expense or looming awkwardness of sleeping arrangements.

To assuage the guilt I felt at leaving him, I resolved to call him every day we were gone. And to buy him gifts. That would have to be enough.

I felt trepidation about leaving for this trip. I feared I would get a call that Dad had passed away while we were gone. He had been declining gradually for the last six years, and severely for the past few months. I had been flying back to see him in Michigan every three to four months. My most recent visit had been three months earlier, in March, and I believed that would be the last time I would see him.

When I first noticed that Dad's gait was awkward, it was hard to believe there was anything wrong with him. Shortly thereafter came a diagnosis of neuropathy. My siblings and I didn't think too much of this, except that it perhaps was a sign of old age. He was in his early seventies by this point. The disbelief came in part because he had been an athlete his whole life, and until now his advancing years had not slowed him down. He had played a variety of sports in high school. When he was in his fifties, he'd run two marathons and participated in countless road races. He had ridden his bicycle from Michigan to Colorado and then participated in the Ride the Rockies race for a half-dozen years, beginning when he was in his mid-sixties. He'd gone on his last ride, the Lewis and Clarke trail from Michigan to Oregon, at seventy-two.

It eventually became clear that Dad had a degenerative neurological ailment, but it was not Parkinson's and it was not Lewy body. He graduated into using a cane. This lasted for two years. Then, he required a walker. Then he could not move independently at all and needed someone else to move him from one chair to another and in and out of bed.

His ability to speak declined gradually, but he was still able to speak somewhat these last few months of his life. He had been such an intimidating parent, I did not miss his ability to disapprove.

My relationship with Dad was rocky and volatile during my teen and young adult years. He never papered over his disappointment. In my second semester of college, I became pregnant. I was eighteen. Mom made plans to quit teaching to take care of my baby, so I could continue on with school, but that turned out not to be necessary because I miscarried six weeks later. When I started hemorrhaging, Dad took me to the emergency room because Mom was teaching night classes. He said nothing during the trip from my dorm to St. Joe's.

A few days later, he stood over me while I lay in bed and said, "I thought school was more important to you."

"It is," I said.

He stood there for a few minutes then walked away.

I had no defense. The one ace I played over and over again was pleasing him by doing well in school, and now he didn't trust this. I didn't do poorly at all that semester—I received A's and B's. Still, the message was clear: having a baby at eighteen was too much of a gamble with my future. Maybe all he could think about was his sister, who'd had her first baby when she was sixteen and three more by the time she was twenty-one. Or his mother, who was also sixteen when she became pregnant with his sister. Maybe he felt it was his failure, too—that he hadn't raised me well enough to avoid this family pattern.

I felt crushed. I wanted him to ask how I felt, or say that he was sorry this had happened, or ask me why I thought it happened. I needed to know I was more to him than just his daughter who did well in school. A friend suggested I see a therapist. I did. I paid for it with what I made working my full-time job at Big Ten Party Store in Ann Arbor, but at $3.25 an hour it wasn't easy. Going to see her every week, I quickly racked up a $500.00 bill—a hefty sum in 1986. I felt like I was staring into a bottomless well.

Mom knew I was going to therapy but there wasn't any mention of money for it. I didn't tell Dad about it. I felt bad about disappointing him. I also felt lost, and for the first time, I could see that it was not safe inside of family to look at a feeling and deal with it. But if I didn't, I felt, I would explode. When this pressure eased and I was able to see my therapist every other week, I focused on making extra payments. I paid off the charges over six months.

I returned to school in the fall and graduated with my bachelor's in music and minor in writing in 1989. Excelling in school was a reflexive habit. I could do it like taking a breath. The invisible shifts in my psyche were much harder to define. What I felt was separated and in disbelief that I'd been abandoned by my dad. Acknowledging anger would have been a luxury. That would have meant someone valued what I felt, that there would have been a forum to express my feelings. Anger would come later.

The biggest falling-out Dad and I had was when he left Mom for another woman. He met her when he and my sister Melanie moved from Michigan to Colorado. Melanie had finished college and didn't know what she was going to do, and Dad's job had just transferred him. Mom stayed behind with my younger brother, Peter, who was about to start his senior year of high school. She didn't want him to have to make new friends and relocate. She decided to join Dad after Peter graduated. It didn't work out that way, though.

After his move, Dad divorced Mom and moved in with Delores. The divorce process took two and a half years. I met Matt in the midst of all of this.

When we were planning our wedding, Mom and Dad were still battling things out, and the money for our wedding became cannon fodder against one another. I hated being caught in the middle and told them they would have to speak to each other about who was paying for what. It didn't work. Disgusted with them both and still fuming at Dad for running away from all of us like a coward, I didn't ask him to walk me down the aisle.

Matt and I had an outdoor wedding at Island Park in Ann Arbor. Each of us came down one side of the gazebo and then met in the middle before walking up together. I thought it was poetic and appropriate: I was giving myself to this marriage, as was Matt.

A few months before the wedding, I was speaking to Dad about money for the photographer and he said that if I had any left over, I was to give it back to him.

"There might be $200.00 left," I offered, hoping to placate him, and hoping more that he wouldn't revisit this.

But he did, after we returned home from our honeymoon.

I wrote him an angry letter stating that if he were my child, I wouldn't be asking for that money back. I included a check for $200.00, money Matt and I needed. He was still in college, and I was working as a secretary.

A week later, I received an envelope containing the letter and the check, both of them torn to bits, along with a sticky note that said he was disappointed in me.

I didn't speak to him for several months—long enough for my siblings to get very uncomfortable and insist I apologize. Instead, I waited. After a couple of months more, I apologized for how things were between us, but not for what I had done. Sometime after this, we started talking again.

I hated him for years for upsetting the sense of stability and structure his marriage to Mom had given me. It wouldn't be until I left Matt that I began to forgive him. We had things in common that we didn't talk about. Each of us had been the one to leave our marriages. Each of us had had an affair as a means of getting out of it. We never talked about why he left Mom, but it became clear over the years that he felt more at ease separated from her. He shifted from being a grumpy, sober man who hated his job to going out dancing, taking Spanish classes at the community college, learning how to carve wood into animals in nature settings, hiking, and riding his bike long distances. Mom would refer to this as his mid-life crisis, but it was obvious he was expanding and reuniting with the desire to be active and involved in life. He hadn't felt he could be that person with her, and similarly, I'd felt invisible when I was with Matt.

Things eased between Dad and me, an unstated truce

created a bridge. A hardened exterior peeled back. I would find myself feeling shitty about my life and leaving Matt and would call Dad. Sometimes I would barely get any words out and would start crying. I expected him to hang up on me or to make up some excuse to get off the phone, but he never did. He listened to my blubbering and said the only true thing worth saying, and that was that he didn't know what to say.

Dad didn't coax anything out of me or ask how he could help.

I began work on this book in 2006 and told him about it.

"Are you going to let me read it?"

"Sure," I said hesitantly.

"Will it make me blush? Surely, it's not G-rated," he said.

I laughed. "No, it's not G-rated."

Once, I told him about liking older men.

"Well, eventually, you will be that age too," he said sincerely.

He said what he meant and meant what he said, and I grew to respect that clarity. He had always been consistent in his support of whatever I did creatively. He was my champion when I didn't know what to major in as an undergraduate student. He said I should pursue a degree in music because I loved to play the piano and I'd been doing it all my life. So, I majored in piano performance and minored in writing.

He kept every craft I ever made when I was a girl, too. Once, I made him a likeness of the Planter's Peanut character with aluminum. It was a six-by-nine-inch raised impression, complete with hat and cane. He loved peanuts and he loved my project. He had it hanging in his closet for years.

As Dad's neurological degeneration advanced, his temperament swung between appreciative and grateful and sharp shot through with fury. We were told it was natural but knowing this didn't shorten the recovery from an outburst. It would take me a minute to remember that I wasn't seven anymore and he hadn't just been yelling at Mom. That this eruption was rooted in frustration at watching his abilities deteriorate, his forced dependency on others. He did everything he could to remain autonomous for as long as possible.

When Dad was seventy-seven, he came down with a fever and this landed him in Bixby Hospital in Adrian, Michigan. He seemed to have no infection and the reason for the fever remained mysterious, but it caused him to stay there several days. Then he was transferred to a nursing home. His roommate, Arthur, was ninety-six and wheeled himself around haphazardly up and down the halls. He carried with him four-by-four-inch laminated notes on a large metal ring that had answers to questions he frequently asked. He had been taught by the nurses to refer to them whenever he asked where his wife was and why he was there.

One of Arthur's other frequent habits was to yell out at night. With only a curtain between them, Dad did not rest.

I visited when he had been at the nursing home for over a month. I spoke individually with one of his nurses, and she said that they were planning on having a care conference the next day to discuss his case. I relayed this casually to Dad's wife Nicole when she came to visit Dad that evening.

"They're going to try and move it up before I have to leave for the airport," I said.

Dad arched his back, his ice-blue eyes widened, and with folded arms he yelled, "You will not change anything! You will work with their schedule! If you can't make it, too bad! They are busy around here!" He looked harmless in his white T-shirt and flannel pajama pants, but his voice undoubtedly carried all the way down the hall.

Nicole watched him, saying nothing at first. Then she said that whenever they scheduled for would be fine. After a few minutes, she said she and I were going to get some water. She led me down the hall by the elbow and walked me to the social worker's office. She explained to her that I had a plane to catch in the morning and asked if there any way they could meet with me and my brother Rich before I had to leave. The social worker moved it to three hours earlier.

Dad detested the nursing home. He made it a goal to do

anything he could to be given permission to go home. He went to physical therapy and exceeded all milestones. They had told him he needed to be able to walk on his own, so he worked at it until he could. After nine weeks, he was allowed to go home.

$\mathcal{I}$ visited him when he had been home for a few months. It was the summer of 2012. One day, Nicole left the house to go shopping and left me alone with Dad. She had prepared lunch for us. We ate at a card table in the TV room, so he wouldn't have to move out of his mechanical chair.

We ate chicken salad, macaroni salad, and veggie sticks. Dad fed himself. At one point, a couple of grapes got away from him and like a trigger, he went off.

I laughed a little. "Don't get sore, Wally!"

"I don't even know who Wally is," Dad stuttered.

"From *Leave it to Beaver*, the TV show," I reminded him.

"Oh . . . haha. I'm not sore," Dad said.

"Okay. You got it. They just got away from you for a second."

Later, on the phone with Melanie, I said, "I thought he would get that reference. You know, that TV show is from his era. Oh well. He probably didn't even watch it. But laughing a little did defuse him. It dampened the rocket."

$\mathcal{O}n$ my second to last trip to see Dad, I went with Melanie and her daughter, Kylie. We stayed in a hotel in Tecumseh and commuted daily during our four-day weekend to the assisted living community in Adrian, Michigan. It was October of 2013, and the fall colors were in full glory. I often missed this illustrious display during September and October; Colorado's autumn paled in comparison to Michigan's. The bright, contrasting flames of yellow, red, orange, and purple were a delightful interruption as we drove. I inhaled the colors, grateful for being able to rest my eyes on something so beautiful. It quieted the murky turbulence of wanting to better

Dad's situation, so we wouldn't have to watch him struggle or suffer. We knew he didn't want to be at the assisted living facility. He wanted to be home, but Nicole could not handle lifting him in and out of chairs and getting him to bed anymore. He needed help using the bathroom, and with bathing, too.

We joined him for lunch the last day we were there. We watched Dad push mashed potatoes and corn with a knife in one hand onto a fork in the other and then slowly, with a quaking hand, bring the mound to his gaping mouth. Melanie had cut his pork chop for him and he stabbed at those pieces easily. He had been given a bib but didn't spill anything the entire meal. It took him forty-five minutes to finish. He ate every crumb.

I was impressed and not one bit surprised. He had always been fiercely determined. He never gave up on anything he tried. It was an old family story that he failed calculus twice in college, and his third time through he wrote out the final exam in ink because by then he knew all of the answers.

Melanie, Kylie, and I watched him patiently as he ate. When he was finally done and it was time to leave, Melanie said, "It's good to see you, Dad. I'll be back again in December."

"I'm glad you came," he said. "I don't plan on being here in two months, so I'm glad you're here now." He looked around at each of us, his eyes wide, glassy, and startling, more blue than usual.

Melanie and Kylie sat across from me. I looked at each of them. I put my hand over Dad's. My face grew hot. I didn't want to swallow. One blink was going to send tears streaming. But there was no use in holding back. We all cried.

I was grateful to not be there alone. Melanie was so good at speaking to the doctors, nurses, aids, and Nicole about Dad. She had been doing this for the last year and a half, ever since it had become clear he was not going to get better.

Dad hung in there longer than he predicted. In March of 2014, I went to see him one last time. Melanie had recently visited with Kylie and didn't want to go again; I wasn't thrilled to go alone, but I wanted to see him.

I only stayed for three and a half days. I rented a car, so I would be free to visit other people too. I did. I needed to.

I felt as though I was in the midst of a white-out blizzard. I couldn't see more than an inch in front of me. I was numb and completely incapable of feeling the impact of what was happening. There were no instructions and no rule book. I would have shredded them anyway. Maybe it would have helped to have someone else there.

Melanie made an effort to answer her phone any time I called. I didn't have to explain what I was feeling to her; she knew. There weren't many words, then, only tiny, kaleidoscope flashes of memory, and most of these I hoarded for myself. It was instinct. In a family of four kids with two parents who fought a lot, feeling alienated came naturally. Any affection and genuine attention was parceled out in pennies, and no one ever quite knew when any one of us would get lucky. But we sometimes did.

For everything Dad didn't know how to do, his core was good. He quit smoking cigars once he found out I'd been born with a heart murmur. He took me to Washtenaw Dairy for ice cream when I was about ten and told me not to tell my siblings, making me feel special that afternoon. He drove Peter and me around on our paper route, located three blocks from our neighborhood, in the winter. He showed up at many of my track and cross-country meets in high school to watch me come in third or fourth from last. He often told me he was proud of me.

There were also important missteps that he didn't ever evolve out of. He was the man who didn't voluntarily hug our mother or say he loved her. His silence oppressed every meal. His guttural utterances were a language we learned to decode. It took effort for him to smile and laugh.

I visited him every day during that last visit. He slept a lot. The TV was always on, and when Dad was out of bed he sat in a motorized chair that would raise him up and put him in a wheelchair either to transport him the five feet to his bed or to attend an event down the hall at Grand Royale. Nicole appeared punctually to feed him twice each day. He sat upright and chewed with his eyes closed. He ate nearly everything she put up to his lips.

One morning, I got there in between breakfast and lunch to spend time alone with him. Nicole always left in between meals to take care of other things.

He lay in his bed. I sat in a chair and meditated for forty minutes. I silently reassured him that it would be okay to let go, that he was going to be fine.

I left for the airport earlier than necessary on the afternoon I was heading back to Denver. I parked in a fast food lot off of US 12 a few miles west of I-94 and called Steve. I had left messages for him over the last couple of days, but he hadn't returned any of my calls. I was surprised when he picked up.

"How are you?" he asked.

"I feel like I'm swimming through Jell-O," I said. "He didn't speak much, slept a lot. A guy from some Veteran's Center stopped by and asked a bunch of questions about his life: where he went to school, what he did, how many kids. They're going to do a ceremony for him and the other vets at Grand Royale."

"Nice."

"Yes, absolutely . . . One of the nurses, Linda I think her name was, told me that she'd seen the type of degeneration Dad has in others. She was such an idiot! She asked if he'd been highly intelligent and I said, yes, he'd been a chemist for twenty-five years. She said that he'd used up all of his good brain cells when he was younger. I couldn't believe those words made sounds to spill out of her mouth. Nicole was sitting there, and she nodded along like a bobble-head. She wasn't even paying attention to what Nurse Linda was saying. Unbelievable! Didn't you know, you only get so many good brain cells and then if you use them all, that's it? Oh well! Country-bumpkin, small-town, mini-mind medicine. Idiot!

Shit. If he were in Ann Arbor, things would be different. Couldn't sway him away from what his crackerjack-box doctors thought, though, even when he could talk and think clearly. God!"

Realizing Steve hadn't said a word, I caught my breath and asked, "How are you?"

"Not good." He sighed. "I saw Paul. He needs to just move out."

"Did you say anything to him?"

"No. He doesn't get it. Who is he to say anything about Vietnam? To me? He has no right."

"I'm sorry," I said. "I hope you feel better. I'll call you when I land." I had learned how to say the right things, but I wanted to get off the phone with him. I felt angry, though I didn't understand why.

"Thanks for calling, Jane," he said. "I'm sorry the visit with your dad was hard."

"Me, too," I said, crying.

I hung up and sat in the car for a few minutes. I was sick of Steve's ongoing upset about Vietnam. I was beginning to think he deliberately sought out people he knew would set him off, so he'd have a reason to remain angry, to not heal, to not be happy, and to not shift his life in any way. It was the first clear thought I'd had since I'd been in Michigan.

Shane and I returned from the Grand Canyon in late June. Dad passed away July 5, 2014. He was seventy-nine. My brother, Peter, and his daughter were on their way to see him when Melanie got the call from Nicole. The funeral was planned and scheduled for July 9, little time to make travel arrangements.

After a lengthy delay at the airport due to mechanical failure and storms, Shane and I arrived at 4:00 a.m. on the ninth. We were supposed to have arrived on the eighth in the afternoon.

The church was full. The minister spoke about how much Dad had volunteered and been a part of making lives better for others prior to his illness. Peter, Melanie, Kylie, and my sister's younger daughter, Lara, delivered eulogies. I did too. I spoke about Dad's inimitable, disapproving stare, our bumpy relationship, and how things had smoothed out as we aged. One of his friends approached me afterwards and said that he appreciated what I had said because it was true and authentic.

Nicole invited us to go through Dad's things and take what we wanted. I only wanted one thing: the needlepoint that he had made when he was twenty-three. It was of a dove and a bowl of fruit. He had been very frustrated then. His mother had suggested he make the piece as a way to redirect, said maybe it would help him get clear. It was framed. To me it represented the importance of creating something different when life seemed overwhelming.

Shane and I returned home, and he went on vacation with Matt and Jill and her family.

I went back to work and felt relief waft into me in tiny flecks, tentatively sprawling, allowing me to breathe deeply for the first time in months. I felt confident there wasn't going to be another planned or rushed trip to Michigan anytime soon. I looked forward to being singularly focused on the capricious dance of grief.

CHAPTER SIXTEEN

First and Final

It was a warm September afternoon. Shane was back in school, vacations were behind us; we had eased back into the routine of week on/week off. Matt pulled into my complex to drop Shane off. His father-in-law, John, was driving.

I leaned near the passenger side window. Matt rolled it down.

"What did they say?" I asked.

"They've got to run more tests. I'm scheduled for an ultrasound in a few days." He shifted and raised himself up a bit from the seat. I looked at the color in his cheeks: pink, ruddy.

"What are your symptoms?"

"I thought it was what I was eating. I just didn't feel good." He shrugged.

Test results came back a few days later. The ultrasound showed an obstruction that needed to be removed immediately. Surgery was scheduled for five days later.

Matt wanted Shane at the hospital.

"I can bring him after school. Let him have a normal day at school," I pled.

"If it were you, you'd want him there, wouldn't you?"

"No. I wouldn't. I wouldn't want him in the hospital all day worrying about his mother. He doesn't need to be there."

"That's your prerogative. I want him there. My family is going to be there."

I talked to Shane and told him that he had a voice in this too. He didn't have to go. He wanted to please his dad, so he went.

On the afternoon of the surgery, I sat at my desk, waiting for someone to call me about what had happened. Finally, Matt's mother, Pam, called and told me to come to the hospital right away. Shane was upset. "He needs his mother," she said.

I drove to St. Joe's in Denver.

Shane's face was a jigsaw puzzle of blanched and hot red splotches. I hugged him.

Matt's brother, Terry, hugged me. "Shane was good. He's a good kid. It's just got to be a lot. Okay, so the tumor was the size of a football. It was malignant, liposarcoma. The cancer he had before in '07 came back to the same place, where they took the kidney. The surgeon said it's spread to his aorta, vena cava, pancreas, and lung." He sighed. "Matt doesn't know yet. Jill lost it and ran out of the room. I went after her and got her calmed down. She's a mess."

"I told Matt I didn't want Shane here for this," I said.

Terry shook his head. "It is what it is."

I hugged Pam and held her face in my hands while she wept.

Except for Terry, I hadn't seen or heard from Matt's family since 2007, when Pam and his brother, Rob had come to town after removal of the first tumor. There was no animosity between us, but the constancy of connection had evaporated. I never knew what they thought or felt about me after Matt and I had divorced. I felt a little uncomfortable about what they knew and didn't know. Did they judge me? Had Matt told them I'd had an affair? Did they blame me for leaving him, and now this? They were devoted to family. They were there for Matt, for Jill and her kids, for Shane, and for me.

I didn't belong, but I was going to be noticed because I was Shane's mom. I didn't want to go near Jill but there wasn't any avoiding it either. It was a soup of awkward.

I followed Terry into Matt's room. He was still doped up from the anesthesia.

"What's that bobble-head doing in my room? Terry, you scared me," Matt quipped.

Terry shook his head and laughed.

Shane stood near me.

Jill looked for a sock that had come off of one of Matt's feet. She mouthed to me that Matt didn't know yet that the cancer had spread. I nodded and looked at him in the bed.

Jill asked a nurse if Matt could have another sock.

"Check my throat," Matt said. "It's so dry."

Terry, Shane, and I chuckled.

9 resisted the habit to call Steve when I got home. It had been a week since I had called, texted, and emailed him, all without getting a response. I knew what this was. This was what he did best: disappear anytime anyone else really needed him. He couldn't handle anyone else's pain, so he avoided situations where he would be expected to do so. A familiar rage surged. I felt tempted to text D O N E to him, but I didn't.

The last time I had spoken to Steve was a week before Matt's surgery. He'd said he had been hallucinating again and could taste blood in his mouth. He usually only tasted blood when he had to go to the VA Hospital. I knew this was serious for him, but I had become so deflated it was difficult to care.

I asked what had become perfunctory: "Do you think you should talk to someone? I'm sorry." I tuned out to his predictable answers of "No" and "No one can help me. This too will pass."

I was tired of being his cheerleader. I was tired of showcasing positive things in his life, like how much Shane and I cared for him. I was tired of waiting to see if he was in a good enough mood to get together and listen to me and dare to tiptoe toward some semblance of normalcy in relating. I wasn't even sure what that looked like, or what I should expect from him, or anyone, anymore. I had dodged and shifted so much in the time I'd known him, having no expectations or anticipation about anything we had planned was normal. Having a Plan B, C, and D was normal.

I needed to talk about what was going on with Matt, but I knew Steve wouldn't answer if I called again—or, if he did, he would be mean and curt, telling me what I already knew: he couldn't be that guy who could be there for me.

I wasn't afraid of being abandoned by him anymore. And I wasn't willing to wait through him failing to deal with my pain and acting like it didn't matter. I wasn't three years old, my mother wasn't threatening to leave our family. I had already lived through that, just as I had lived through a miscarriage, a divorce, and the death of my dad. Now I was standing before this. I wished I were in a stable, loving, established relationship. For the first time in my life, I knew I deserved that much. I wished I hadn't spent all of that time hoping Steve would wake up to realizing his life didn't have to be stuck in 1969, that I was right here: a caring, loving woman who was willing to help him through accepting losses and creating again. I wished we had made it far enough through his struggles to establish a stable pattern.

A tidal wave had come in and frozen in front of me. I could only watch and wait.

It was decided that Matt would undergo aggressive chemotherapy three weeks post-op. The doctors would not wait the recommended four to six weeks. The regimen required four days on, ten days off.

My new habit was to drive Shane to the hospital a couple days per week to see his dad. I sat in the first-floor lobby and corresponded with students in my online class. I didn't feel welcome in Matt's room in the oncology unit.

The cooler air of October asserted itself and whisked puffs through the revolving door on the first floor of St. Joe's. Occasionally, I would visit the cafeteria. I sat alone. Shane usually didn't stay much longer than an hour. I didn't restrict his time.

One night, he stormed ahead of me down the street toward the car. I let him walk ahead. When I caught up to him, I said, "The doctors are doing everything they can. Your dad's family and Jill, everyone is trying to find the best treatment." I felt helpless to say anything that would soften the reach of this for him. But I could drive him to the hospital. I could let him spend as much time with his dad as he wanted. I could stand up or sit or lie down with him. I could be there. This wasn't my devastation; I wasn't grief-stricken.

There was no controlling this. I didn't want to believe it. I needed to be more than a mother to a son whose father was gravely ill. I wanted to be wanted. I wanted to be strong, and not return to calling Steve once there was a resolution with Matt. I didn't trust myself. I had repeated that pattern so many times before. But this time, I wasn't just telling myself it was different; it was. Between losing my dad and handling this, I had reached overflow.

I needed support. Steve couldn't give that to me. I didn't know if I wanted him in my life at all. I couldn't make any decisions about that right then, though. I just needed someone to hold me. That was simple. I could find someone to do that. I could, and I would.

$\mathscr{I}$ created a new dating profile. The first couple of dates were reminiscent of the summer of one-date wonders, minus the ebullient curiosity I'd felt then. I was much more capable of saying no now. Steve and I hadn't been intimate in a year and a half. I had gotten used to not hungering for sex. I also no longer felt my breath catch as though icy wind had slapped my face at the thought of being alone.

In the normal course of Q&A on a first date, I couldn't help myself: I shared that my ex-husband had cancer and it didn't look good. I teared up. I said I shouldn't be dating because there was too much going on. Of course, I said this as much as an excuse to get away from guys I never wanted to see again as I did because it was true.

I wanted someone to hold me, but I wasn't sure that I

wanted to date someone to get that. I couldn't think that far ahead, and it was easier not to think, period. I wanted to be small, to be picked up and rocked because someone had the good sense to see that I needed that.

I decided to stop announcing that my ex-husband was dying. It was an unnecessary detail. If things worked out, I could say it later.

I met Joe after about three weeks of dead-end duds. He had a flare for adventure. The more he talked, the more a fairy tale came to mind of a princess locked in the tower, suitor after suitor soliciting her. She passed on all of them except for one who made her laugh. My Achilles' heel.

Joe's humor wasn't rooted in wit but rather awkward circumstances and flappable humans. I didn't want to scare him off, so I said nothing about Matt; I needed one person in my life who was not going to ask about him every time I got on the phone. Joe was plenty busy as a contractor and didn't ask a lot of questions. He was my vacation from the reality of Matt's illness, and I was going to stay on that beach as long as possible. So I dribbled out my life to him in pieces, volunteering only the ones that I wanted him to see. I felt contorted and frayed. Nothing fit together neatly, but I at least had someone to hold me.

9 called Matt from work one afternoon. He was home but was getting ready to go back to the hospital soon.

"I have questions about what plans you've made for Shane," I said. "Do you have life insurance?"

"Yes."

"What about the college fund?"

"Yes. Look, I've got to go soon, but I'll call you back," he said.

"I'll be home tomorrow," I said. "I'm taking the day off to get some things done."

I concealed my pleasant surprise when he really did call the next day. I hadn't felt happy about him calling me in years.

"I'm calling because you said you had questions," he said. "But you have to promise that you won't tell Jill I told you."

"Okay." I felt deflated but determined to hear what he had to say.

"Jill went home to get some clothes, so I have some time here. I don't want you ever telling her that I told you this stuff because . . . it just . . ."

I visualized him shaking his head and shrugging his shoulders.

"I won't say anything," I said, knowing it was a promise I wouldn't keep if she made things difficult for Shane.

"Jill is the executor and so all of the decisions will be made by her. I thought about making my brother Rob executor, but he's so busy. Jill's a good person, and I trust her to make good decisions. By the way, I think between the two of us Shane has turned out to be a pretty great kid. He'll be fine."

"Yes, he will." Tears stung my eyes.

"Anyway, I have a life insurance policy, and Jill and Shane are the beneficiaries. Jill will get 83 percent and Shane, 17 percent. It's about $100,000, so that's not too bad for him. I have the 529 college fund. There's not much in there. I split that with Jill's daughter, Jackie, because she was starting college last fall, and when I was out of work Jill used a lot of her savings to pay bills, so I said that I would split this with her to kind of make up for that. But I don't know, depending on the market, there might be as much as $7,000.00 in there by the time he starts. That's a semester's tuition, which is more than what I had when I started."

I kept my mouth shut and listened closely. I didn't protest this even though I thought it was cruel to Shane.

"My car, I'd like for Shane to have it, but Jill's kids are all young and will need a car. I don't know what will happen with that. Shane has relationships with everyone out there, especially Lance and Jackie. He likes Ian, too. He'll always have a room out there. If he could still come out every other weekend or once a month, you know."

I'd been crying a little as he talked but at this request I snapped back, angry, "I know he has formed relationships with everyone there. I am not going to interfere with that."

"Okay, good," Matt said.

"You don't have to worry about that," I said. "Can you put what you just said in an email or on a piece of paper, so I have it?"

"No! I don't want you showing up in probate with some piece of paper contesting the will."

"All of this will be in the will, won't it?"

"Well, yes. Look, Jill is a good person."

"It would still be better if I had this in writing," I said. "But okay."

I didn't like leaving things loose. Maybe Jill would be all right—Matt wasn't a horrible judge of character—but I didn't have any reason to trust her, either.

$\mathcal{G}$ saw Matt twice more after that. He was in the hospital undergoing chemo one of the times. The TV was on. Jill was on her phone but looked up momentarily to smile at me. Matt was talking to the doctor, who was busy adjusting the chemo solution, when I arrived. With effort, he leaned forward and then leaned back and closed his eyes. He looked laden; his legs were puffy and swollen, his cheeks sallow, downy sprigs of hair jutted up on top of his head. Matt said he was cold, and the doctor said they'd get him another blanket. He turned his head in my direction but didn't nod or say anything.

The last time I saw him, he was in hospice. Shane skipped, bounced down the hall. It was a Thursday. I walked casually after him, not wanting to catch up.

Jill and all of her kids were in the room, surrounding Matt's bed. He sat up and turned a large bottle of pills in his hand. His Adam's apple protruded and reminded me of a turkey's neck. He looked like Tweety Bird, his glasses too large for his sunken, emaciated face. His skin had the gray-yellow tint that only comes from cancer.

Jill showed him something on her phone. He nodded. He didn't acknowledge me, just turned to Shane and asked how his final exams were going. I pivoted and headed back down to the lobby.

Disgusted at having to walk past walls in a medical facility again, I wanted to scream. When was I going to get a break? Dad had passed away in July. I had just begun feeling the earned, real sigh of being relaxed again in September, and then Matt's tumor had engulfed him, scrambling pink-blushed cheeks to gray, ballooning his thighs and arms, stripping his head of hair. After six years of watching my dad deteriorate and be moved in and out of his house, and now to deliver my son back and forth, watching his father's demise, I hated the pastel paint and inspirational artwork, industrial carpet, and faux-everything furniture. I hated the smell, IV drips, adjustable beds, sterile sheets. I wanted to say I hated it. I wanted to tell someone I resented all of it without the cost of reprimand or judgment.

I was everything, I was going to be everything, to Shane, and in Matt's room I was nothing. I wanted five minutes with him. I didn't know what I would say or if I would say anything. I wanted it to be okay to hold his hand, or his face, and tell him that everything was going to be all right. Everyone else needed to clear out and acknowledge that I had a right to be there, that we had a few things to say about Shane, or about us. I had spent twelve years married to him, three times the amount of time Jill had been married to him, and we'd spent the last twenty-five years in each other's lives. We had had a child together. The one person who appreciated my son as much as I did was leaving. He wasn't going to ever look up at me again, requesting a second chance.

I would never forget standing in the courtroom on the morning we finalized the divorce. The legality of it took all of two minutes. The judge read off the declaration and asked if this is what both parties wanted. Matt looked back at me and waited. I nodded. He turned back to the judge and said, "Yes." He didn't ever want it, even after I'd hurt him. He didn't believe I would leave. I didn't want to, but there was no way I could stay. How was it possible to hold opposing sentiments so close and not implode?

My looking at him no longer commanded his attention. I needed him to look at me once more. I wanted reassurance. I wanted safe passage. I wanted to be told that I would find a way, that I would not be left alone, that Jill would be pleasant and easy to approach. I felt foolish for dreaming. It was wasteful; I had no room to wallow in that hope. The ubiquitous unknown rolled in like beach fog. Someone needed to promise it would burn off with the persistence of a rising dawn.

I texted Matt the next day, telling him everything would be fine. Jill's family, his family, and my family would take care of Shane. He didn't need to worry. My friend Whitney had advised to leave nothing unsaid so I wrote this. I didn't have the luxury of ambivalence.

The gesture assuaged little for me. Doubt ushered itself in: What if we hadn't divorced? What if I had still been with him? Would he have been able to beat this the second time through? Would he have listened to me about his health if I had chosen to go back to him, proving that he was the one for me, the one I wanted to be with? Could I have prevented this loss for Shane? My stupid little text message was not going to change a damn thing.

Matt didn't text me back.

Shane finished his final exams on Friday, the day after I took him to hospice, and he was picked up to spend the weekend in Aurora that afternoon.

On Saturday, I was off and on the phone with Terry and Matt's sister, Lorraine, who had flown in to spend the weekend, trying to arrange dinner plans. In the end, they decided to stay at Matt and Jill's. I told them that was fine. I silenced my cell phone and closed my bedroom door.

I woke up with the image of Shane's head on Matt's chest. I went downstairs and saw that Shane had called the landline twice, the cell phone once. He had texted me. Terry had texted me to call when I could.

I called Shane. He didn't answer. I called Terry and he said that Matt had passed at about two thirty in the morning.

Shane called a little later and told me to come in a while. I went for a walk and called Joan and my counselor, Thomas. It was December 21st.

I felt forced to act, to be in motion. I had no sense of what I needed.

Jill was flanked by two of her sons when I pulled up. They were returning from a walk. I gave her a hug and said I was sorry.

"Now we have to get along," she said.

It wasn't appropriate then to say that I had always wanted to get along, that she'd made that impossible with her whimsy and control of family activities.

Pam met me on the sidewalk. I hugged her and followed her into the house. Jill looked at me, hesitating.

I knew I was not welcome in the house, but I kept stepping through the front door.

The family dog, Sam, a German shepherd/lab mix, lay with her head on her front paws. Her eyes were downcast, sad. She barely lifted her head when I petted her. Matt and Shane had taken care of her the most. I thought of her as Shane's dog. Matt and Jill had adopted her from Dumb Friends two and a half years before, three days after Shane fell in love with a stray that had come into my neighborhood. When Matt picked Shane up from my place that evening, he helped Shane and his friends find the owner. Shane launched into a relentless campaign to get his own dog, and by the weekend, they had acquired Sam.

I petted her while I waited for Shane.

I heard Jill mutter about having gotten donuts for breakfast because she was a "nutritious-focused mother." One of her sons laughed a little.

I saw the pink box on the counter. I had no delusions that I was invited to have one. I didn't want one anyway. The thought of grease and sugar coating my teeth made me queasy. Junk food was a staple in their house. Shane had told me that. I'd never spoken to Matt about it because I knew it wouldn't do any good, but I'd told Shane to make good choices and to eat fruit, yogurt, and vegetables whenever they were available.

I silently accused Jill of killing Matt. I cursed him, too, for not taking better care of himself. I hadn't paid much attention to what liposarcoma was when Matt had it in 2007. I hadn't wanted to know, and I hadn't believed it was serious. The kidney stone that had precipitated the discovery of the benign tumor attached to the kidney that was removed all led me to believe that it was simply an inconvenient, treatable detour. I'd felt annoyed, then.

It was only after the tumor was removed that the liposarcoma was discovered. At that time, Matt said it was one of the rarest cancers, that it attacked the fat cells of the body. I remembered thinking that was interesting, like a detached scientist who had no interest in following up with a study. I remembered attending doctor's appointments in 2007 and the oncologist saying that there were new studies being done, different proteins being used to combat cancer, with some success. His statements hadn't sounded any alarms in me. I remembered that radiation should have eliminated the possibility of a return. I hadn't done any of my own independent reading on liposarcoma until this recurrence.

Now I knew that getting this type of cancer in the abdomen was more uncommon than on a limb, and the morbidity rates in cases like Matt's were higher. Research showed statistics on occurrences where an injury had occurred previously. If this occurred on a limb, it was easy to excise the tissue, and sometimes radiation wasn't necessary. A soft-tissue appearance made it more challenging, but since Matt had had radiation the first time, there had still been an 85 percent chance of it never coming back.

Matt attended his biannual check-ups, but he had also reverted to lousy eating habits. They ate take-out frequently. Jill didn't cook; Matt did, but he had a heinous commute—from his work in downtown Denver to picking up Shane in Lakewood and then home to Aurora. Oftentimes, he picked up their dinner on his way home.

Matt didn't pay close attention to discomfort, either. He'd told me he thought he was having digestive problems in June. In retrospect, it was probably the tumor beginning to press against his colon.

Shane put on his jacket. As we got into the car, he told me to drive away from there. "I don't care where," he said.

I drove down Arapahoe until restaurants popped up on both sides of the road.

Shane cried as he talked. "I didn't know what to do but to lie next to him and rub his back. I thought that would help him, and I think it did. Then, he'd lean up and cry out, 'Help me!' I just kept rubbing his back."

"You'll always be happy you were there, buddy. You will never regret that," I said.

"I know. I got up and went to sleep and then I woke up to hearing everyone crying. I missed it, but I think he wanted that too. He was waiting for me to go to sleep, then he was going to go."

I looked at the lavender and pink splotches painting his face. His eyes were wide and red. "Do you want something to eat?" I asked.

"Yeah, but I'm not going in there looking like this," he said. "Bring it out to me. We'll eat in the car."

The sky was pregnant with gray clouds, but no rain or snow would fall.

We ate in the car and then he wanted to go back.

The funeral was scheduled for December 27th. Jill didn't want to remember burying her husband right before Christmas.

I asked Shane if he wanted to speak and he did. He sat at my computer and wrote what he remembered best about his dad. I asked him to read it out loud to me until he was comfortable. "Slow down for the funny parts," I coached him. "You don't want people to miss that."

I took him shopping for a suit. While we riffled through pants and jackets, rage welled up. I didn't want to be there shopping for funeral wear for my son's father's funeral. Some-

one else should do this. His father should be there to do this.
I hated Matt for leaving me to be the only one there for
Shane.

Terry called while Shane held up pants and a jacket.

"I didn't want to say anything, but Jill didn't want any of
us to be pallbearers. I told her that Matt's brothers would be
carrying the casket, end of story. She didn't want Lorraine to
be a pallbearer, so Lorraine backed off. But I don't want Shane
to know about this. She only wanted her boys and Shane to
be pallbearers. I yelled at her that that wasn't going to happen, so we're all going to do it whether she likes it or not."

I stepped away so Shane wouldn't see my face.

"And, the obituary," he continued. "Rob and our mom
wrote about Matt's life before he knew her and told her to
write about his life after they got together. She didn't like
what Rob gave her and completely changed it. You're not in
it. It's all about her and after they met. But Rob is going to
include you in the eulogy, so you won't be completely left out."

I laughed. "That's perfect. You know what? Obituaries
are fictions. They're whatever the person writing them wants
to say. My stepmother completely butchered my dad's obituary. She had the names of the universities he attended wrong
and didn't include my mom. It doesn't matter. Jill needs for it
to go this way. The rest of us know the truth."

I believed most of what I said. I mattered. That was the
running subtext that imprinted the future. In the longer view,
Jill did not matter. She could be petty and publish an obituary about her husband that only reflected the last four years
of his life. If I blew up about it, that would seep into Shane's
relationships with her kids and the rhythm of visiting at their
house. Now was not the time to let loose my fury. Everything
I did for Shane and for myself could not be cloaked anymore.
We could not hide in the shadows. I was intent on showing
up and stepping into this, even if rages of resistance exploded
here and there. I knew I would be the only one with an eagle
eye on Shane in the coming months, watching for wayward
acts and helping him build a toolbox for how to navigate the
impact of losing his dad at fifteen.

ℒ

Whitney insisted on driving me to the funeral. "You don't know what you're going to feel like that day," she told me. I resisted and then decided she was probably right. It was okay to let someone else—someone who was not invested—worry.

I dressed in a gray suit and pink turtleneck. Whitney arrived early. The church was in Parker. I was glad she was there, ready to drive, ready to wait through whatever was coming. I could have driven myself, but it was nice to be waited on.

The room where the service was to be held was not the sanctuary. It was an extra room of the church that held hundreds on Sundays. It was drafty, anonymous, and sterile. Nothing in there represented the denomination or affiliation of the church where Matt had embraced God in the final weeks of his life. He was not religious, and neither was Jill. We were Christmas and Easter attendees to a church when we were married.

I choked up when I walked in. A silent video of Matt's life in pictures played on a large screen. Jill's daughter had assembled this, Shane told me later. I had been the photographer for several photos: when he graduated from the University of Michigan; playing with Shane when he was an infant; when he dressed as a woman for a Halloween party we attended while he was getting his master's in public administration at Syracuse University.

My sister and brothers and their families arrived and sat on the right side of the aisle. Whitney, Shane's friend Zuban, my friend Karen, and I sat together behind Jill and her family on the left.

I leaned over and told Karen and Whitney that I was on the other half of that Halloween photo of Matt dressed as a woman. I had been cut out. They laughed and said they assumed that was the case.

The minister knew enough about Matt to speak about him because he had met with him several times in recent weeks. His memorial of him was thoughtful, highlighting Matt's accomplishments and his love for Jill, her children, and Shane.

Jill's brother Jeremy spoke, then Rob, and then Shane. I had told Shane to tell Jill that he wanted to speak last. I thought that as Matt's son, his words should be the last ones anyone heard.

After Shane sat down, he turned around to look at me, three rows behind him. I smiled, looking steadily at him, nodded, and made a big "okay" sign with my fingers.

He smiled and shrugged. "Was it good?" he mouthed.

I nodded more vigorously and kept smiling at him until he leaned back into the pew and turned his head toward the front of the church. I resisted the urge to get up and sit next to him in that front row for family. The biggest event of his life, a devastating loss—I should have been allowed to sit with him, to let him cry on me or hold my hand. His step-family was not going to envelop him. I watched, draping him silently with tenderness. Unexpectedly, I noticed panic and disbelief churning on low. This had to have happened to someone else, not me. I was only watching it, wasn't I? Whatever dock I had rested on knowing another adult was responsible for my son had disintegrated. I wanted permission to leave and to be forgiven for not wanting Shane to need me. How was I going to be his only parent? I felt alone and knew I was alone, and this was daunting. I didn't want to be a hero. I didn't want to rise up and do the right thing. I wanted to run. I wanted to fall.

We drove to the cemetery. The funeral director took the longest route imaginable to the Elizabeth Veteran's Memorial Cemetery. It took us forty-five minutes through back roads, not all of them paved.

Terry joked with Shane at the cemetery because he wandered off to pee near a cluster of trees. I envied him. I had had to pee before the end of the funeral and hadn't gone at the church because I'd felt nervous about missing the caravan to the cemetery.

❧

Whitney blazed down the highway to get back to the reception at the church. No more dirt back roads on the return trip.

I ate and visited with Matt's family. I looked across the amply seated room for Shane. He sat with his friends. I wanted to say good-bye to him before heading back home. I knew he would want to stay at the house in Aurora for a few days longer, while Jill's family was still in town.

Jeremy, Jill's brother sidled up to me and put his hand on my shoulder. I didn't like that. I had just met him. He had no right to assume such familiarity. My own family didn't hug freely. Besides, prior to all of this, despite my efforts to the contrary, I had not been welcome in Jill's family, or kept apprised of the happenings that involved Shane while he was over there. All of what Matt and I had created in the spirit of congeniality and trying not to mess up Shane emotionally prior to Matt's union with Jill had been whittled down to angry deference.

"You and Jill will work together to raise Shane now," Jeremy proclaimed. I didn't take my eyes off of him. I refrained from yelling that he was full of shit.

Whitney dropped me off at home and said I could call her anytime.

I sat on my favorite blue chair in the living room and noticed how soft it was. I could sink into it. I sat until I made myself go to bed.

I wanted Steve to call. I thought about calling him and letting him know Matt had passed on the one-year anniversary of his mother's passing. We would have that in common—another pedestal of pain. But I didn't call. And I knew he wouldn't, either. He had run away again and by this time recognized it was wrong to do that, felt ashamed, and couldn't come back. I had made it easy before by calling him and forgiving his missteps.

At his best, he reminded me of me and he knew how to sing my song back to me, so I wouldn't forget who I was. I ached for that. But I would not allow myself to call him. I could not forget or pretend this time. I had reached the threshold of what I could tolerate. It wasn't that I was better or stronger or had finally come to my senses. For the first time, I could say out loud to myself that what I needed counted more than his fragile, wounded, tormented self. I couldn't wait any longer. I couldn't turn around and give my hand back to him.

I had a son. I was all he had right now. I didn't have room or time for a man whose grievances were nearly fifty years old, who didn't want to look at any of it, who preferred to recreate misery by pushing those who loved him away.

I had lived so many different versions of not enough, almost there, and "no" with him. I didn't hope, and I couldn't tolerate the thought of opening up one more time to him. If he called, I imagined that I would answer. I would speak. I might even act like it hadn't been hours, days, and months since we last talked. I might pick up where we left off.

Or I might scream at him a litany of reasons why I hated him and how frustrated and disappointed I was that he couldn't show up for me. After I had worked so hard to prove how much I cared for him. I wanted what I gave. I wanted all of it from someone who was incapable of delivering it. Steve was different from Matt. He could see and hear me. It was genuine. But the ever-present tripwire of his pain would forever keep him from stepping into a cohesive us.

My dad's and Matt's deaths were beyond my control. Their absence allowed my internal strife about not feeling seen in their presence to fade. The years of weaving, dodging, negotiating, and blundering had left ineffaceable imprints, but from now on I would no longer be forced into the tension of getting along for my family's sake.

As the reality of the end of this struggle settled, a question arose: Why was I still willing to put up with someone who constantly made me feel insecure? I had never known what it felt like to be authentically seen and heard before I met Steve. I would miss that part of him. When he was available, he fed that desire to bloom, to show my self-worth to the world. I mattered. I wasn't insignificant. But every time he retreated and stepped away from me, I doubted and felt diminished. It was not trivial to let go of him, but the truth of the matter was that there was nothing more to say. It was no longer about yelling at him or accepting him but rather about setting myself free.

Who we were together brought me into the center of simultaneously hoping for nurturance and a hand to hold and fearing abandonment. With him, I repeatedly lived through that moment at age three when my mother threatened to leave. I felt both drawn in by the hope of a different outcome and repelled by the pain of impending disappointment. I kept stepping back in hoping for the ending that would feel right, where I would feel vindicated—but I was never going to arrive at that with Steve, or anyone else. I couldn't change the fact of witnessing my parents' argument or the reflexive habit of freezing in the face of rejection. Just because something felt familiar didn't mean it was right. I knew now that conflict didn't have to mean abandonment, and I didn't need to fear what would happen if I said what I felt in the midst of it.

Space and opportunity danced, escorting in the possibility of dreaming. I had stood in the center of losses I never imagined, and I was still here. I was lovable. A desire to trust myself to find someone I could be vulnerable with began to bud. I knew how to be alone. The revolving door of men I had encountered in my life, especially over the last dozen years, had taught me well. They reflected that frozen fear of moving forward, the inability to break free and create a new way. I felt terrified of trusting someone to be there in a continuous, supportive way, but I was now more afraid of never allowing myself to have the experience of being loved for all of who I was. I was whole. I had earned that. I was more than I could measure, and no one would compromise that truth for me again. The most important relationship I was ever going to have was the one with myself, and I didn't have to choose to spend time with anyone who made me feel uneasy, brash, or sad.

Boundaries melted away. I could create and sculpt without chains. I was afraid of making mistakes with Shane, but I was committed to figuring out how to move forward. This was the most important job I had. I would rewrite the script of how to be his mom. I would be a clean slate; what lay ahead would braid itself into paths unknown.

EPILOGUE

My sister Melanie and I had been on the phone for a while when I asked her if she remembered that horrible fight between Mom and Dad when we were little. "You must have been about eight, I think," I said.

"Oh yeah, I got in the middle of it. I tried to stop it," she said. "I begged Mom not to go. I sometimes wonder what would have happened if I hadn't."

"Me too," I said. "But Dad would have been bad at parenting. Mom was all we had."

"Dad once told me he didn't like parenting. He didn't think he was good at it," she said. "There were other fights, too. Not as bad as that one. When Dad threw the chili at the wall behind the stove."

"I remember that too," I said. "I was in the kitchen when Dad did that. I remember him cleaning it up."

Numb, vacant, I went through the motions of errands the rest of that Saturday. This wasn't the first time we had ever talked about the dynamics of our childhood, but it was the first time I had shared with Melanie about that memory. I had no answer for why I hadn't brought it up sooner. I trusted what I had experienced to be real—it was too vivid to not have happened—but hearing her relate her version without hesitation made mine palpable, tangible. Any doubt about the horror of that threat of Mom leaving was justified. I had a witness. The fear, so early imprinted, had lines and edges. I could see it, I could hold it, and because it was now defined, I no longer needed to be ruled by it. Unmasked, it held no more power.

ACKNOWLEDGMENTS

Every story needs readers and listeners. We all need an audience. I am grateful to everyone who leaned in, listened intently, and laughed when they caught the live show of these stories. My friends, I am beholden to you: Jeff Berg, Lee Christopher, Anita Clark, Linda Coppard, Ruth Hidalgo, Juliet Hubbell, Candace Kearns Read, Bonnie Kenny, Sandy Kerr, Lindsay Lewan, Sharon May, Josie Mills, Reina Payne, Kelly Phillips, Wendy Talley, Kristi Thorland, Donald Walker, and Kathy Winograd.

My long-time kindred spirits from Writing and Poetics at Naropa: Jen Asteris, Lisa Birman, Jimmy Gleacher, and Lisa Trank-Greene, I have appreciated our connection and your words of encouragement. A special commendation goes to David Madgalene, who has offered generous feedback and has always been a beacon for my literary life. I am grateful to my writing group, the Visceral Realists: Jeff Becker, Jenny Cookson, Brian Dickson, Bret Hann, Aaron Leff, Pete Lindstrom, Nicole Servino, and Ian Tyson for insightful feedback and direction. I am especially grateful to Annie Howley, who asked the critical question that every writer must answer: what is at the center of this? It caused me to reintegrate what I had originally written in the very beginning when this book was scraps of paper and journal entries.

I am thankful to my teachers who provided exercises, ways to practice writing, and who offered praise and critique honestly: Keith Abbott, Jack Collom, Arthur Flowers, Kristen Iversen, and Michael Martone.

Thank you to She Writes Press: Brooke Warner for finding my book worthy of the light of day and for developing such a wonderful supportive community through She Writes; Krissa Lagos for gently suggesting edits and places to cut that were not moving the story along; Julie Metz for designing a beautiful cover that truly matches my intention and message;

Crystal Patriarche for organizing a dynamic publicity campaign; and Maggie Ruf for designing a beautiful and sleek website.

I am deeply indebted to my long-time friend and editor, Natascha Bruckner, who has been willing to read every tiny and long-winded word-smithing I have ever sent her way. She read this book in all of its smaller and larger iterations several times over, enthusiastically and compassionately, always carrying the torch when I felt lost, fearful, and full of doubt.

Last though not least, I am thankful for my family and especially my parents. From my father, I learned stoicism, perseverance, and the value of creativity, and from my mother, to take time to stare out the window, to have many friends, and to laugh at myself.

ABOUT THE AUTHOR

photo credit: David Lara

Jane Binns grew up in Ann Arbor, Michigan. She holds a BS from Eastern Michigan University, an MS in education from Syracuse University, and an MFA in prose from Naropa University. In 1998, she was awarded the Jack Kerouac Award for Prose. She was the managing editor of *Bombay Gin* with Lisa Birman from 1998 to 1999. She is an English composition instructor at Arapahoe Community College in Littleton, CO, and has worked in online learning assisting faculty, students, and staff with the online platform since 2006.

SELECTED TITLES FROM SHE WRITES PRESS

She Writes Press is an independent publishing company
founded to serve women writers everywhere.
Visit us at www.shewritespress.com.

Daring to Date Again: A Memoir by Ann Anderson Evans. $16.95,
978-1-63152-909-2. A hilarious, no-holds-barred memoir about a
legal secretary turned professor who dives back into the dating pool
headfirst after twelve years of celibacy.

*Where Have I Been All My Life? A Journey Toward Love and
Wholeness* by Cheryl Rice. $16.95, 978-1-63152-917-7. Rice's
universally relatable story of how her mother's sudden death
launched her on a journey into the deepest parts of grief—and,
ultimately, toward love and wholeness.

Loveyoubye: Holding Fast, Letting Go, And Then There's The Dog by
Rossandra White. $16.95, 978-1-938314-50-6. A soul-searching
memoir detailing the painful, but ultimately liberating,
disintegration of a twenty-five-year marriage.

Seeing Red: A Woman's Quest for Truth, Power, and the Sacred by
Lone Morch. $16.95, 978-1-938314-12-4. One woman's journey
over inner and outer mountains—a quest that takes her to the holy
Mt. Kailas in Tibet, through a seven-year marriage, and into the
arms of the fierce goddess Kali, where she discovers her powerful,
feminine self.

Miracle at Midlife: A Transatlantic Romance by Roni Beth Tower.
$16.95, 978-1-63152-123-2. An inspiring memoir chronicling the
sudden, unexpected, and life-changing two-year courtship between
a divorced American lawyer living on a houseboat in the center of
Paris and an empty-nested clinical psychologist living in
Connecticut.

Not a Perfect Fit: Stories from Jane's World by Jane A. Schmidt.
$16.95, 978-1631522062. Jane Schmidt documents her challenges
living off grid, moving from the city to the country, living with a
variety of animals as her only companions, dating, family trips,
outdoor adventures, and midlife in essays full of honesty and humor.